# Q ON PRODUCING

**QUINCY JONES**
with Bill Gibson

# Q ON PRODUCING

## QUINCY JONES
### with Bill Gibson

## HAL•LEONARD®
Hal Leonard Books
An Imprint of Hal Leonard Corporation

iv

Published in 2010 by Hal Leonard Books
An Imprint of Hal Leonard Corporation
7777 West Bluemound Road
Milwaukee, WI 53213

Trade Book Division Editorial Offices
33 Plymouth Street, Montclair, NJ 07042

Book design by Adam Fulrath

Photo credits:
Front cover, rear cover (top), and rear-flap; color insert, pp. i, xi, and xvi; p. 248; and p. 256 by Jeff Katz Photography for Quincy Jones Enterprises. Copyright © 2010 Quincy Jones Enterprises, LLC (*www.quincyjones.com*).
Rear-flap photo featuring Quincy Jones Signature Line Q701 reference-class studio headphones by AKG®.
All rights reserved. AKG is a registered trademark of AKG Acoustics GmbH (*www.akg.com/quincy*).
Title page, Photofest.
Rear cover photo of Michael Jackson and p. xii, Getty Images.
Color insert, pp. ii–iii, viii–x, and xii–xv, Bill Gibson; pp. iv–iv, Lorie McKloskey, pp. vi–vii, Quincy Jones collection.
All other photo credits noted on individual pages.

Grammy® is a registered trademark of the National Academy of Recording Arts & Sciences.

Printed in the United States of America

Jones, Quincy, 1933-Q on producing/ Quincy Jones with Bill Gibson.
    p. cm. -- (Quincy Jones legacy series)
1. Jones, Quincy, 1933---Interviews. 2. Sound recording executives and producers--Interviews. 3.
Popular music—Production and direction. I. Gibson, Bill (William A.) II. Title.
ML419.J7A5 2010
781.64092--dc222010032871
ISBN 978-1-4234-5976-7

www.halleonard.com

# ACKNOWLEDGMENTS

Bill Gibson would like to express sincere thanks, gratitude, and appreciation to:

Lynn Gibson, my wife and the love of my life.

Quincy Jones for leading the way in the music industry. You have been the leader and teacher that so many of us needed, and you are the most sincere and loving dude I've had the pleasure to meet. Your care for great music is motivational; your great care for people inspirational!

John Cerullo, Group Publisher for Hal Leonard Publishing, for entrusting me with such a fantastic and important book. Thank you.

Chairman and CEO Keith Mardak and President Larry Morton of Hal Leonard Publishing for setting the industry standard for publishing excellence and integrity.

Rusty Cutchin, senior editor for Hal Leonard Books, for your tireless efforts on this book. Your hard work in the trenches made this book come together with excellence and on schedule. Also, thanks to Christine Corso, for transcribing hours of recordings, Patty Hammond, for her top-notch copy editing, Adam Fulrath, for a great design and his long hours fine tuning the results, and Diane Levinson, for her hard work on the publicity end.

Mike Lawson, Lawson Music Media, for originally including me to help Quincy with this book. Your professionalism has always been exemplary and you are a true friend.

Kristi and Paul Zimmerman for your absolutely crucial assistance. We would have never kept this on schedule without you. And, thanks for providing Noah.

Noah Zimmerman for being born right in the middle of the writing of this book. There is nothing like the perfect grandson to keep things in perspective. You are very loved by your Grandpa.

Adam Fell, Vice President of Business Development Quincy Jones Productions, for being the link to all things Quincy Jones. You define professionalism, hard work, loyalty, and class.

Rebecca Sahim, Quincy Jones Productions, for helping faithfully and cheerfully with searches for photos, documents, and other materials. You are a gem.

Yue-Sai Kan, You-Sai's World television program in China, for your help documenting the production of the World Expo 2010 theme. Thank you!

JoAnn Tominaga for arranging so many interviews with the Quincy Jones family and for always being a source of cheer and joy.

Debborah Foreman, Coordinating Manager for Quincy Jones Productions, for making the schedule work. Your job is formidable and you handle it with grace.

Clarence Acox, Band Director at Garfield High School, for continuing a standard of excellence in the Seattle Public Schools and for an insightful interview about Quincy's impact on music education

Mark Freed, Owner Action Video, Las Vegas, for going the extra mile to maintain a high standard of excellence in the video component of this book

Martin LaPire and Andrea Estalio, Action Video, Las Vegas, for your camera operation

Rita Montanez, makeup

The members of the Quincy Jones musical family who I was so fortunate to interview. Your love for each other and for Quincy is obvious, and it was an honor to speak with each of you:

▶ Alfredo Rodriguez, Pianist/Composer

▶ Bernie Grundman, Bernie Grundaman Mastering

▶ Bruce Swedien, Engineer/Producer

▶ Ed Cherney, Engineer/Producer

▶ Francis Buckley, Engineer

▶ Greg Phillinganes, Keyboardist

▶ Jerry Hey, Trumpet/Arranger/Producer

▶ John Robinson, Drums and Percussion

▶ Louis Johnson, Bassist

▶ Nathan East, Bassist

▶ Ndugu Chancler, Drums and Percussion

▶ Neil Stubenhaus, Bassist

▶ Paul Jackson, Jr., Guitarist

▶ Paula Salvatore, Studio Manager at Capitol Records, Los Angeles

▶ Peter Chaikin, Engineer/Director of Recording and Broadcast at JBL Professional

▶ Phil Ramone, Producer/Engineer

▶ Siedah Garrett, Vocalist/Songwriter

▶ Rod Temperton

▶ Steve Burdick, Studio Owner Westlake Studios, Los Angeles

▶ Steve Ferrone, Drums and Percussion

▶ Steve Genewick, Engineer at Capitol Records, Los Angeles

And special thanks to:

Harman/JBL Pro for equipment and technical support

Avid for equipment and technical support

And extra special thanks to the production staff at Hal Leonard Publishing for all your help in putting this book together and for your continued adherence to the highest standards of excellence.

# PREFACE

by Bill Gibson

*Quincy Jones is one of the best friends
a song ever had.* —Whitney Houston

Music coexists in space with inanimate objects that contain and reflect it, but when music reaches a human being, the soul absorbs its magic, refracting it into the listener's spirit. The artist's vision touches the senses of all who truly hear—there's a connection that surpasses biology and logical science. Quincy Delight Jones, Jr., is that powerful music echoing throughout our world like the sound of an orchestra throughout the concert hall, infusing love, passion, and excellence with every carom.

Quincy's words form a complex harmony—thematic undertones and nuanced overtones—yet Q is focused, purposeful, driven, energetic, and intensely passionate about people, life, and music. He is a true master at his trade, complete with all the essential tools: solid education, rich experience, relentless pursuit of excellence, and an acknowledged God-given gift.

Quincy's influence has been ingrained in our culture since shortly after he joined Lionel Hampton's Big Band in 1951. His groundbreaking work as an executive with Mercury Records and his relationships with Frank Sinatra, Michael Jackson, and an impressively diverse group of artists have spanned musical, racial, and cultural chasms. Often, he has been the bridge enabling the connection between diametrically opposing forces, inspiring respect and reconciliation.

As the preparation of this book unfolded, it became much more than a technical how-to manual on producing records. At its core, it provides a prescription for excellence, a guide to creative effectiveness, and a roadmap to success. I invite you—actually, I'm excited for you—to enjoy and share in the musical journey, the call to excellence, and the wisdom in the words of Mr. Quincy Jones.

# CONTENTS

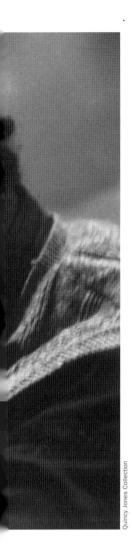

ix

## See DVD menu for content of included disc.

# INTRODUCTION

*Q on Producing* is one component of the Quincy Jones Legacy Series. This book reveals the methods and mind-set behind the creation of the most wide-ranging, respected, and successful music of the last half-century, music that has touched the lives of countless people around the world. It is inspiring and instructive to see the way Quincy works, how he thinks, and how he builds winning teams.

Quincy's body of work has been indisputably successful, and his list of megahit productions reflects not only his musical genius but also his intuition and creative vision. His work has crossed generational, stylistic, racial, and socioeconomic boundaries; it has had global impact. Quincy's hits range from Lesley Gore's "It's My Party" to Michael Jackson's Off the Wall, Thriller, and Bad, and from *Sinatra at the Sands* to Quincy's latest release, *Q: Soul Bossa Nostra,* which includes contributions from Usher, Ludacris, Akon, Jamie Foxx, Jennifer Hudson, Mary J. Blige, Amy Winehouse, T.I., B.o.B, and many others.

# THE SCOPE

Many people don't realize the scope of Quincy's work. In addition to his impact as an iconic music producer, he has set standards in the areas of film scoring, songwriting, composition, concert production, business, education, and global humanitarianism. A complete account of Quincy's experiences, techniques, and knowledge could fill many books—and his legacy continues to expand.

Young Quincy Delight Jones, Jr., triumphed over poverty and pain, and he was changed in a single compelling and revealing moment, as we shall see. As a result, Quincy Jones the man had a dramatic impact on jazz, pop, rock, and hip-hop music, integrating musical styles successfully and powerfully throughout his career. Quincy also discovered many of the most influential and creative artists of our time and became a global ambassador of goodwill, compassion, and tolerance. He also became an advocate for (and provider of aid to) those in need.

# THE STRUCTURE

Herein you'll discover Quincy's belief that true freedom ultimately exists in well-defined structure. In assisting Quincy, I have tried to adhere faithfully to that premise. This book fundamentally is about music production, and if it doesn't relate to that subject, it's not within these pages. However, from that adherence has evolved an interesting dichotomy. The information that Quincy shares is, on one hand, rich in musical insight, and, on the other, about everything other than music. It's about finding your individual road to success. It's about developing a mind-set that is ageless, passionate, and caring. It's about learning the right way to develop wealth and the right way to use that wealth. It's about investing life  life. It's about finding meaning and sharing love. It's about recognizing talent and knowing how to develop it.

Quincy's story is also about family, love, conflict, and resolution. It's about generosity and lending a hand to the fallen. It's about having an insatiable thirst for knowledge and understanding. It's about embracing your heritage and understanding the heritage of others. But it all circles a single focal point: the legendary work of Quincy Jones.

## THE PROCESS

In this book, Quincy generously shares, through a series of personal interviews, the thoughts and techniques that have resulted in a body of work unparalleled in scope, sophistication, and commercial impact. He recounts in his own words what he has learned and what continues to shape his expanding legacy.

The musicians with whom Quincy works reflect the spirit of family, caring, and love that we see in his words. The accompanying interviews (in the "On Q" sections) by those in his creative family help us see him from another angle. It's inspiring and revealing to hear what some of the most talented musicians in the world say about Quincy Jones. These people have worked with countless producers and music-industry professionals at the highest level, and the perspectives they bring are poignant.

## THE DVD

The accompanying DVD contains never-before-seen video footage, including

- Quincy's guided tour through the actual multitrack masters of some of his hits as he dissects his work, taking a microscopic look at the individual ingredients in a Quincy Jones production.

Co-author Bill Gibson with Quincy.

xvi

- Personal interviews with Quincy
- Interviews with members of Quincy's musical family
- Quincy, in the studio at Capitol Records, producing his newly discovered Cuban pianist, Alfredo Rodriguez.
- Quincy, in the studio at the famous Westlake Studios, Studio D, producing the theme for the Shanghai's World Expo 2010. This session includes several of Quincy's musical family members including: Greg Phillinganes, Paul Jackson, Jr., Nathan East, John "JR" Robinson, Siedah Garrett, Alfredo Rodriguez, Francis Buckley, and also Antonio Sol.

In the DVD, Quincy provides powerful insights as he shares many of the methods and means that he has employed in the creation of his work.

## THE LEGACY

If you read and absorb what Quincy has to say, you are likely to be a changed person. You may look at music, relationships, business, success, spirituality, family, and life from a different perspective. Quincy's words are encouraging, motivational, and inspirational; his methods are original, efficient, and effective. His legacy is powerful, and so are the lessons he shares about life and making music.

xvii

Bill Gibson Collection

## Chapter 1

# THE MAN

Within this chapter are revealing insights into the mind and actions of a musical genius, a consummate producer, and a truly caring and loving man. Q, the producer, is best seen through the filter that is Q, the man. We can much more easily understand the actions of the producer when we realize the underlying forces that drive and compel the man, Quincy Delight Jones, Jr.

I was seven years old and on the wrong street. They nailed my hand to a fence with a switchblade and put an ice pick in my temple. They don't play.

During the Depression in the 1930s, Chicago had the biggest black ghetto in America—makes Compton and Harlem look like Boys Town. At the time, there were 5 million black people who were buying music before they bought clothes or food, just to keep their souls together. Going to school each day was a life-or-death experience, with kids shooting teachers and other kids in the halls, even in grade school! And there were gangsters everywhere you looked; it was rough—everybody on the block was in the gang. There were always fights at night, and man they were rough. They had everything from switchblades to zip guns. Until I was 12 years old, I wanted to be a gangster just like the Scorpions, the Vagabonds, the Giles AC, and all the others—that's definitely where I was headed. I was on a crash course with hell!

2

Every street had a gang. Each gang had an identifiable yell, like an African call. All the alleys were cobblestone; the junkmen—rags and old iron guys—would have one raggedy horse and a big wooden wagon with big steel wheels on it. People threw their bottles out in the alley, and these big metal wheels would grind them down into a fine powder. Every part of the ghetto was the same way—the streets were shiny from all the glass that was crushed under those steel wheels and ground into the pavement.

I was just wandering around. All of a sudden I realized I was on the wrong street. At age seven you don't know what you're doing. I was just messing around, and I hear their call and I don't know how to respond! I knew I was in big trouble, but they grabbed me. I put my hands up and they put my hand up against a fence and stabbed the switchblade straight through it into the fence! Then they jabbed the ice pick into my temple; that's when I thought for sure I was gonna die. You never forget something like that as long as you live.

(Left to right) Mother (Sarah), Lloyd, and me in Chicago, 1936.

Quincy Jones Collection

My daddy and Julian Black, who was Joe Louis's manager, found us. They were mad! Daddy even hit a couple of them in the head with his hammer! I don't remember much about what happened next.

Everybody was a gangster back then. Daddy wasn't. He was a master carpenter for the Jones Boys, one of the most notorious groups of black gangsters in the history of America. The gangsters of this era are referred to by the modern hip-hop community as the "Triple OGs" because they're some of the pioneer gangsters. "OG" stands for "original gangsters." But these guys are really old, so that that's why they're called "triple" OGs. They ran the first black businesses, the policy racket, and the five and dime stores—they called them the "Xs and Vs."

On the streets you had to be clever—you always had to outguess the status quo. That's why, with my kids, I've always wanted them to be well rounded, including understanding what the street's about, too. And they know—all of them.

## Q TOUCHES THE PIANO and Music Touches Q

What I'm about to tell you is extremely important in my life, because it shaped my relationship to and connection with music and people. I had a mother who was absolutely brilliant. She spoke and wrote 12 languages, and she was a student at Boston University in the '20s! By the time I was seven years old she was showing signs of dementia praecox, a condition that is now treated with vitamins. Her condition worsened quickly; my brother Lloyd and I watched them throw her on the bed, tie a straitjacket around her, and take her to Mantino State Hospital. For me, that was the end of what "mother" meant. Whoever's had a mother doesn't know what I'm talking about, and I don't know what they're talking about. I don't know what it means—it's just M-O-T-H-E-R. I have no association with a mother, none.

By the time I was ten years old, I thought I wanted to be a gangster. That's what I saw when I was growing up in the ghetto in Chicago—dead bodies, tommy guns, and piles of money on the table under lights. It's what I knew and it's where I was headed. The Jones Boys were the biggest and most prosperous black gang in Chicago. One day in 1943, Al Capone's gang ran the Jones Boys gang out of town (Capone was in prison, but his gang

Quincy Jones Collection

Mother, Sarah Jones

had continued on) so we left everything behind and got on a Trailways bus to get away from some bad stuff that was going down with the Jones Boys. My dad wasn't one of the Jones Boys gang; he was a master carpenter and built their homes. But because of his association with the gang, we left Chicago and went straight to Bremerton, Washington, just across the water from Seattle. They put all the black people up on the hill in Sinclair Heights, away from everyone else. You'd have to take a bus up to that hill, and then walk up three more miles.

My brother Lloyd, my stepbrother Waymond, and I knew everything. We had jobs in all the stores, and we were stealing everything in sight. We'd steal cases of honey. We took a whole case out in the woods and drank the thing—every bottle. I didn't want to see honey for 20 years! We broke into homes and even burned down dance halls. I'm telling you, we were trouble! However, living and working on the streets during that time is when I learned that excellence isn't an act; it's a habit. I wanted to do everything as good as it could possibly be done, whether it was shining Stacy Adams shoes for pimps, picking strawberries, setting bowling pins, or working in locker rooms at the country clubs. I carried that ideal into everything, even when much later I was babysitting for the director of the Navy dance band (and the former director of the Wings over Jordan Choir), Joseph Powe, which I really did so I could study his Glen Miller arranging books.

One night, when I was 11 years of age, we broke into the armory. We were well informed and had heard there was a shipment of lemon meringue pie and ice cream coming in, so we hit it that night at midnight. We broke in and had so much lemon meringue pie you can't believe it. We had a pie fight after we got full, and then individually we went around and broke into all of the rooms.

I broke into the supervisor's room—I met her later, Mrs. Ayers, a wonderful old lady—and there was a spinet piano inside in the dark. I almost closed the door, but God said, "Idiot! Go back in that room!" And that saved my life. I walked over, and when my hands touched that piano, every cell, every drop of blood in my body said, "This is where you will live the rest of your life." The concept of a human being playing an instrument had never occurred to me. I was around music all my life, but I never thought I understood or felt it. I hit that piano and I knew instantly what I would be doing for the rest of my life.

*... when my hands touched that piano, every cell, every drop of blood in my body said, "This is where you will live the rest of your life."*

I started to practice all day on piano and stay after school playing all the percussion instruments, sousaphone, tuba, B-flat baritone sax, E-flat peck horn, and French horn. I wanted to play trumpet, but I was practical! In the marching band you could be up front next to the majorettes if you played trombone, because the slides needed more room than the rest of the instruments. So, I waited until later to get to my trumpet.

As soon as I picked up a horn, I started to hear French horn parts and trombones and everything else—that's when I knew it was in my DNA to be an arranger, orchestrator, and composer. I just knew it. And that was when I was 12 years old!

Garfield High School in Seattle, Washington.

5

Bill Gibson Collection

# RESPECT ALL GENRES

In the '40s and '50s, Seattle was one of the hottest cities in the country because everybody in the military had to pass through on their way to the Pacific theater. There were 900 nightclubs! From the time I was 13 years old, I absorbed everything musical that happened around me. Very quickly, I'd be able to participate and not be afraid. I met Ray Charles when I was 14 and he was 16. I was in Charlie Taylor's band first, and then Bumps Blackwell's band. Ray had his own group called the Maxim Trio. Ray was singing and playing piano like Nat Cole and Charles Brown and playing alto sax like Charlie Parker. Ray and I would play "To Each His Own," "Room Full of Roses," and all that stuff at the white country clubs dressed in our little white cardigans. Then we'd change our clothes and go play at the Washington Education and Social Club, a black club with strippers, rhythm and blues,

Parker Cook: My music teacher and choir director at Garfield High School in Seattle from 1947 through 1950.

Bill Gibson Collection

6

and "There's Good Rockin' Tonight." Its proprietor was Reverend Silas Groves. After that, we'd go down to the Elks Club in the red-light district and play bebop for nothing. So, we were playing Sousa and schottisches at bar mitzvahs, bat mitzvahs, or anywhere we could play for money, and then we'd play bebop later. A lot of times we'd just play for "the kitty," which was a big wooden box with a cat's face on it, a lightbulb inside, and a hole in the top where people would put money when they wanted us to play something like "Big Fat Butterfly." We were at three or four clubs a night until 6:30 in the morning, and then I had to get to school! Thank God I had Parker Cook. He was my music teacher, but he never even looked twice when I came dragging into class. He never once reprimanded me. He'd just say, "This is what you're doing because this is what you're going to be doing the rest of your life." Parker Cook came to my 50th birthday concert that we held at The Paramount in Seattle. We had the original Bumps Blackwell/Charlie Taylor Band, Ray Charles, Henry Mancini, Alex Haley, Nancy Wilson from Heart, and a lot of other people—it was a great evening.

My home in Seattle, where my father, step-mother, siblings, and I lived while I was attending Garfield High School in Seattle, Washington.

7

Bill Gibson Collection

The Garfield High orchestra during my sophomore year.

8

My senior class picture, 1950

Quincy Jones Collection

QJ collection (from 1948 Garfield Yearbook)

# Parker Cook, 85, Music Educator at Garfield High School for 43 Years

(Seattle Times, July 16, 1991)
By Melinda Bargreen

Over four decades, Parker Cook became an "institution" in Garfield High School's music department, where he made an enduring mark on the music community through several generations of students, including music luminary Quincy Jones.

Mr. Cook died Sunday (July 14, 1991) at age 85.

A Seattle native, he was a graduate of Franklin High School and the University of Washington, where he received a B.A. and M.A. in music education. He began his career as a law student but switched to music on the advice of his glee-club director and performed for many years as a singer. Mr. Cook sang bass on tour with Fred Waring and his Pennsylvanians, a legendary choral group.

… Dr. Forbes Bottomly, then Seattle superintendent of schools, said at Mr. Cook's retirement festivities, "I don't know how many thousands of young people have gone out into the world better equipped because of the care and consideration given them by Parker Cook."

In 1983, jazz performer and producer Quincy Jones, Mr. Cook's former student, returned to Seattle for concerts at the Paramount Theatre in honor of Jones' 50th birthday. Jones honored Mr. Cook as a "major influence" on his career.

"Parker Cook is a man who had my life in his hands," Jones said then, "and treated it very gently."

Always modest, Mr. Cook responded: "How do you teach a genius? I just stood aside and watched him develop."

I was fortunate to learn, at the very beginning, to play all kinds of music. That was one of the best things that ever happened to me, because I learned that music has a very sincere purpose: to lift the spirit. We used to try to make the schottisches and bar mitzvah music, like "Eli Eli" and stuff, sound like bebop in Seattle, but Ray would say, "Goddammit, don't! Play it true to the spirit of the music! Let each song have its own soul—its own truth." That was the best advice. Ray was only two years older than me, but he was like a hundred years smarter.

*Ray was only two years older than me, but he was like a hundred years smarter.*

Those are great lessons, you know, because lots of guys are snobbish in this business. They think everything should be in one bag. That's BS, man; you play whatever you're capable of playing. If you're true to it, each style of music has its own spirit and it deserves the dignity of having its own space.

There is a huge amount of diversity in all the things we deal with in music. It's really amazing, but it's good. I like it. It's the way I live. It's been wild, man. I think of all the things that have happened because I've kept an open mind—it's just incredible.

# MUSIC WAS MY MOTHER

Lloyd and I had a stepmother that that I don't even like to think about. She was illiterate and mean—just the opposite of our mother. She had three kids of her own, my father and she had three together, and then there was my brother and me—she just called Lloyd and me "Jones's kids." She never even called me by my name until I was 57. When she finally did say, "My son, Quincy," I cried.

But at a young age I said, "I don't have a mother, I don't need one. Music will be my mother." If I had a good family, I might have been a terrible musician. We'll never know, we'll never know. Music never let me down. I went after it, studying with all the passion in my soul.

# WISE OLD ROAD WARRIORS

I learned a lot from the guys in the old-school bands. When I was in Lionel Hampton's band, I'd watch them all the time. We were making $17 a night and I'd watch everything they did. We could go to Father Divine's and eat for 15 cents. You could go in and say, "Peace," and you'd get veal stew and apple pie or something. I learned that I could neatly fold my pants and put them under the mattress at night so they'd be ready to go in the morning. I learned that

WHEN I WAS 15 YEARS OLD, EXCITED ABOUT JOINING THE LIONEL HAMPTON ORCHESTRA, MRS. HAMPTON SCREAMED, "GET THAT CHILD OFF OF THIS BAND BUS AND LET HIM FINISH HIS EDUCATION".

5 YEARS LATER ON A TRAIN LEAVING OSLO, NORWAY, MRS. HAMPTON SCREAMED "IF THEY WON'T LET MY PARROTS ON, THEN TAKE THE WHOLE BAND OFF" (P.S. WE GOT OFF, AND IT WAS COLD!!

THERE WAS ALWAYS A DEPTH & WARM GLOW OF ADMIRATION SURROUNDING THIS STRONG-WOMAN— I'LL NEVER FORGET HER STRENGTH—

LADY GLADYS HAMPTON, A PROUD LADY, WITH VISION WAY AHEAD OF HER TIME. FOR HER LOVED ONES, HER CO-WORKERS, AND HER BLACK BROTHERS & SISTERS. HER SPIRIT IN APPROACHING A DIFFICULT TASK WILL ALWAYS BE FELT IN ALL OF US AS SIGNIFICANT & PROGRESSIVE.

Quincy Jones

11

**12**

Paul Dorpat

The Palomar Theater, where I spent a lot of time with
Basie and the guys, hosted some of the best bands
ever. It was at 3rd and University in downtown Seattle.
It's a parking garage these days!

Quincy Jones Collection

With Billy Eckstine in
the Bumps Blackwell,
Jr., band, 1949.

Quincy Jones Collection

On the road with Lionel Hampton. Hamp c
ould drive a crowd better than anybody.
(L-R) Me, Art Farmer, Hamp, and Gigi Gryce.

14

Clark Terry and me in 1987. Clark was my mentor in the very beginning, and we've always remained close.

Quincy Jones Collection

"Kingfish" was Quincy's first recorded composition and arrangement. It included a rare Quincy Jones trumpet solo. Quincy was heavily influenced by Miles Davis.

Bill Gibson Collection

Quincy Jones Collection

Young Quincy on the road with Lionel Hampton (left to right: Art Farmer, me [18 years old], Hamp, and Walter Williams).

15

a wash-and-wear shirt could be washed and hung up over the tub, near the shower, along with your suit coat—the steam from the hot water did an acceptable job of pressing both. And, if you wash your handkerchief and put it on the mirror wet, the next day it would be dried almost like it had been pressed. I watched all the old guys—they knew all those tricks, man, they knew. I watched them carefully, and they showed me what it was like to survive—they'd been out there 30 years.

I talk a lot now, but I used to sit down, shut up, and listen. I learned a long time ago that there's a reason God gave us two ears and one mouth—it's so we can listen twice as much as we talk. Basie practically adopted me when I was 13. I would play hooky and go down to the Palomar Theater where he would be with Serge Chaloff, Dexter Gordon, Bobby Tucker, and Clark Terry. Basie was my manager and consultant and everything. Ben Webster was also an important influence. When he wanted to share some wisdom with me, he'd say, "Youngblood, step into my office." That's the way they used to talk. "Step into my office, let me pull your coat" was like "Come over here, I want to teach you something." Then he'd tell me something that I needed to know at the time. Basie was also very important in my growth. I specifically remember one time when he pulled me aside and said, "This business is all about hills and valleys"—being the metaphor for good times and bad—"... you find out what you're made out of when you're in the valleys." And I was very lucky to have guys like that put me on their shoulders and tell me about the results of their experience. That's why it comes easy for me to help young guys, because I was given a hand up when I was young.

# FASCINATION WITH SCIENCE

I'm telling you! We used to laugh at Buck Rogers! We don't laugh any more—he's old-school now. Guys in space... you've got to be kidding. Dick Tracy with those funny watches and stuff ... just like cell phones! Everything that happens in a movie is gonna happen in real life—that's for sure. Conventional wisdom at MIT predicts that the first application of nanotechnology will be a $1,000 computer capable of 1 trillion transactions per second. That's a lot, man, compared to silicone microchips that we have now. They predict that by 2019 it'll have the calculation equivalent to one human brain, and that by 2029 it'll have the equivalent to 1,000 human brains. They also predict that by 2099 we won't be able to differentiate between a biological human being and a machine.

Along with Seymour Papert and Jerome Bruner, I'm a board member on Alan Kay's organization called Viewpoints. They made Squeak to be a programming language and a curriculum designed to teach kids math and science. They built Squeak eToys as a learning tool for young children. These guys are the ones building our future, man. Alan is also a board member on my Musiq Foundation, and he is known as the father of the personal computer. At the Xerox Palo Alto Research Center in the early '70s, he invented Smalltalk, the first completely object-oriented programming, authoring, and operating system, including overlapping windows. He also instigated the bitmap screen, screen painting and animation, desktop publishing, and other desk-top media. Along with Robert Taylor, Butler Lampson, and Charles Thacker, Alan developed the first modern networked personal computer, called the Alto, and his work formed the basis of what became the Macintosh and Windows operating systems! And he's one of the midwives in the birth of the Internet, through his work at Palo Alto Research Center. He told me about the Internet 30 years ago. I thought he was smoking Kool-Aid!

## THE DRIVING FORCE

Love, laugh, live, and give; that's what it's about. There's nothing like it. Just to be fortunate enough to help kids and people who are in trouble is a blessing— it really is. I am extremely passionate about that! Whether I'm in the favelas or the Gulf Coast following Katrina or Compton or Soweto or Angkor Wat or South Side of Chicago or Watts, it's all the same. It's the haves and have-nots—I come from the latter. I feel for people in need of help; it's deep in my soul, and I'll never give up doing everything I can to help. People ask me when I'm going to slow down and rest. Rest! I've got a lot that I want to do. You can rest when you're dead!

*Love, laugh, live, and give; that's what it's about.*

## GO TO KNOW

To see these little kids over in Ankor Wat, Cambodia, with no parents and their legs blown off by land mines just destroys me. It's ridiculous for them to suffer for something they didn't have anything to do with. We're gonna do a concert in Columbia this year to raise money to help with the land mines down there. We'll do the same going to Cuba, and Haiti, too. But I love it. It's just like when we went to Iraq in 2003 and Rome in 2004. You've gotta go to know. You've gotta go to see, and to understand it. You have to experience the psychology behind it and feel what the natives feel. And you need to see how they interpret us. It's very important. We can't grow without the knowledge of who the people really are. My friend [auto magnate and philanthropist] Mohammed Jameel commissioned the Gallup Poll people to do a representative survey of 1 billion Muslims regarding how they feel about the West and Europe and vice versa. I think we totally misunderstand each other. No wonder there's a conflict. Again, if you don't have the diagnosis, you can't write a prescription. If you don't know what's wrong, how in hell are you gonna fix it?

# MONEY AND PASSION
## Are Not Enough

On our first real effort to help, we sent over a million dollars' worth of food to a tribe in Ethiopia—this was our three-toes-in-the-water test. The impetus for our first attempt to provide assistance was Live Aid. Harry Belafonte had called Ken Kragen and Lionel Richie and said, "Live Aid is doing something to help, and we're doing nothing." They called me to produce a song to help raise funds because I had just finished a song with Donna Summer called "State of Independence," in which I had put together one-third of the choir that we used on "We Are the World." I'd said I wanted to have the best choir in the world on that tune, so we used Stevie Wonder, Michael Jackson, Lionel Richie, Diana Ross, Chris Cross, and went on to build a great choir sound. So that's why we put "We Are the World" together in the first place, and that's where the money came from to fund this first attempt. Marlon Jackson, Belafonte, and Kragen took all the food over to Ethiopia, but we didn't understand the ground rules, or the ground for that matter, or anything like that. We turned everything over to the government and they tossed it on the desert during the Eritrea conflict and just said, "If the people want it, let them come get it." So it sat there for four days and a million dollars' worth of food spoiled!

Then Bono and I met, and we realized that it was time to go to school, so we just said, "Let's go do it." I introduced him to a lot of the people here in the States, and he did the same for me in Europe. We went to meet Pope Paul in 1999, and he ended up giving us his affirmation that he totally agreed with what we wanted to do with HIPC Third World debt relief! This time, after we had done our homework, it was announced in the *International Herald Tribune* that because of that trip, we got $27.5 billion in debt relief for Mozambique, Bolivia, and the Ivory Coast. That means 20 million kids can go to school now that could have

18

never thought of going to school before. That's a serious accomplishment, man, especially for two raggedy dudes from Ireland—Bono and Bob Geldof—and a brother from Chicago with no agenda other than to help some people who could use a hand.

Up until "We Are the World," we didn't really have a clue about how to go about helping. We had money and we wanted to help, but money and passion aren't enough. We had to learn; we had to study it like a science; we had to figure out how to deal with politics and heads of state and everything. And now we know everybody, and we can really get some stuff done. We're also working with Luis Moreno, who is

Bono and me at the Vatican.

the former ambassador to Colombia and head of the Inter-American Development Bank, to build the most transparent Website ever built. It will tell where every cent goes for all of our upcoming humanitarian efforts.

# WORDS TO LIVE BY

We think we have so much to do with stuff; we aren't in control of anything! Art Linkletter, who passed away recently, has told me for years, "Quincy, if you want to make God laugh, tell him your plans." It's so true, man. I was so blessed to have Art as a friend. In his obituary they mentioned another quote from Art about longevity. He said, "You live between your ears. You can't turn back the clock, but you can rewind it." Art was a very smart man and a good friend.

When I see how everything has turned out, sometimes I just want to pinch myself to see if it's a dream. I think much of our progress though life is based on our attitude about fear and love—on how we choose between them all the time. We choose whether we take a step of defeat or a step of victory. Taking a step of defeat makes you cautious and reticent about everything. That step causes a response of defeat, caution, and fear. A step of victory gives you the energy to take a bigger step next time. Take a giant step and, if you fall on your ass, get back up, quickly. When you keep going with steps of victory, you eventually find that nothing scares you. That's where I am now—absolutely nothing scares me. I've had a lot of chances to make mistakes, but at one point it all turns into experience. You know what to look out for; you've already seen what you should avoid. And don't keep doing the same thing over and over expecting different results—that's insanity. There's really not anything I'm afraid of, because I've been dedicated and I've learned my core skills. I use that as the basis for whatever else I do. I pay attention!

## THE GARFIELD PEN

JUNE 1948

BARBARA FISLER

### At a Glance

...nd one of the clouds, came the moon, lik...
...through the haze.

JOYCE MURRAY, JUNI...

...ser dreams on and on
...are hopeless, it seems,
...n't listen,
...k God for his dreams.
QUINCY JONES, SOPHOMORE

...hioned by God.
CAROL JACKSON, SOPHOMORE

...ls. Instead it is a pattern
...working together.
...RD MITCHELL, JUNIOR

...s mind.
...K SAFLEY, SENIOR

...HOMORE

...IOR

But as a composer dreams on and on
And his dreams are hopeless, it seems,
Even if people don't listen,
He can always thank God for his dreams.

QUINCY JONES, SOPHOMORE

From "The Garfield Pen"
at the end of my sophomore
year. I started dreaming then,
and I still dream now.

## Chapter 2

# SOUL AND SCIENCE

## WHAT IS MUSIC?

Music is all about soul and science. It is the only thing that simultaneously engages both the right brain (emotion) and left brain (intellect). So, when somebody listens to music, their emotion and intellect are both active all the time—you cannot use one without the other.

Music is played in free style from the soul, but it is based on mathematical relationships between pitch and time. I love bebop because the beboppers used every exercise and trick in the book to create a statement that was musical but also intellectual. Bebop was all about getting away from being an entertainer. It was about being intellectual. There is a lot of stuff going on in jazz, but it isn't music until it comes from the soul.

Nicolas Slonimsky and Joseph Schillinger were Russian mathematicians who both studied and documented the mathematical components in music. Both music and math are considered absolutes. Before Berklee I had a scholarship to Seattle University. When I went to Berklee, it was called the Schillinger House of Music after Joseph Schillinger. I studied Schillinger and discovered Slonimsky's *Thesaurus of Musical Intervals and Scales*. I didn't know why it was important at the time—didn't know what it was—but you know, those mathematicians were proving the relationship of absolutes in math and music. When you listen to the patterns in there, you hear Charlie Parker all over the place. Coltrane always had Slonimsky's book with him. Always! I don't know why, but when I saw it I said, "Something is going on here." It grabs your curiosity—gets your attention real fast.

Nicolas Slonimsky's book *Scales and Intervals* is now called *Thesaurus of Scales and Melodic Patterns*. This book completely caught my attention. Coltrane had it with him all the time.

Quincy Jones Collection

24

## Berklee School of Music

**LEARN MUSIC THE WAY QUINCY JONES DID. AT BERKLEE.**

Quincy Jones Collection

Berklee, then called the Schillinger House, was the only college with a jazz curriculum when I attended in 1950. Whatever you do, you need to get an education.

## Milestones

**1945**  Founded by Lawrence Berk, Schillinger House is the first U.S. school to teach the popular music of the time, jazz.

**1950**  Quincy Jones graduates from Garfield High School in Seattle, Washington, looking forward to taking advantage of his music scholarship to Seattle University. Shortly after the start of his first semester at Seattle U., Quincy reads about the jazz program at Schillinger House. He applied by sending them his composition "The Four Winds" and is immediately accepted and given a scholarship. Quincy catches the first train out of Seattle.

**1951**  Quincy leaves Schillinger House to play in Lionel Hampton's band.

**1954**  Schillinger House changes its name to Berklee School of Music.

**1960s**  Berklee recognizes guitar as a principal instrument, and rock music hits the campus.

**1966**  Berklee graduates its first fully accredited baccalaureate degree class.

1970    Berklee School of Music changes name to
        Berklee College of Music.
1971    Duke Ellington receives the college's first
        honorary doctorate.
1979    Berklee establishes the world's first
        undergraduate degree program in film scoring.
1983    Quincy Jones receives honorary doctorate degree
        from Berklee.
1984    The school launches the world's first college-
        level major in music synthesis.
1986    Quincy's son, QD3, attends Berklee.
1987    Berklee begins offering the world's first college-
        level songwriting major. Students spend several
        days in Nashville, attending clinics, concerts,
        and jam sessions, giving birth to an annual
        pilgrimage to Music City.
1991    City Music, Berklee's program to make music
        education available to underserved youths, is
        launched.
1993    The school establishes hand percussion
        as a principal instrument. Founds Berklee
        International Network to support contemporary
        music education globally.
1994    Berklee Center in Los Angeles opens in order
        to build strategic relationships for the college
        throughout the music industry.
1995    Student-run Heavy Rotation Records is launched to
        promote student rock, pop, and hip-hop talent.
1996    Berklee establishes music therapy major.
1999    Hip-hop is incorporated into the curriculum.
2002    Berkleemusic.com, an online music school, is
        launched.
2003    Students found the college's second label, Jazz
        Revelation Records.
2005    Music business/management becomes the most
        populated of the college's 12 majors.
2006    Increases presence of bluegrass on campus
        as mandolin and banjo become principal
        instruments.
2007    The school increases presence of bluegrass
        on campus as mandolin and banjo become
        principal instruments.

# THE WORD OF GOD

I think music is the word of God. I really do. You can't taste it, you can't touch it, you can't see it, and you can't smell it; all you do is feel it. I think it's the most powerful of all the arts.

There are techniques for creating counterpoint, harmony, and so on, but melody comes straight from God—*straight from God!* There's no technique or science for that. I studied with Nadia Boulanger in Paris for about five years. She always said that although music is made up of rhythm, harmony, and melody, melody is king. Counterpoint is a science—it consists of retrograde inversion, or you can play twice as high or low and twice as fast or twice as slow. I've studied every aspect of the science of music—it's an absolute—right alongside mathematics.

It's astounding, because the universe operates at 450 cycles a second. The universal tuning for every orchestra in the world is 440 cycles, which is [the pitch of] A. When an orchestra tunes up, they reference A. It's not an accident that A-440 is so close to 450, which is the rhythm of the universe. So it's a very spiritual thing, you know. It really is.

It's absolutely amazing. Most people remember the song they fell in love to. It sticks in your mind. No legislation can say "It didn't happen then, it happened ten years later." It happened then, and it's just hanging in the universe. That's the way music rolls.

The world has never experienced a period when they had no music—no iPods, TV, radio, CDs, elevator music, nothing. Can you imagine a world like that for a whole month? Not a drop of music? You'd go crazy—you'd go absolutely nuts! I truly believe that the last things to go on this planet will be water and music.

Nadia Boulanger was an amazing teacher, conductor, and musician. I studied with her a few times a week for nearly five years while I was living in Paris.

27

# CORE SKILL

I devoted 28 years of my life developing my core skill and learned all of the principles of music. You have to develop your skills until you really know what you're talking about—really know deep down inside. It's about learning your craft so you have something to offer. It really is about soul and science.

This is Aretha Franklin in 1971. She would sit at the piano and go over and over a line until it would be in-grained in her soul. She worked hard!

The old cliché about success being 10 percent inspiration and 90 percent perspiration is true—you have to know the science. Granted, music is ruled by the soul, but you have to back it up with science. I've had people tell me, "If I could play piano, man, I could be as good as Herbie Hancock." But if you can't really play piano, you can't sound like Herbie Hancock, because Herbie Hancock can play anything, and could since he was six years old. It's really the same with anybody who is truly great— Frank Sinatra, Marvin Gaye, Aretha Franklin, Patti Austin, Stevie Wonder, or anybody. I've seen Aretha sit at a piano and sing a line over and over again. She might sing it 20 or more times, exploring her voice, developing it, finding out what its capabilities are. It's a science, too, and if you don't deal with the science, the soul can't play or sing the way it should. It's astounding!

People ask me how they can get better or be good. I say, get your ass to school and force-feed it! Force-feed it! I really believe that. Parents who have kids that want to do music need to make them get to school. If they don't want to go, make them do it! Because you know, they can't give it back. If you make kids play their scales four hours a day, they're gonna become proficient eventually and then have something to work with.

Even the great jazz musicians who started with music deep in their soul eventually had to learn what they were doing. Nadia Boulanger had really figured the jazz musicians out. She always said, "Jazz musicians are wild, because they shack up with music first and then they court it and marry it later," which is true. Look at any of them—John Lewis, Gil Evans, Bird [Charlie Parker]—they all did the same thing. They'd go out and play for a while, but then they'd go back and study the basics.

It was Nadia's [belief] that "Until they get 13 notes, [they should] learn what everybody out there has done with these 12."

Remember one thing, though: you have to treasure the opportunity to make a lot of mistakes. Because the more mistakes you make, the more you're going to learn. And at some magical, unexplained moment, all of those mistakes, with Band-Aids all the way up to your neck, morph into experience. When you have a lot of experience and have made a lot of mistakes, you have something to offer.

# LIFE FORCE MUSIC
## Versus Classical Music

There's a difference between European classical music and life-force music from Africa. Life-force music from Africa isn't written for virtuosity or concerts or any of that stuff. It's written as an expression for virginity rites, or elephant hunts, or circumcision rites, or just for something to help ease the burden of hard work. Also, life-force music imitates sounds in nature—crickets and monkeys and birds and so forth. It comes straight from the ground—straight from God. That's the power of it and that's why it took over the whole world.

Toscanini told me once after he went to the Amazon and heard real life-force music, "One day this music will crush the hallowed halls of classical music." And he was right! He was right, man.

# AFRICAN INFLUENCE

The two most powerful African influences on American musical culture are: antiphony and significant tone.

*Antiphony* is simply call and response. Components of the African call and response are included in everything from Lester Young and Basie, to doo-wop and the Ink Spots, to hip-hop, to country music. Look at the lyrics to the chorus of "Swing Low, Sweet Chariot."

Swing low, sweet chariot (call)
Comin' for to carry me home (response)
Swing low, sweet chariot (call)
Comin' for to carry me home (response)

In a lot of blues songs, there are three lines in a verse. The first two are the same or similar (the call) and the third tells a little more about the story (the response). Call and response can also be as simple as improvised horn licks in between lyrics of other musical phrases. It's everywhere! Its origins are in African musical culture.

## Significant Tone and Antiphony

by Amiri Baraka

Melodic diversity in African music came not only in the actual arrangements of notes (in terms of Western transcription) but in the singer's vocal interpretation. The "tense, slightly hoarse-sounding vocal techniques of the work songs and the blues stem directly from West African musical tradition. (This kind of singing voice is also common to much other non-Western music.) In African languages the meaning of a word can be changed simply by altering the pitch of the word, or changing its stress— basically, the way one can change the word *yeh* from simple response to stern challenge simply by moving the tongue slightly. Philologists call this "significant tone," the "combination of pitch and timbre" used to produce changes of meaning in words. This was basic to the speech and music of West Africans, and was definitely passed on to the Negroes of the New World.

Another important aspect of African music found very readily in the American Negro's music is the antiphonal singing technique. A leader sings a theme and a chorus answers him. These answers are usually comments on the leader's theme or comments on the answers themselves in improvised verse. The amount of improvisation depends on how long the chorus wishes to continue. And improvisation, another major facet of African music, is certainly one of the strongest survivals in American Negro music.

—from *The LeRoi Jones/Amiri Baraka Reader*, William J. Harris, ed. (Thunder's Mouth Press, 1960)

Africans were also masters of rhythm and tempo. They might play six rhythms in one piece, simultaneously! American audiences have never understood polyrhythm like African audiences. Slave owners took the drums away from the slaves because they were using them to write music and because they were using them as communication devices. When the slaves were freed, in 1865, they got their drums back. As they incorporated them into their music, they often ended up playing in 6/8 or 12/8 with the shuffle, walking, boogie-woogie feel that was the origin of so many blues and rock 'n' roll songs.

While Americans and Europeans were calling the African slaves "savages," they were actually the most rhythmically sophisticated people on the planet. Igor Stravinsky knew it. Claude Debussy knew it. Edvard Grieg knew it. Dvorzak knew it. Picasso knew it. They got it. It's fascinating. There are only 12 notes, and what each culture does with those notes is definitive to their sociology—our music is mostly sociological.

We also thank the early American Africans for the sock cymbal, the drum set, and many new ways of using traditional instruments. It was all very new—that's why it was able to so powerfully impact American music.

# THE PSYCHOLOGY of Music and Sound

There's a reason that Beethoven lasted so long. In addition to the science of music—retrograde inversion, and all that—he used thematic development. Leitmotifs were always recurring and being developed throughout his music. That's very important. It's subconscious and people aren't even aware of it. There's a similar thing in movies that I discovered a long time ago from Robert McKee. It's an imaging system similar to what Edgar Allen Poe used in his writings. Musical ideas and images recur throughout the song, movie, poem, or whatever, and people latch onto them without even knowing it.

In the movies, *Diabolique* and *Casablanca*, there were constant recurrences of images that set the tone for the scenes and developed throughout the story. They acted as counterpoint throughout the movie in the same way Beethoven used musical counterpoint and thematic development in his compositions. The listener, reader, or viewer doesn't really know what's happening most of the time. They just know that they are pulled in farther and farther. It's not loud; it happens way down in the subconscious mind.

I asked [Steven] Spielberg, "Have you known about this stuff for a long time?" and he said, "Yeah." I said, "God damn!" It shocked me, because it immediately reminded me of musical counterpoint. It's the same stuff.

# LISTEN TO GOD'S WHISPERS

I honestly feel that we are a terminal for our higher power. You might say we're a vehicle or an instrument for a higher power. When we write or play music, we're being used by that higher power. Music comes *through* you, not *from* you. Sometimes I've felt it physically. If you believe that music is all about you, then you're not going to do it for very long.

Quincy with
Henry Mancini

You need to trust the whispers of God. Victor Young and Alfred Newman used to tell me, "Don't ever look back. Just write and turn the page and keep going." I also had some other great mentors, including Henry Mancini and Armondo Traviolli, who told me the same thing. And you know, they're right. We're 88 percent subconscious mind and 12 percent conscious mind. It's really all about intuition, our subconscious, and our ability to hear the whispers. Our conscious mind is full of it, because it's all about making judgments like, "Oh, this is gonna be great," or "People are going to hate this," and all that kind of crap. It's not about that. Just go with the truth, go with God's whispers. Believe that you are a terminal for a higher power and you're letting it come through you, that's all. There's no

Quincy Jones Collection

more mystery to it than that. It is not about you.

I really learned this for myself writing for movies. I had to write the main title theme for *The Out-of-Towners*. I was writing for 108 musicians and I was tired. I used to just lie on the floor and put my feet up on the bed to let the blood come back the other way. Or, I'd put my wrists under cold water to help wake up. But what really happens, as you get tired, is you're feeding the problem down to the subconscious mind, which is being affected more by images than literal verbal orders.

On this project, I laid down with my score paper and my pencil and pen but I ended up falling asleep and woke up two hours later than I should have. I had a 10 o'clock session with all 108 musicians and the producer and director and not quite enough time to finish the piece, but you don't show up late for a session like that or you'll never work again. I woke up and didn't even look back. I just let it flow—it's like you can feel it coming through your arms to your mind to your heart to your hand. It's amazing. Just write and listen and let it come through you.

## The Out-of-Towners

**Producer** Paul Nathan
**Director** Arthur Hiller
**Screenplay** Neil Simon
**Cinematography** Andrew Laszlo
**Art Direction** Charles Bailey, Walter H. Tyler
**Music** Quincy Jones
**Film Editing** Fred A. Chulack
**Cast** Jack Lemmon (George Kellerman), Sandy Dennis (Gwen Kellerman), Sandy Baron (Lenny Moyers), Anne Meara (robbery victim), Robert Nichols (passenger), Ann Prentiss (airline stewardess #1), Ron Carey (Barney Polacek), Carlos Montalban (Manuel Vargas), Graham Jarvis (Murray the mugger)

PARAMOUNT PICTURES PRESENTS JACK LEMMON and SANDY DENNIS in A Neil Simon Story • "THE OUT-OF-TOWNERS" Director of Photography ANDREW LASZLO, A.S.C. Film Editor FRED CHULACK • Produced by JALEM PRODUCTIONS, INC. Music by QUINCY JONES • Written by NEIL SIMON Produced by PAUL NATHAN • Directed by ARTHUR HILLER
© 1969 Paramount Pictures Corp. and Jalem Productions Inc. All Rights Reserved.

# WRITING MUSIC

When you've got a great melody and great lyrics, that's when you really have something to offer. All the production in the world isn't going to make up for a bad melody and lyrics. Alan and Marilyn Bergman used to live next door to me, and I did one of their earlier films. When *Heat of the Night* came up, Ray Charles was supposed to do the music, but he just wanted to sing. I took the job and immediately called the Bergmans and said, "We got a gig here!" They don't mess around. They wrote the lyrics for four songs in that picture: "Fowl Owl on the Prowl," "Heat of the Night," "It Sure Is Groovy," and "Bowlegged Polly." It was so much fun.

*You have to go with your instincts. You can't suffer from the paralysis of analysis!*

You have to go with your instincts. You can't suffer from the paralysis of analysis! Studying with Nadia, we'd see seven or eight versions of the same melody with the best composers in history, including the three Bs [Bach, Beethoven, and Brahms]. There is logic in the construction of a melody even though it isn't a science. There's power in octaves and fifths, and in tendency, active, and passive tones. Because there are only 12 notes, there are naturally going to be some similarities between many compositions.

Melody is the power of God. It's crazy how much we don't have to do with a lot of this. The more you learn to listen—to trust your instincts—the better off you'll be. Because it's not all about you—it's just not! In our 12-note system, there are only so many possible combinations of notes and rhythms, but it's not about mathematical predictions regarding pitches and durations; it's about the way those notes reach into the soul of both the listener and the composer. It's about a melody composed out of deep pain and sorrow stimulating that same kind of deep pain and sorrow in the listener—spontaneously or a hundred years later. That's the power of melody!

Listen to music from other cultures. You'll learn a lot about the cultures and the souls of their peoples. Our tonal system contains 12 half steps per octave—the distance between any two adjacent notes is one half step. The tonal systems in the Middle East and some other cultures utilize 24 quarter tones per octave. That opens up a new realm of possibilities.

The people in the Middle East need music. I used to sit in the Sophia Mosque and the Blue Mosque in Istanbul, Turkey, sometimes all night, listening to the singers. The acoustic reverberation in those buildings was incredible, and their songs just made my soul sing. Middle Eastern music is like the blues in so many ways, and, just like the blues, it comes from deep pain. I met Arif Mardin in Ankora, Turkey. He came from one of the wealthiest families in Turkey, but when I was playing there with Dizzy, Arif came up to me and told me that he wanted to do what I did—that he wanted to write bebop. He did a tune called "Schumate's Delight," which we recorded with Dizzy, and then sent it to Schillinger House with a letter of recommendation. He got a scholarship and eventually ended up being made a vice president at Atlantic by Ahmet Ertegun, who knew the Mardin family. I knew he was talented. He went on to create the Bee Gee's sound for *Saturday Night Fever*, write arrangements for Aretha, record Phil Collins's "Take a Look at Me Now," Bette Midler's "Wind Beneath My Wings," Norah Jones, and a lot of other great music. He was the real deal!

It's the pain and emotion in American music—blues, jazz, and rock 'n' roll—that reaches into the deepest part of the soul. That's why every country on earth has pushed their indigenous music aside to make way for American music. It hits the bottom of the soul because it is born out of the emotion and desperation that resides at the bottom of the soul. It's the connection to American music that opens the door to the American culture. I've been watching this development in Europe and all over the world for a long time; you can't tell what country you're in. Whether I'm in Europe, Abu Dhabi, China, or Soweto, I hear American music and I see American culture: cell phones, hip-huggers, flip-flops, and Adidas. It's the same all over the world. It's astounding.

Americans don't have a clue about the rest of the world. Only 12 percent of Americans have passports, and only 6 percent use them. Twenty-five percent of Senate and Congress have passports, and only half of them use them. World-wide, we are viewed as an isolationist country; most Americans don't know about the other places, and most of the time they don't care. It's myopic.

I was going to Europe with Lionel Hampton in 1953, and Ben Webster gave me some of the best advice I've ever had. He told me that the soul of a country is identified by its music, its food, and its language. "Wherever you go, eat the food the real people eat, listen to music the real people listen to, and learn 30 or 40 words in every language." I took Ben's advice very seriously. You don't have to learn the whole language, or eat all the food, or hear all the music, but when you open up to the food, music, and language, you start to understand the people. Start small; learn three or four words and then add a few more, and so on.

When I was in Las Vegas with Frank Sinatra in the '60s, and he assigned bodyguards to every member of the Count Basie Orchestra. My goombah was a

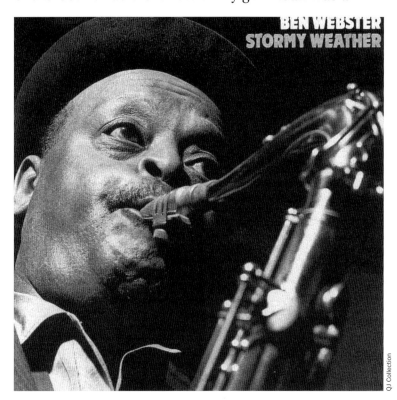

QJ Collection

70-year-old Croatian. Man, he was so tough he could drown a glass of water! He taught me a little Serbo-Croatian, and then I started to study it.

An interest and fascination with different cultures is an important aspect of our humanity and our musicianship. When we learn how other peoples live, we understand them on a new level and we benefit from the new depth they add to our soul. Who you are as a person determines who you are as a musician.

## Chapter 3

# EVOLUTION OF Q: THE MODERN PRODUCER

To follow Quincy's musical history is really to follow the evolution of the modern producer. His growth through the big-band years as an arranger and bandleader set the bar for the expectations we place on anyone claiming to be a producer. It is amazing that through his formative years, Q absorbed and transferred the standards, expectations, and genius of many of the very best musicians of an era. In a single echo of Quincy Jones, we also feel Count Basie, Duke Ellington, Clark Terry, Clifford Brown, Charlie Parker, John Coltrane, Sarah Vaughn, Ella Fitzgerald, Nadia Boulanger, Igor Stravinsky, Maurice Ravel, and the list goes on and on.

## EARLY LESSONS

Quincy is an avid learner. Just spend some time studying him, and you'll soon understand and feel his passion for knowledge and his intense curiosity about everything. In this chapter we see several examples of experiences from which Quincy learned important lessons. Listen closely, and you can almost hear Quincy say, "Oh, I get it!" He doesn't tend to make the same mistake twice.

# LIFE THROUGH THE
## Big-Band Prism

We were junkies; I'm talking about big-band junkies. There's no question about it. We wanted to see every band that came through Seattle. We would have our little bebop leather bags and our cigarettes—I didn't even smoke then, but we were trying to look older because we were only 13 or 14 years old. We would go to the back door, and the bouncer would say, "Where you guys going?" We'd lie, saying, "We're with the band!" It usually worked out fine, because almost all the bands were mixed at that point. Then sometimes we'd say the same thing and they'd go, "No, you're not with the band. Get out of here," because there would be an all-white band like Claude Thornhill or Les Brown.

Sitting next to Art Farmer. We were all big-band junkies.

Quincy Jones Collection

The world of big bands literally became my vocabulary. I lived, breathed, and ate big band! Even at that age, I saw everything through the actions and structure of the band. Four trumpets, four trombones, five saxes, drums, piano, bass, and guitar, all doing something different but doing it together with a common purpose. And to this day, I look at politics, music, and everything from that perspective.

When I put an album together, I look for just the right players at every point—people who are excellent at their core skill. I might have 120 people, including the band, singers, orchestra, and engineers working together. They're all doing different things, but they're all working toward the same result—the creation of a great piece of music. I used exactly the same approach in 2004 with the We Are the Future event in Rome, or at the Clinton inauguration, or on the recording I just produced for the World Expo in China. It's all the same to me—talented people doing what they're good at to realize the common goal in the best way possible.

## BASIE AND THE POCKET

Basie taught me the importance of paying attention to the details a long time ago. He was at Birdland on a Monday rehearsing the band. All of the best arrangers—Thad Jones, Neal Hefti, Johnny Mandel, Ernie Wilkins, and Frank Foster ... the best guys in the business—would show up with new charts for the band on Monday, because the show opened on Tuesday. At that time, getting Basie to play your arrangement was as good as it got. Everyone wanted to be writing for Count Basie or playing in his band.

Neal was the hot guy then. He was the most popular and the best paid—while we were getting $50 for an arrangement, he was getting $125 to $150. He brought in "Lil' Darlin," which he had just recorded on Coral Records with Bob Thiele. Neal passed out the chart and says, "All right guys, here we go," and he counts the band in at about 220 beats per minute. Right away Basie stops the band and says, "Unh, unh ..." and counts the band in again at about 65 beats per minute! And it was magic!

I said, "Man!" One tempo change, and it's like a different tune! At the right tempo you hear those big

STEREO

li'l ol' groovemaker....BASIE!

Basie could put it in the pocket like nobody else. He was the master of finding the right groove.

42

fat harmonies, but at the faster tempo they were just moving by too quickly. Basie went the opposite way than you would have expected. That was a huge lesson for me. That's where I learned to put it in the pocket. There's a pocket where God wants it. There's no other place for it to be—not faster or slower. That's when emotionally it hits you—when you've got it just right, when the tempo is where the tune needs it to be. And Basie got it right away. I was very young then, and that was definitely one of the biggest lessons I ever had on tempo.

Now, as a composer and an arranger who's been going at this a long time, I know that when it's in the pocket, there's nothing to talk about. When it's not working, everybody will say, "Oh, the bass is too high or it's too low or it's too fast or too slow," but when it's right, everybody just sits back and grooves by nodding their heads in tempo. They don't need to say anything, because you've got it—it's stone in the pocket.

## NADIA BOULANGER

Early in my career [1957], there was a great arranger that I really wanted to meet named Sy Oliver who had written several classic charts for Jimmie Lunceford and Tommy Dorsey. I finally got the chance to meet him at the Brill Building, the home of Tin Pan Alley [1619 Broadway in Manhattan]. I told him, "I sure would like to see some of your scores." He said, "I can't do that, I'm the greatest Negro arranger in the world." And I said to myself, "That's exactly what I *don't* want to be. I just want to be the greatest *arranger* in the world." I'm serious. It was a big statement, and it never left me. I said, "Negro? I don't think so." Notes can't tell what color you are, and there are only 12 of them!

I wanted to be a real musician, I really did. I wanted to go all the way with music. At one point everyone needs to decide what he or she was made to do—I knew I was made for music. I didn't have a clue what was coming; I just knew I wanted to be as good as I could possibly be. In those days, the last thing we thought about was money and fame. That was not on our list at all. All of our idols were broke! Charlie Parker died at 35 years old from heroin without a quarter to his name. We didn't come up with a quest to be rich and famous and all this stuff everyone worries about now. We just wanted to do what we wanted to do.

In 1956, George Avakian (from the State Department) sent Dizzy's band to Argentina. While we were there, I had fallen in love with the sound of strings.By 1957, I had done a lot of playing and arranging already, but I knew that without the fundamentals there would be limitations on how good I could become. Although I was ready to go, in the U.S. there were really no steadily working black string arrangers, with the exception of Sy Oliver.

Lalo Schifrin, from Dizzy's band, told me about this great composition teacher in France, who had mentored Igor Stravinsky, Aaron Copeland, Maurice Ravel, Michele Legrand, Philip Glass, and Virgil

When I was on the U.S. State Department Tour with Dizzy Gillespie, Lalo Schifrin told me I should study with Nadia Boulanger in Paris.

43

Quincy Jones Collection

Thomson. He said her name was Nadia Boulanger—the name just resounded in my soul.

Because of my encounter with Sy Oliver and the limitations on black arrangers in the United States, I knew the time had arrived for me to take the next step. Almost at that very moment, I got a call from Nicole Barclay in France. She asked me to come and be the musical director for Barclay Records [Disques]. I said, "Hell yeah! Can I use strings?" and she said, "All you want." I said, "You've got a deal." And I went over as musical director of Barclay Records, which gave me the perfect opportunity to study with Mademoiselle Boulanger.

Eddie Barclay asked me to come to Paris and be his arranger for Barclay Disques. I asked if I could arrange for strings, he said yes, the rest is history. L – R: Henri Salvador, Eddie Barclay, and me.

Nadia changed my life! She was Rumanian, Russian, and French, and she was a really brilliant and strong woman—she was the first woman to conduct the New York Philharmonic. She took me to school, man! You don't just walk in and say, "I want to study with you." She auditions you! So, the first thing she asks me is, "What's the distinguishing feature to the C scale?" I said, "A half step between 3 and 4 and between 7 and 8." She just threw it right back at me and tricked me. She said, "Oh, how about starting on E and coming down, descending?" And that shocked me, because I'd never thought of that in my life! Same rule but backwards! She really opened my mind.

She accepted me as a student, and I signed up for three months—I ended up studying with her for five years. Nadia said, "Learn and listen! Until they find another note, learn what everybody has done with the 12 we have." It's true. I listened to everybody and tried to figure out what they were doing: Alban Berg, Stravinsky, Ravel, and Ellington. I learned from everything.

We studied counterpoint, retrograde, inversion, and harmony in *Histoire du soldat*, *The Rite of Spring*, and other Stravinsky compositions. Eventually I said, "I'd love to talk to you about orchestration," and she comes right back with, "Fine, but before we talk, I want you to take the first 25 bars of Ravel's *Daphnis et Chloé* and, from the transposed score, reduce it back to a six-line concert-pitch sketch." I found out how helpful that was later, because that's what you have to do in film scoring—get everything in a symphony on six lines, plus the percussion line.

So, after I finished it, I took it to her and she said, "Now transpose it up through all 12 steps." I said, "Holy moly!" But she was so right. As I worked through it, I found myself thinking, "I wonder why he added double-stop pizzicato violi, celli, and sometimes harp to the French horn attacks." Well, it was because the French horns don't have any attack. They have incredible sustaining power but no attack. I learned all sorts of lessons working through that exercise—it was just astounding. When I was through, she said, "Now we can talk." And she was right, because I understood so much more than when I first asked her about it. A lot of questions just answered themselves. She knew how to put me through the paces so I'd get it without even talking about it. It eventually became instinctive. This all fit together perfectly with my work at Barclay Records. They had an excellent 55-piece house orchestra that I could use to practice everything I was learning!

Nadia Boulanger always used to say, "Quincy, your music can never be more or less than you are as a human being." And she's right! If you want to be a great musician, start by becoming a better person: really care about people, be loyal, kind, and honest. It's important. It's at the core of what you have to offer as a musician.

In the five years I studied with Nadia, we worked a

lot at her home at 36 Rue Ballou, and in the summers we would go out to the American Conservatory in Fontainebleau. She'd always set up my lesson for last because, she said, "You've already been corrupted, playing jazz in the nightclubs with Ray Charles since you were 13, so I can't treat you like a classical student!" She used to enjoy saying that as a joke, but she also had the insight and instinct to realize the difference between the ways that classical and jazz musicians typically got into music. Later I read that she had said that the most influential students she worked with were Stravinsky and me. I couldn't believe it!

## BREAKING BARRIERS with Duke

One of the greatest memories I have happened during one of my first TV productions, *Duke ... We Love You Madly*. It was a tribute to Duke Ellington, and none of the networks wanted to do it at that time. We searched around and found some footage of Duke receiving the Medal of Freedom at the White House to try to sell the special, and eventually we got CBS involved and it aired in 1973. After it was finished, Duke signed a picture for me that read, "You be the one to de-categorize, American music."

I never forgot that. I feel like somebody has to stand up for what's right. When I was young, I used to say "You can't play this" or "You shouldn't play that," but now I understand that you should just play anything you are able to play. Just be sure to put everything you have into everything you do. I don't like categories, and it really bothers me when I hear people saying they hate this or that kind of music. It's all music! It uses the same 12 notes! I love it all.

*... it really bothers me when I hear people saying they hate this or that kind of music. It's all music! It uses the same 12 notes! I love it all.*

Duke Ellington and me preparing for
*Duke … We Love You Madly.*

## Disrespect for Jazz

My mother once sent me the War Department Education Manual EM 603, *Discovering Music: A Course in Music Appreciation*, by Howard D. McKinney and W. R. Anderson. She was trying to convince me that jazz music wasn't worth pursuing. It didn't work.

From *Discovering Music: A Course in Music Appreciation:*

"Some may start with an enthusiasm for music of the jazz type, but they cannot go far there, for jazz is peculiarly of an inbred, feeble-stock race, incapable of development. In any case, the people for whom it is meant could not understand it if it did develop. Jazz is sterile. It is all right for fun, or as a mild anodyne, like tobacco. But its lack of rhythmical variety (necessitated by its special purpose), its brevity, its repetitiveness and lack of sustained development, together with the fact that commercial reasons prevent its being, as a rule, very well written, all mark it as a side issue, having next to nothing to do with serious music; and consequently it has proved itself entirely useless as a basis for developing the taste of the amateur.

The ambitious listener might better start from the level of Chopin's melodious piano music, or Grieg's northern elegiacs or Tchaikovsky's gorgeous colorfulness."

This second edition military manual had been published in 1943 by the United States Armed Forces Institute, and it was indicative of the attitude toward jazz music for a long time. Imagine how that would make you feel as a kid! It's crazy! It amazes me that, because jazz and the blues evolved from plantations and jook joints, our country treated it as an unworthy and uncivilized form of expression. However, the power and potential it possesses is mighty, and I've been able to witness how it has touched people all over the world, including in America. The transformational effect of our gospel, blues, and jazz music undeniably transcends geographic and cultural boundaries, and it has a profound ability to touch the souls of those who experience it.

## Duke ... We Love You Madly

An all-star tribute to musician
Duke Ellington
CBS-TV, February 11, 1973

**Executive producer** Bud Yorkin
**Producer** Quincy Jones
**Director** Stan Harris
**Music director** Quincy Jones
**Music supervisor**
Luther Henderson, Phil Moore
**With** Count Basie, Sammy Davis,
Ray Charles, Billy Eckstine,
Joe Williams, Tony Bennett,
James Cleveland Choir, Sarah Vaughn, Peggy Lee, Aretha Franklin,
Roberta Flack, and Chicago

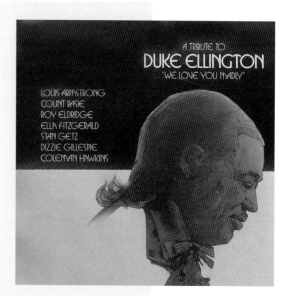

A TRIBUTE TO
DUKE ELLINGTON
"WE LOVE YOU MADLY"

LOUIS ARMSTRONG
COUNT BASIE
ROY ELDRIDGE
ELLA FITZGERALD
STAN GETZ
DIZZIE GILLESPIE
COLEMAN HAWKINS

## On Q

# Phil Ramone

We were doing "It Don't Mean a Thing if It Ain't Got That Swing," and Billy Eckstine and Sarah Vaughn were cursing because they couldn't get the lyrics out. There were cue cards, but it was live and it was in front of the audience and things weren't going so well. They'd sing things like, "I don't give a crap, I can't read the lyric," or "I can't see the words, doowah doowah doowah." So when the director yelled "Next!" I jumped into his truck and I said, "You can't just let this stuff go; these are things we can't fix later." I ran out and told Q, "It's terrifying; we've got to fix it." He said, "Okay, well what do you want?" I said, "We've got to do another take." Anyhow, the second take had a lot of problems, too, so I told Q

I had to get to a studio the next day before the final was handed in. We needed to get a couple sound-alikes so we could do some word fixes, and so on. We had to make changes, but these stars were *gone*. Sammy had to get on a plane after the first two numbers and head to San Francisco for another gig—that's just how it was.

# THE PRICE PAID
# for Modern Musicians

I guarantee you that very few young people in our country know about John Coltrane, Charlie Parker, Duke Ellington, Ella Fitzgerald, or Sarah Vaughn. If you mention any of them, most people don't know what you're talking about, man! It's the hip-hop performers who have the entrepreneurial spirit today. But the American educational system hasn't provided them with a way to learn about the music that preceded them—to understand how many people had to bleed and get beaten and die so they could be where they are today. They don't know anything about the music that preceded them—they just use samples. We used to get 36 requests a week for the rights to use samples. I mean, Tupac's biggest record, "How Do You Want It?" is a sample from *Body Heat.* Ludacris did "Number One Spot" from a sample of "Soul Bossa Nova," which was also the *Austin Powers* theme. And from his album released in 2007 called *Graduation*, Kanye West's "The Good Life" was based on a sample from "P.Y.T." It won awards on MTV and BET, including MTV Jams Jam of the Week Award, Best Hip-Hop Video at the BET Hip-Hop Awards, and Best Special Effects in Video at the MTV Video Music Awards, in addition to reaching No. 4 on the VH1 VSpot Top 20 Countdown.We went through hell and there was a lot of blood laid down—that's what brought us all to this place in time.

# KNOWLEDGE BY FIRE

I never thought I'd ever consider suicide, but I was close, man. One night in Finland, when I was 26 years old, I thought it might be time. I just wanted ten minutes of peace. The pressure was immense, and I had been an idiot to attempt to support 33 people in my band in Europe for ten months—I don't know how we did it!

It was a great band. *Please!* The greatest honor I've ever felt in my life was when Clark Terry and Quentin Jackson left Duke Ellington to come with my band. Can you imagine what it felt like to have the guy who I idolized, and who taught me when I was 12 years old, leave Duke Ellington's band to come play with me? It was incredible! And I had Phil Woods, Sahib Shihab, Bud Johnson, and Buddy Catlett. Buddy and I played our first musical notes together when I was in school. He played sax and went on to be a fantastic musician, playing with Basie and Louis Armstrong and everybody. This band had the best players in the world, and it was very well received all over Europe.

We met up with Harold Nicholas to do performances of the musical *Free and Easy* in Utrecht, Amsterdam, Brussels, and Paris. Harold had also been in *St. Louis Woman*, the original version of *Free and Easy*. Sammy Davis was then supposed to meet us in London to take over for Harold. We would then tighten the show up, and ultimately take the production to Broadway. However, the Algerian crisis happened just as we were opening. It was a very tense time. We could hear machine guns firing during our rehearsals, and several of us were stopped on the streets by police with cocked machine guns. People were afraid to leave their homes at night, so the show quickly lost money. We were told by the producer on Thursday that the show was cancelled and that the following

This road case travelled all over Europe with us, holding the charts for one of the best big bands ever assembled. There are a lot of memories in that case.

Saturday was our only chance at getting guaranteed transportation home, and this was just two weeks before we were to meet Sammy in London. The whole plan had fallen apart. I couldn't stand to see this band, which I considered to be as good as any band in the world, just dissolve. I gathered the band together to propose that we stay in Europe. We knew that this was a great band, and I told them I thought I could line up a tour. They all agreed! For that group of musicians, it was all about making great music. Today, most people care about fame and fortune more than excellence in music. It was different then. So, I had 33 people, 18 band members along with spouses and kids, and two dogs on the road in Europe, with a weekly payroll of over $5,500 to make. It was tough! The band was like a family and they were great, taking any gig we could get just to survive. My life was full of trying to find work for the band, advancing everybody money in whatever currency we happened to be using and getting paid back in another currency. I never missed a week—the band always got paid. That went on for ten months and I was broke. Finally, I found a promoter in Francewho

Now with Mercury Records, I'm standing with Brice Somers, chief executive of the Swiss office of Mercury Records International. Brice and his wife, Clare-Lise, bailed my band and me out by paying for a train—out of their own pocket—to get us out of Yugoslavia. I'll never forget them as long as I live.

52

Quincy Jones Collection

said he could book some gigs for us. He booked 16 gigs and we headed to Paris only to find out that he had taken all the advance money and split!

That was the last straw—my lowest point! I just said, "Enough already!" I called my friend, Irving Green, who founded Mercury Records, and said, "This is it! I'm stuck. I've got 33 people and two dogs and I don't know what to do." Irving advanced me monies against my royalties, I sold my publishing rights for $14,000, and brought the band home by slow boat, on the USS *United States*.

In hindsight, I learned a *lot* from that experience, but it was a close call for me personally. Irving gave me a job at Mercury Records in A&R and as an arranger. Within a year I was vice president and I was on to the next phase of life. I'm just glad now that I didn't do anything stupid when I was really down!

I'm gonna say one thing, though: you have to treasure the opportunity to make a lot of mistakes, because the more mistakes you make, the more you're gonna learn. Experience is a very valuable thing.

3

## On Q

# Phil Woods

Quincy Jones discovered me in the '50s when I was with the Birdland All Stars: Al Cohn and me on saxes and Conte Candoli and Kenny Dorham on trumpets with Sarah Vaughn's rhythm section. Q hired me to be part of the Dizzy Gillespie band that was getting ready for a Middle East tour for the state department. I did all of Quincy's early recordings and took part in the band that went to Europe with the ill-fated show *Free and Easy*, a remake of Harold Arlen's *St. Louis Woman*. Quincy lost a bundle during that year in Europe. When the show folded, Quincy kept the band in Europe booking it himself. Read his [autobiography] *Q* to learn more about this. One time I called him and told him I did not have enough money to buy groceries for my family. He said, "Come over and I'll give you half of what I have." He had 200 francs. He gave me 100! When people say he has too much, I tell them they don't know squat about this great man! His first album was called *This Is How I Feel About Jazz*. I just did a

CD of some of his great tunes and did this one original to be included. The CD is called, appropriately, *This Is How I Feel About Quincy*. It was done for Graham Carter's label, Jazzed Media, and is a heck of a good album if I do say so myself.
—*Reprinted from a post at philwoods.com*

# THE HIT RECORD
## Challenge

Mercury was happy with the music I was putting out, but they said I was a budget buster. Sarah Vaughn, Nina Simone, Dinah Washington, Billy Eckstein, Shirley Horn, and all the other artists I was working with were great musically, but they weren't making hit records.

Everyone else passed on Lesley Gore, but I heard something in her voice that I liked.

In the early '60s, jazz record sales were down and Shelby Singleton at Mercury challenged me to make a hit pop record. I told Shelby that it shouldn't be that big of a deal, and I didn't think it would be.

It was actually more work than I had originally imagined. It was tedious, listening through piles of tapes of really bad singers and terrible songs. I knew how to make something sound good, but I wasn't willing to cross the line, musically, and accept something that wasn't high quality.

One day in an A&R meeting, we listened to a submission from Lesley Gore. Everyone else passed on her, but I heard something in her voice that I liked—she had a mellow distinctive tone and she sang in tune.

Lesley's first single was "It's My Party." When we finished the recording, I went to Carnegie Hall to see Charles Aznavour—we had worked together in France. On the way in I saw Phil Spector, and he mentioned that he had just finished recording "It's My Party" with the Crystals and that it was going to be a smash hit! Freaked me out! I went in

54

Quincy Jones Collection

and said hello to Charles and then hauled booty to Bell Sounds where we cut, packaged up, and mailed 100 acetates to the top radio stations around the country, as fast as humanly possible.

I had to leave the next day for Japan on business, and before I left, I called Lesley to let her know that the next step was to change her last name—I didn't see how the name Gore would work on a hit record. Three weeks later, Irving called me in Japan and let me know that it was too late to change Lesley's last name. "It's My Party" was No. 1! He told me to get my butt home immediately to do an album!

Before "It's My Party," I didn't know that producers got a percentage of the record sales. We sold millions of units on Lesley's first record. Instead of making a lot of money, I made the arranger's fee and my regular salary. My contract with Mercury Records stated that my annual salary as vice president could in no event exceed $40,000! I learned quickly that I wanted to be the producer and that I wanted in on those percentage points! Lesley was 16 when this all happened, and we were blessed with 17 more hits together!

## On Q

# Phil Ramone

He looked at me the first time we recorded Lesley Gore, and he said, "You know, she should double-track this." And I said, "I don't have another machine. We're poor kids here. We have one big multitrack and that's it, we're out of tracks." We had already used all three tracks!

Well, I pulled the erase head off the machine and I said, "You get one chance. You're gonna record on top of your other vocal." By removing the erase head, as soon as you go into record mode, the new vocal records over the existing vocal but nothing is erased—you can hear them both. The only problem is that there is no way to fix a mistake; there's no way to undo it. In addition, if the new part is flawed, you need to rerecord the original part, too, because it has been permanently joined with the new track.

I did things as a child and knew it would work. I wasn't going to bounce the two vocals to a 2-track, mix it, and then fly it back in by hand—there would be no sync, and it would take forever.

We couldn't have tried this if Lesley wasn't really good, but she rehearsed it a couple of times and we knew she could double-track. She's one of those musicians who *knows* what she just sang and she can duplicate it. Some singers know what they sang but aren't able to match it closely enough when they double it on tape. Lesley got it right on the first take, and that's what you hear on the record.

# THE BIRTH OF
# the Producer

When I started as an arranger, I learned to do a lot of the things that a producer does today. The expectations were different then. The producer would tell the arranger, "Call the engineers, get the musicians, write the arrangements, and I'll see you Thursday."

It all started to make sense after our hit with Lesley, when I found Cannonball Adderley and got him signed. On his first album, I called the producer, Bobby Shad, and he said, "I don't need to hear him, I trust you."

I said, "This is the greatest artist I've heard since Charlie Parker." He just said, "I'll see you Tuesday in the studio." And when he got there he just sat down and said, "Take 1."

He was the producer, and I'd just done all of the heavy lifting. So I learned most of the basic fundamentals of producing as an arranger and a conductoron a lot of sessions. One thing led to another, and I started to be the producer.

As the producer, you've got to call a lot of shots. Sometimes you have to bring good or bad news. No matter what you do, it needs to be delivered in a loving and gracious way. You need to know when it's time to push the artist or give them a break. You need to love the person enough to understand their mind-set and, whether they're an instrumentalist or a vocalist, how much stress they've been putting on their chops. If you love the person and you're open and really listening for

God's whispers, you'll be received well and you'll be building the relationship rather than tearing it down. You can simply say, "You know, it's time, I think we need to take a break," or "It's time to play," or just, "Let's relax for a while. Be cool." Nine times out of ten they'll come back and get it done in one take. It's different every time, though. There are no rules; you just have to go with your instincts—the instincts (soul) that you've developed by really knowing your craft (science).

## Chapter 4

# TOOLS FOR SUCCESS

When Quincy Jones starts talking about what it takes to succeed at something, it's time to step up and listen! The following principles and guidelines can be life changing and transformational.

**M**y daddy used to say to my brother, Lloyd, and me, "Once a task is just begun, never leave it 'til it's done. Be the labor great or small, do it well or not at all." *Every* day he said that. That has stuck with me through everything I've done.

> *"Once a task is just begun, never leave it 'til it's done. Be the labor great or small, do it well or not at all."*

## PREPARATION AND LUCK

There's nothing in the world worse than having an opportunity that you're not prepared for. Good luck usually follows the collision of opportunity and preparation—it's a result of that collision. You've got to be prepared. So, make your mistakes now and make them quickly. If you've *made* the mistakes, you *know* what to expect the next time. That's how you become valuable.

One day, when I was working in Paris for Eddie Barclay's record company, Barclay Disques, Eddie's secretary walked in the room and said, "Grace Kelly's office called today and said Mr. Sinatra would like you to bring 55 musicians to the Sporting Club in Monaco for a charity fund-raiser." He wanted me to bring my house band, which included Kenny Clarke, Don Byas, and Stephan Grappelli along with the Blue Stars, who later became the Double-Six (Mimi Perrin, Christiann LeGrand, and Wards Swingle). Obviously, I said, "Hell yes!"

We played with Frank that night. I think maybe six or eight words were exchanged between Frank and me the whole night. I'd never seen anything like him before— he was like something from another planet. It was so magical. That was 1958, and I didn't hear from him until 1962; he called me from Kauai, where he was directing *None But the Brave*. He says, "Q!"—nobody had ever called me that before—"I just heard the record that you arranged for Basie. I've always wanted to do Bart Howard's "In Other Words" ["Fly Me to the Moon"] the way you arranged it, instead of like the original 3/4 version. Would you consider working with Basie and me and our band?" I couldn't have said *yes* fast enough! Especially

**This was our first meeting with Frank Sinatra at the Sporting Club in Monaco (1958). L – R: Eddie Barclay, me, Frank Sinatra.**

Quincy Jones Collection

since I had come up with that arrangement in my hotel room, without a piano, when I couldn't get the notes on the page fast enough.

It all just came together. After Basie practically adopted me when I was 13 years old and we became so very close, who would ever have guessed that I'd be writing hits for him later and working with Frank Sinatra and all that? You can't control it, you know, you can't pick it, that's for sure. It's not in your hands. You're judged on the last thing you do, and you need to just keep on doing your thing, developing your skill, and then let what happens happen. I was just fortunate that I was able to work with, I think, the greatest artists from the last 60 years of American history. All of them: Lionel Hampton, Louis Armstrong, Billie Holiday, Basie, Duke, Ella, Michael, and everybody else, all the way up to the rappers today!

It would have never happened if I wasn't ready—if I wasn't prepared for what was to come. If I wasn't ready, I wouldn't have lasted 20 minutes with Frank. Trust me! Frank would either love you or he'd run over you with a Mack truck. There was no in between. And if you ask Frank Sinatra to jump without a net, you better have your stuff together!

# CORE SKILLS
# of a Musician

On one of my first compositions/arrangements, entitled, "The Four Winds," which got me in the door with both Hampton and Basie, I printed an asterisk with a little note on the Bs throughout the chart that said, "Attention! Play all of these a half-step lower because they sound funny if you play them natural." The guys in the band said, "You just put a flat on the third line at the beginning and then you don't have to write all that stuff all day." But you know, I was 13 years old—I didn't know what I was doing. Passion for something is just not enough. You need to put your time in on the core skills—there's no way around it.

In Malcolm Gladwell's book *Blink,* he talks about knowing something instinctively about a person or a situation. He calls them *slices* of insight. He followed that book up with *Outliers,* in which he makes the important point that the secret to making those instinctive determinations resides in 10,000 hours of study—10,000 hours of practice. So, your insight is guided by your experience. I believe it! I don't care what you do, whether you're a doctor or a carpenter or a musician, if you don't have the science together (practice), your soul (passion) just doesn't have a clue how to get where it wants to go!

If you want to be great, put your time in on the fundamentals. Learn the basics of music and build on that. Learn how to read music. Learn about harmony, counterpoint, leitmotifs, constructing a melody, and definitely orchestration. If it has to do with music, learn it! Learn everything about the kind of music you're into and about every other kind of music. Master your craft. Put your time in!

Some of the rappers are coming to me for help. They're already making money at music, but they're not totally satisfied artistically. I tell them the same things: Learn the fundamentals! Great musicians put a lot of energy into what they do. They put their 10,000 hours in, and more, practicing scales and developing their skills. They learn about music and songwriting and arranging. They study the thing they want to be great at. Then, all of a sudden their soul is released to express itself. Music engages the left and right brain simultaneously without fail. It's an absolute, right along with mathematics. Music affects the emotions and the intellect; always, it pulls at each side. That's why music has a healing effect. Music can positively affect people with Down's syndrome, autism, dyslexia, and more, because it stimulates both right and left sides of the brain, simultaneously.

# CORE SKILLS
## of a Producer

The producer has to be able to take charge of virtually every phase of the creative process. He or she must be able to find and recognize a good song, get the right instrumentalists and background singers, and find the right engineer and studio. You have to be the conductor of everything from the bottom to the top of the project. And, you have to be able to help the artist realize their musical vision and personality while you do everything else. You have to learn about marketing, covers, liner notes, and you have to know enough about all of the instruments to be able to communicate effectively with the players. On top of everything, you need to be a psychiatrist in the studio so you know when to tell the artist to take a break or to keep pushing through. You have to push them, but you can never let them fall. If you have studied and know what you're doing, you can be confident that you can handle whatever comes up.

As a *music* producer you have got to be extremely proficient with *music.* If you expect to have the kind of confidence you'll need as a producer in the studio, you must be proficient in your core musical skills in addition to being able to handle all of the organizational and relational demands placed on the producer.

Whether it was Michael or Frank or Ray Charles, I had no insecurities—I was ready because I had worked so hard. When Frank would say, "That's just a little too dense up front in the first eight, Q," in five minutes I'd fix it. That's what I was born for, man. I'd go to flügelhorns so the high end would mellow out and get out of the way of the vocal or go straight to one of my favorite sounds: four flügelhorns, three alto horns, double bass, four French horns, four trombones, and a tuba. I'd have them all play soft, with no vibrato. That's sexy, man. It's the warmest sound on the planet. It's like painting, man, and you have to be able to respond on a dime.

# SUCCESS AND INTEGRITY

There are many kinds of success. There's the one where you reach your musical goals, and another one where you reach your financial goals—they're different. Reaching musical success involves everything we've been talking about—soul and science. Reaching financial goals involves exposure and fame and everything that goes with that.

When we were young, we didn't want to know about money or fame. You couldn't be playing bebop and looking for those things, that's for sure! Money and bebop had nothing to do with each other. The beboppers were all about revolutionizing music—and that's just what Charlie Parker, Dizzy Gilespie, Miles, Coltrane, and the rest of the guys did.

My financial success just happened to come around because I did some projects I believed in, like Michael Jackson and *We Are the World.* A lot of kids think I started with Michael Jackson. They don't know about Billie Holiday, Ella, Sarah, Sonny Stitt, Cannonball Adderley, Clifford Brown, and all those jazz artists that I worked with for so many years. They don't have a clue that I played with Duke Ellington or that I wrote for Count Basie until he died.

On the other side, the jazz cats looked at me like, "What the hell are you doing." I don't give a rip! You think I'm ashamed of *Thriller*? No! Listen to "Baby Be Mine," the second track on *Thriller.* Rod Temperton wrote that song and it is pure Coltrane. The production has a bass line on it and pop lyrics, but the essence of the song is Coltrane. Rod is just such a great songwriter! He has absorbed music to such an extent that great music comes straight out of him as if it were second nature. That's as hip as you can get!

# CHARCOAL, Watercolors, and Oil

I used to do cartoons and sketches—I was really a junkie and I was actually into art before music. Producing music always reminds me of painting. I would always start with charcoal sketches, then I'd add watercolors, and finally oil. The charcoal sketch defines the basic shapes and proportion in broad terms—that's the way I like to start a production. The trick is to not get locked in right away—that mind-set draws from the jazz mentality. Go with what you feel, but then give everyone else the same canvas. Benefit from the creativity that they bring to the palette. Find the structure on the canvas by defining dynamics, colors, density, and so on.

Sometimes people have a hard time getting started. Steer clear of "paralysis from analysis." Just get started. A lot of times, you just need to stop thinking about it and get started with a contour or a shape or something like that. Start with an image in your soul, and let it out. As the sketch takes shape, we can lay on the watercolors. Charcoal and watercolors can always be changed, but as the structure becomes more established, when the background lines and other basic components are nailed down, it's time to commit and put it in oil. When you get to the oils, that means you've got the background nailed, you've got the melody nailed, you've got countermelodies in place, and you're able to commit. Once it's in oil, it's final—you're closing in on it because you know where you're going. It's just a psychological trick, but it works.

## Monoprint

The people in China wouldn't like a painting of a bowl of fruit, even if Rembrandt or van Gogh painted it! I find that fascinating. I noticed that the longer I looked at many of their paintings, the more things I'd see. For example, what seemed at first to be an organized pattern of small oblong shapes, could turn into a rabbit, or a little girl's faces, or any number of things. Everything was intertwining to form one piece of art, but it was built from connected individual pieces.

I knew there had to be some science involved, so I asked Nate Giorgio, an artist that I deeply admire. He told me that it's called *monoprint* and that it is indeed produced using a scientific process. The Chinese think art should come from the abstraction of the artist's mind, which I love because that's the same way I think about musical voicing and color.

If you take your music from charcoal to watercolors to oil, you leave room for creativity. One of my favorite sayings is "Let's always leave some space for God to walk through the room." I believe in that. The studio is a sacred place, which is why I never wanted a studio in my home. You're looking for something very special to happen in that studio, very mystical and special—something spiritual. That special thing has to happen for the music to be really powerful—for it to have a powerful effect on the listener.

I can't think about what the listener is going to say or about focus groups and all that nonsense. I don't want to hear about what 40 people who are not even involved in music think. Can you really tell me you're going to go against what you feel in your soul and make changes based on that? I don't think so. Go with what you feel in your gut. Listen to the whispers from God. I just go by the goose bumps I get when I hear the music. If the music moves *me*, it'll move somebody else, too. If it doesn't move you but you think it might move someone else, that just doesn't work. On every project I've produced, from the biggest-selling to the least, I just started out saying, "Let's do the best we can." Nobody knows what's gonna happen, ever. All we can do is use everything at our disposal, all of our resources, to make the best music possible—music that touches our soul and our mind.

*I can't think about what the listener is going to say or about focus groups and all that nonsense. I don't want to hear about what 40 people who are not even involved in music think.*

# PRODUCTION STYLE

Always be aware of how the finished product represents the artist. Make the record organic to the artist. The producer should help the artist do a better job than they've ever done before, always making sure that it's still the artist's musical personality portrayed on the record—not the producer's.

You can go into the studio and tell every player exactly what to play. I know how to do that, and sometimes that's what needs to be done. But I've always loved introducing the framework and giving room for creative input from the musicians. Steven Spielberg works exactly the same way. He says, "Let it be everybody's movie." Let the people you work with add their musical personalities over a creatively conceived and grounded structure. Producing music and movies is much more complicated than just letting a bunch of studio musicians loose on a song; however, to me, if you don't find a way to include other musicians' personalities, it's very stiff and limited. I love it when everybody is working together and making a valuable contribution—when I'm getting collective input from all of the players and singers. That's creative power you can't touch. That's what you can't even get with a symphony orchestra.

Each case is different. Sometimes if you're working with someone you don't respect musically, or if you're under major time constraints, you have to call all the shots. If you don't have a mutual respect with the musicians, nothing will ever get done if the producer doesn't jump in and get it done.

When it's right, you can feel it—it just flows. I don't need yes-men. People I work with need to tell me what they feel. I don't need to work with people who just tell me that everything I do is right. That's a waste of time; I don't believe in that BS.

Every time I've ever seen Nelson Mandela, he makes me write down this phrase: *Umuntu ngumuntu ngabantu*, which means "I'm a person, you're a person, because of other persons." I've been involved with Mandela and doing whatever I could with South Africa for close to 40 years—we've grown very close. The overriding survival cry and mantra for South Africa is *ubuntu*, which means that the collective is always stronger than the individual. It's true. That's what music is all about—many people working together, sharing a common creative goal. It's deep and it's ancient.

When you find a way for people to be who they are and still be a part of the whole, you've got something going on. The best music is made when that happens in the studio. Everybody is shocked when they see and feel it happen. It turns me on; it melts me; I love it! And it's the same with all types of music. That's what happened on *Back on the Block*. We had Zulu music, gospel, hip-hop, jazz, and everything else. It's amazing when you're in the middle of it, and it's amazing to hear the music later, too. That's how I like to work, and that's how we like to roll.

## Umuntu Ngumuntu Ngabantu

**Nelson Mandela** explained *ubuntu* as follows:

A traveler through a country would stop at a village and he didn't have to ask for food or for water. Once he stops, the people give him food, entertain him. That is one aspect of ubuntu, but it will have various aspects. Ubuntu does not mean that people should not enrich themselves. The question therefore is: Are you going to do so in order to enable the community around you to be able to improve?

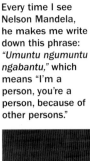

**Archbishop Desmond Tutu** offered a definition in his book, *No Future Without Forgiveness* (Image, 1999).

A person with *ubuntu* is open and available to others, affirming of others, does not feel threatened that others are able and good, for he or she has a proper self-assurance that comes from knowing that he or she belongs in a greater whole and is diminished when others are humiliated or diminished, when others are tortured or oppressed.

**Archbishop Desmond Tutu** further explained *ubuntu* in 2008:

One of the sayings in our country is *ubuntu*—the essence of being human. Ubuntu speaks particularly about the fact that you can't exist as a human being in isolation. It speaks about our interconnectedness. You can't be human all by yourself, and when you have this quality—ubuntu—you are known for your generosity.

We think of ourselves far too frequently as just individuals, separated from one another, whereas you are connected and what you do affects the whole world. When you do well, it spreads out; it is for the whole of humanity.

Every time I see Nelson Mandela, he makes me write down this phrase: *"Umuntu ngumuntu ngabantu,"* which means "I'm a person, you're a person, because of other persons."

68

Quincy Jones Collection

Producing is a spiritual event that is made up of love and connection. When you love somebody, you know their range and what kind of substitutions and chords they like, and you can easily relate to what they're going through. When you love, you go all the way inside the person's creativity. You can help them do their best. It's about love. My Belgian brother Toots Thielemans has always told me that I know how to jiggle his molecules and make him play his booty off.

I've worked with a wide range of people. Each one has a different place on the planet—a different perspective on life. Listen to God's whispers and love the people you work with. Open your soul and listen to the whispers. It's beautiful; it's a great feeling. When everything is right, you can almost see a great performance before they deliver it.

It's the arranger's dream to create an ambiance with each arrangement that's better than the last. The producer must provide a creative environment in the studio where the musicians will contribute the best that they have to offer. If they're not comfortable and if they don't feel love in the room, they won't be able to feel the spirit of the music. The smallest details can be extremely important, even down to the level of the lighting in the studio. I've always tried to create the right environment for the artist to feel comfortable enough to give his or her best performance. On "Secret Garden" we had the lights almost all the way off except for dim lights in the control room just to create an ambiance that could match Barry White's low, sexy tone. The producer has to understand what it takes to provide an atmosphere (lighting, temperature, smell, all of the aspects of the environment) to get the most out of the artist.

## MUSIC AND ARCHITECTURE

My father wanted me to be an architect, which, if you operate on my friend Frank Gehry's premise, I did. He contends that, "If architecture is frozen music, then music must be liquid architecture." And it absolutely is. It *feels* like architecture. The structure of an orchestration, composition, or arrangement is just like the framework that the architect starts with. If the framework, the charcoal, isn't right, the final product will be weak and lack integrity.

Music requires structure—you can't do music without it. Musical structure consists of loud, soft, high, low, fast, slow, verse, chorus, and so on. Freedom is realized within a well-defined structure. Lack of structure might seem like ultimate freedom, but, in most cases, it really leads to disorganized mayhem.

Nadia always told me, "The more restrictions you can find, the more freedom you'll have." It took me a long time to get my arms around that, because it sounded like it was too much restriction, but it's not. If you've got total freedom, you won't write anything; however, if you determine that it will be slow here and dense there, or loud or soft, the music will start to take shape.

*The more restrictions you can find, the more freedom you'll have.* —Nadia Boulanger

The freedom displayed by a brilliant jazz musician seems very spontaneous, and it is in a way, but he or she still relies on chord structure, tempo, and dynamics. The ability to spontaneously improvise, or for the rhythm section to flow smoothly through dynamics and texture, relies on emotion, insight, and experience hanging on structure, framework, and stability.

# DYNAMICS AND COOKING

Dynamics are extremely important. Always remember that it can't be loud unless it gets soft! And after you get the loudest you can, you have to go back down and get quiet—fortissimo doesn't mean a *thing* without pianissimo! It's just like breathing or making love or anything else. Also, you don't start out with the dessert; you have an aperitif and gradually build up to an entrée.

*After you get the loudest you can, you have to go back down and get quiet—fortissimo doesn't mean a thing without pianissimo!*

I have an amazing analogy that ties cooking together with orchestration. The loudest and most prominent instrument in the orchestra is the piccolo. Its equivalent in gustatorial hierarchy is the lemon.

I don't care how much hot sauce and garlic and everything else you include in a dish, lemon will take them all out, just like the piccolo will in the symphony orchestra. So the flavors of food and music are very closely related. In my experience, each different culture is defined by its food, music, and language—these three things tell what the culture's about. It can't be hidden.

When I cook I think about orchestration. Food and music are just very closely intertwined to me. I love cooking! I was blessed to work and hang with Eddie Barclay in France. In addition to being the head of Barclay Records, he was one of the top 40 wine tasters and leading gourmet chefs in France. He had me eating a lot of stuff that this brother from Chicago had never even heard about before, like escargot and frog legs and steak tartare. I learned so much about cooking and technique. The fundamentals of excellent cooking are a great chef and good fresh produce. Neither one works without the other. I used to bring a lot of food into sessions. I make a mean chicken sandwich and a nice lemon meringue pie—I put lime in the meringue and make my own crust and everything. I love music and, as much as I love cooking, I love to eat.

71

## Thriller Ribs

This is one of my recipes for ribs that Oprah has at the top of her list. She's had them on her show a few times! It's her favorite rib recipe of all time. They can make you cry, they're so good. You use baby back ribs and three colors of peppers, minced garlic, lemon, and Spike seasoning, and so on. It's quite a process to put them together, but oh, man—they're worth it!

Take a rack of baby back ribs. Cook slowly—we're talking eight hours. Serve to your best friends on earth.

## Quincy Jones's Thriller Ribs

**Ingredients:**
- [ ] 2 teaspoons Spike seasoning
- [ ] 1 teaspoon Accent seasoning
- [ ] ½ teaspoon freshly ground black pepper
- [ ] 5 racks baby back ribs (about 5 pounds)
- [ ] 6 cloves garlic, minced
- [ ] 2 large jalapeno peppers, minced
- [ ] 2 large onions, halved and thinly sliced
- [ ] 2 green bell peppers, thinly sliced
- [ ] 2 red bell peppers, thinly sliced
- [ ] 2 yellow bell peppers, thinly sliced

**Directions:** In a cup, combine Spike and Accent seasonings and black pepper. Sprinkle ¼ tsp seasoning mixture on each side of the rib racks. In a small bowl, combine the minced garlic, jalapeño peppers, and remaining seasoning mixture. Rub the garlic mixture on the top and bottom of the ribs. Line a large roasting pan (1⁷/ x 11½ inches) with enough foil to wrap all the ribs. Spread a layer of onions and bell peppers on top of the foil. Place two rib racks, side by side, on the vegetables. Continue to layer the onions and peppers and the ribs. Tightly wrap the marinated ribs in the foil and refrigerate for two days.

Remove the pan from the refrigerator and let it sit at room temperature for 30 minutes. Preheat the oven to 400°.

Before placing the ribs in the oven, reduce the temperature to 300°. Bake the foil-wrapped ribs for 6 to 8 hours. Remove

the ribs. Spoon off the fat from the liquid in the pan and discard, reserving the pan juices. Cut each rack into three sections and serve with the vegetables and pan juices, plus sides of rice and chopped tomato-and-cucumber salad.
Serves eight people.

**Recommended ingredients:** Spike seasoning is a special blend of 38 herbs, vegetables, and exotic spices, combined with a bit of salt. It can be found in most major grocery stores with the spices or salt. Accent seasoning is also called MSG (monosodium glutamate). It is not a favored seasoning or enhancer in the United States, because many people are allergic to it. It is an optional seasoning and can very easily be left out of recipes. —*Recipe from oprah.com*

# GREATNESS

To be great, a musician should discover everything that happened before them—*that's* what's really important. When singers come to me and say, "Mr. Jones, how can I become a great singer?" I advise them to collect one song from each of their ten all-time favorite singers—singers that they really love and respect with all their heart and soul. Listen to those songs, focus on the vocals, and copy every note. At some point, you internalize the musical attributes of the artists you study. Through that process, the singer or instrumentalist's musical soul is released to express itself in a related but unique way. You get the chance to walk in the shoes of the giants and inhale the air at 50,000 feet. The end result will enhance your own creativity and give you more freedom of expression.

We see that process manifested over and over throughout the evolution of musical styles and genres. For example, check out Buddy Bolden, King Oliver, Louis Armstrong, Roy Eldridge, and Dizzy Gillespie. They're a perfect example of the genesis and evolution of a particular style of jazz trumpet. Buddy Bolden's band started playing in New Orleans in 1895. He's credited as the first bandleader to play the improvised music that later became known as jazz. King Oliver copied Buddy Bolden, Louis Armstrong copied King Oliver, Roy Eldridge copied Louis Armstrong. At each step in this evolutionary process, the student learns from—and absorbs elements of the creativity of—the master. He is then able to release his own unique, yet influenced, musical soul and personality. Dizzy Gillespie copied Roy Eldridge, but then turned the corner to bebop with Charlie Parker, playing faster, higher, and also extending outside the more traditional harmonic and melodic boundaries of his predecessors.

Musicians are all connected to the viral evolution of what preceded them. You can't get to where you're going if you don't know where you came from. That's the driving force behind the new curriculum we're developing in the Quincy Jones Music Consortium. You've got to understand the journey from African life-force music to the far-reaching influence of the Spanish Inquisition on the Moores/Berbers, which influenced everything from the flamenco dances and music in Spain to the Moorish architecture of the Kremlin in Moscow. Meanwhile, the slave trade ignited through the middle passage from West Africa to Brazil to Haiti to Cuba to Puerto Rico to the Caribbean, and finally with the slave ships arriving in Virginia and Louisiana. It's all tied together; it's what has delivered us to where we are right now; it is some juicy global gumbo!

Jazz absorbed everything in its path: quadrilles, marching bands, and classical music, whatever, just like the jig from Ireland evolved into tap dancing. In the mid 1800s, when Adolphe Sax invented the saxophone in Brussels, he had no idea how that instrument would be used by Chu Berry, Coleman Hawkins, John Coltrane, Lester Young, King Curtis, or Charlie Parker—not a chance! Ravel saw the future in *Bolero*, but he still had no idea what was going to happen when the sax hit America.

Through the evolution of the modern singer, vocalists weren't anything unless they could sing and phrase like great jazz musicians. Ella, Sarah, Peggy Lee, Sinatra, and even Bessie Smith had their thing together, which explained why they could have careers that spanned 70 years! It's an ongoing saga, in which we're all connected to what came before us. It's amazing!

# ALBUM SEQUENCING

Two of the producer's jobs that are incredibly important are picking the songs and sequencing the album. To sequence an album is to determine the order of its songs. Sequencing is fundamental to an album's success; it can determine whether the listener progresses through the entire album, or becomes distracted and moves on to something else. Once you find the right sequence, each consecutive song draws the listener forward—they're compelled to keep listening.

People ask me about this all the time. They say, "What's your formula?" Hell, there's no formula! You go with what's real, with what fits, with what your instincts tell you. Each situation is different, so you could never make a template. It's different every time—every album has its own personality. You couldn't use a formula if you tried. But you almost always know immediately when it's right.

The singers I worked with, prior to Sinatra, would have their secretary write the setlist down on a legal pad, including 14 songs, followed by false bows and encores. When the singer wanted to change the order of songs, the secretary would need to rewrite the whole list. Frank had the moxie to use 3-by-5-inch cards with one song title written on each card. To try a different sequence, you just needed to shuffle the cards around. As soon as I saw that, I said, "Now you're talking! That's how to do it!"

I put this technique to use right away when we opened at the Sands with Count Basie. We had to reorchestrate all of Nelson Riddle's arrangement to adapt to the instrumentation of the Count Basie band. That's not easy. To duplicate the effect of the string section, I used the brass in buckets, with a melodic top line doubled by three flutes in unison. I finished "My Kind of Town" last. I was really trying to leave no prisoners with this arrangement—nothing could follow it. When Frank made up the list, he opened with it! I met with him in private and showed him how we could shuffle the cards to end with "My Kind of Town." He was able to instantly see it; that's the order we went with for the show, and that's the order that went on the album. The rest is history.

## LEAVE ROOM
## for the Vocals

Arranging so there is room for the vocals is not just a trial-and-error process. You have to draw on your knowledge and experience to build the pieces of the arrangement so they work together instead of fighting against each other. I take it as far as I can, every time. I go after it! That's how it works. If I slip and miss a few things, I just go back in and fix them. And then if I find something else that needs to be changed, I'll go after that. Every time, though, I go for the throat. It has to be right! That's one of the reasons our work with Michael was so powerful. In addition to Bruce Swedien's sonic expertise and Michael's talent, I had Jerry Hey, Rod Temperton, and Greg Phillinganes who also thought through the arrangements and helped me build parts that worked powerfully together.

You have to adjust the density throughout the song to make room for the vocals. When the voice is happening, drop something out of the texture or change a voicing so the notes in the background are out of the melody's range. Control of these details was very important when I was writing for a vocalist with big-band accompaniment, because it had to work well live! It's tricky because, if you do it right, you'll make sure that the instrumental parts aren't walking all over the vocals. It's worth structuring the arrangement to make room for the voice. The trick to making space for the vocals is in the arrangement and the mix, but if the arrangement is right, the mix will come together with a lot less effort.

## CREATIVITY AND
## Alpha Brain Waves

We're born in an alpha brain-wave state—it's the most creative state of mind—and we spend much of our time there in our first few years of life. Leonard Bernstein, who was a close friend, told me time and time again that he and Sondheim wrote *West Side Story* in the alpha state. Bernstein said he would lie on his couch, put one leg over the side, and relax until he reached the point just between being asleep and being awake. That's when you're most creative.

I function in the alpha state when I'm producing. That's something I've been doing for more than 60 years, since I was 13. I can't help it. So, when some clown would say, "Quincy doesn't do anything! He just sits there holding his head in his hands," I knew they were just unaware of what was really going on. Sometimes I didn't know what they were talking about and they didn't know what I was talking about.

Technically and medically, if you want to achieve an alpha brain-wave state, you must concentrate on stopping your heart. You can't really stop your heart with your mind, but the fact that the mind is trying to stop it will put you in an automatic alpha state. I learned that in 1974 when the doctors were helping me to keep from getting too excited and rupturing my second aneurism. It works! It's where your creativity can flow.

# IT'S NOT A BLOCK—
## It's a Process

I've been asked if I ever get writer's block and how I motivate myself to keep going. It's not about a block. It's about programming the 88 percent of your mind that is subconscious; the remaining 12 percent is the conscious mind—it's full of doo-doo. It's the subconscious mind that you have to try to engage. Take yourself further down into the subconscious, alpha, state of mind, and bring the task with you. It's not a block; it's a process. And so you relax and think about the problem, and then you just try to see the end of it—where you're going and everything else. Sometimes I put my legs up on the bed and I lie on the floor. With my back on the floor and with my music pad and pencil ready to go, I can relax and find the alpha state. I'll wake up four hours later, man, and there are ten pages of music I'm writing— that's the way the subconscious mind works. Victor Young used to tell me, "Man, don't even look back. Just keep going, keep writing it, man, because it's coming

77

from a higher power, you know. It's not you."

You've just gotta get out of your own way. I actually feel it sometimes. I feel like somebody takes over my arms, my heart, and my head. That's how I put my deepest feelings down. When you orchestrate a lot of music, you learn how to put anything you feel down on paper—you learn how to express yourself. I used to always test my stuff to make sure it sounded like it was just thought of, that it was fresh, and that it didn't sound contrived. All of the other composers and arrangers were doing the same kinds of things: crossing bar lines, stretching out the syncopation, the duration of the notes, and all that. It's mandatory that you have complete control over the science aspects of music. That's what supplies the subconscious mind with a sufficient and acceptable range of options.

## BUSINESS

I wish I had all the answers to the current state of the music business. One thing is for sure, though, we have got to change everything, because the old way of doing things is over. I'm sorry, but we're down 44 percent this year, and that doesn't leave us very much time until it's all gone! The problem really hit when we made the switch from vinyl to digital CDs. Would you believe that binary numbers started in Egypt in 3500 BC?!

When the music business was a viable business, the producer made money on a percentage of the album sales. One percent was called a *point*. Depending on the level of the artist, he or she might get 15 to 25 points on an album and from that, would typically assign between 2 and 6 points to the producer. I would get 5 or 6 points, which is very good, but the producer deserves that. If the album doesn't do well, everyone will look to the producer and say, "It was your fault." So if it does well it should be your fault, too. Please! The tracks don't just jump onto the recorder. The producer has to have skill and experience along with the ability to guide the vision to completion. Nobody knew what we were doing on *Thriller*, man. Not even Michael.

Somebody who is new to the business should start by reading Don Passman's book, *All You Need to Know About the Music Business* [Free Press, 2009]. It will provide the complete catechism into the business. You have to put your soul in it and learn how these deals work. You need to know about publishing deals and how to function in the music business. It's very important, and it's all changing. Don is brilliant and he's been deep in the music business for a long time. He is with the Los Angeles-based firm of Gang, Tyre, Ramer, and Brown, Inc.

# ADVICE

Work hard and learn everything about your core skill—everything! Once you've done that, you can trust your instincts because they'll be fed by what you have absorbed and internalized. It wasn't until I'd studied conventional orchestration and really had a solid understanding of what it involved that I started to mix it up. Experimenting with different textures and voicings became a part of my production and arranging style. I mentioned previously that my favorite instrumentation combines just the right balance of flügelhorns, flutes, French horns, trombones, and tuba. To me, that is the most beautiful sound in the world. It's not a traditional instrumentation, but I needed to go through everything else I had done previously to discover it.

Maintain a very open mind and an intense curiosity. Just be curious about stuff and be a learner. Your instincts reflect your background and who you've become—learn to feed them with new experiences, and learn to trust them!

# Chapter 5

# THE ENGINEERS

**I**equate the recording engineer with the DP (director of photography) in a film. If the DP doesn't do his job, everything you do doesn't mean a thing. If he doesn't capture the performances with the personality and quality you had in your mind, you have nothing—you're wasting your time! The engineer is an extremely important part of the production.

I've been blessed to work with the very best engineers from New York to Europe to L.A.: Rudy Van Gelder, Phil Ramone, Bruce Swedien, Al Schmidt, Francis Buckley, Mick Guzauski, Tommy Vicari, and Gerhard Lehrner, who did a lot of the stuff in France. The engineer is as crucial to the final outcome as any instrumentalist or singer. Again, I look at the production in the same way I look at a big band—it's about getting just the right players in all the chairs. The tracking engineer, mixing engineer, and mastering engineer are fundamentally important to the production. Like the instrumentalists and singers, the engineers must be operating at peak levels in their area of specialization—they must be fully versed, technically proficient, creatively free in their particular core skill, and last but not least, visionary.

The musicians, songwriters, background singers, engineers, and so forth are like the cast in a movie—it's true. Each player has his or her own part that is crucial in the big picture. The producer must keep an open mind in order to get a project done in the best way possible because things are always changing—they're fluid. But, what the engineer provides is structural; it's foundational; it's very important.

# PHIL RAMONE

Phil Ramone is like my blood brother. We spent so much time in the studio that it's impossible to describe. Everything: Lesley Gore, Shirley Horn, and everything you can imagine. We did just *hundreds* of sessions. All of those amazing sessions and Jim & Andy's bar downstairs were incredible! It's unbelievable.

## Jim & Andy's

Jim & Andy's bar hosted the best jazz musicians of all time. It was like home to many. A&R Studios was just upstairs, and Phil Ramone had an intercom wired directly into the bar, just in case someone needed another player.

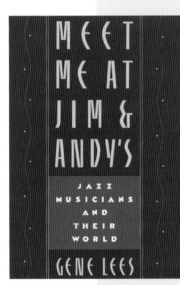

Jim & Andy's was one of those New York bars that become centers of an art or an industry. Jazz musicians had Jim & Andy's, located about 60 paces west of Sixth Avenue on 48th Street.

Its entrance was obscured by a flight of steps rising to an adjacent building. It was easy to pass by, particularly at night, for the small pink electric sign in its window, *Jim & Andy*, was muted by the more assertive neon voices around it. You descended into Jim & Andy's on a slight ramp with a fall of about a foot. The place had a curious cavelike sense of safety about it that, to men in an insecure profession, was undoubtedly part of its appeal.

It was not uncommon to walk into Jim & Andy's in the late afternoon and encounter Gerry Mulligan, Lalo Schifrin, Alec Wilder, Eddie Safranski, Marion Evans, Mundell Lowe, George Barnes, Carl Kress, Clark Terry, [or any other great jazz musician]. Occasionally Harry Belafonte, Lena Horne, Sarah Vaughan, or Tony Bennett would drift in …

A postcard-covered bulletin board near the front door kept everyone up to date on friends who were out on the road. The coat closet was so jammed with instrument cases that nobody was ever able to hang a coat there. The jukebox had probably the best selection of any in the country but it was rarely played.

—from *Meet Me at Jim & Andy's: Jazz Musicians and Their World*, by Gene Lees (Oxford University Press, 1988)

Phil's a master of the studio, and he has been since the first time we worked together. And we didn't have any technology back then. With Lesley Gore, it would take us four hours to get one voice-over done. Double the lead vocal in four hours? *Pleeze!* Today you can layer 200 vocals in Pro Tools and not even think about it! But back then all we had was Sel-Sync, and we had to take the stereo pair and sync up a separate mono tape *with* that. I knew George Martin then, and he was in England starting the Beatles up at EMI. We used to break champagne over the phone, excited because, "Man, we got the voice-over, the double voice!" Lesley Gore was the second person to double-track. Steve Lawrence double-tracked "Go Away Little Girl" about three years earlier.

Phil was an excellent violinist, a fine musician, and he really knew what was going on—he has great ears. He captured sounds that you can't replicate. They tried to replicate "Soul Bossa Nova" for the *Austin Powers* movies but just couldn't do it, largely because of the sound that Phil got back in 1962 at A&R Studios in New York City!

Phil is a producer, too. I think *Smackwater Jack* was one of the first albums that he had coproduction credits on. He started producing and coproducing a lot after that. We've been friends through everything.

## On Q

# Phil Ramone

A&R was this big funky room on top of a building, what I called the basement in the sky. I think the first job we did together was a big-band ad in 1959, with Andy Williams singing Quincy's arrangement about joining the army or something like that. It was very swinging; we got along really well. My lifetime friend Dave Grusin was on piano.

The next time we worked together, still in 1959, was when Atlantic booked A&R to record *The Genius of Ray Charles*. That album became iconic and Quincy had written most of the charts. We were originally going to record Ray's eight- or ten-piece horn section with his rhythm section, but on the day of the session I kept seeing more guys walking in. I said to Q, "What happening?" and he said, "Oh yeah, most of Basie's band's gonna show up, too." I laughed and said, "Oh cool, I'll start working on how we're gonna do that." I was like the second assistant at that point. The head engineers were Bill Schwartau and Tom Dowd. You know … the elite. By the time the album was done, Q and I had become really close friends.

In a session with Phil Ramone (left) and remixer Don Hahn (center).

Q just had this amazing relationship with musicians. You really saw it as he was working with these two bands mixed together. The charts were incredible; they're historic; many of them were Quincy's.

Sometime within the next year, Q became the vice president of Mercury Records. Irv Green, who was the owner of the company, loved Q, just loved him. Mercury had two kinds of music: R&B and jazz. Mercury had a great jazz catalog that was released under their jazz label, EmArcy.

## Finding the Niche

There were a lot of guys finding their niche in the '50s and '60s. Quincy had something in his charts that other people didn't quite have. Billy May had a huge sense of humor in

Quincy Jones Collection

Conducting a session at Phil Ramone's A&R Studios in New York City.

his writing, and Quincy did too, but Quincy just had something intangible that was his alone.

We were two raggedy guys, there's no question. Between his friends and mine, there was always an opportunity to party—we enjoyed life. We weren't bad guys by any means; we just enjoyed the joy of people. We always had too many people around us, having fun, but it wasn't like the posse of today. It was a different kind of posse.

There was a famous bar next to the studio: Jim & Andy's Bar. There's been one book written about it but it needs more, because every player, every writer, everybody came in: Cosby, Bob Hope, and all the musicians. I had a talkback system from the control room straight into the bar. I'd just push the button and say, "I need a trombone player. *Now*," or "Is there a guitar player in there? The chart says two guitars and the other guy didn't show up," or "Is Snooky there? Great. Snooky, what are you doing? Well, come up for an hour."

[Trumpeter Snooky Young was one of the premiere session musicians in New York for many years. He eventually moved to Los Angeles, became a mainstay session player, and was a regular in the *Tonight Show* orchestra during Johnny Carson's tenure.]

It was something very special. There was nothing that existed in New York like it. The studios were so busy that the musicians would just run from one studio to the next.

We had to have drums and all of the big instruments in the studio, because there was no time to get everything torn down and set up at the next session.

## Q Special

When Q went on the stage, there was no discussion, just as there was no discussion with the Basie band or Duke; the audience knew something special was about to happen. They skyrocketed, in the early '60s, into the icons that they became, but Quincy was the youngster in that group. He was very young, even at that time, and he represents a cross-culture in a record company that was steeped in *old* tradition. He woke everybody up. I mean, he woke *everybody* up.

The minute he made a pop hit, they said, "What is that? Who? Why would he be called for that?" It's the same thing they said at Columbia Records when Michael was gonna work with Quincy Jones. "You're crazy. Michael's a pop artist. What's he doing with Quincy Jones? Quincy's a jazz guy!" They weren't jumping up and down about Quincy.

One of the things I learned from Quincy was to not let people put you in a pigeonhole. In all the years I've ever had any kind of success, I've tried to be open to new ideas and experiences. I was a classically trained kid who broke every rule at 11 or 12 years old to play jazz. If they caught me in school playing jazz, they'd say, "No, no, no, no, no, you must play the classics. You're

Quincy woke everybody up in the record business as soon as he had a hit with Lesley Gore. They kept saying, "Why did he get called for that kind of record?"

a violinist." I'd say, "I'm a fiddle player, man." I just have always wanted the freedom to experience different things in life without someone else trying to put restrictions on me.

## Swagger

Quincy brings energy to the room that's magnetic; people play differently when they're around him. Inside, the musician says, "Wait a minute. What is it I'm doing here? I'm playing a Quincy Jones chart and Quincy is conducting and ..." There's a lot that goes through the player's mind, but it's not about playing on top of the beat or behind the beat or wherever. It's about the swagger. Quincy writes for swagger—he *creates* swagger.

# BRUCE SWEDIEN

When you record the music right—get the right amount of reverb on it, blend it just right, and pay attention to the right things—people don't know how to reproduce it. Everywhere I go in the world—Jimmy's in Monte Carlo, Abu Dhabi, Cairo, Rio, Shanghai, or wherever—they play all our music: "Ai No Corrida," "Give Me the Night," the Brothers Johnson's "Stomp!" and they play all of Michael's stuff. It's incredible. I mean 30 years later! It really shocks me. The DJs know the sonic power of what Bruce put on there. It's amazing and very powerful.

Bruce is absolutely fantastic—the best! No matter what they do today, with the Pro Tools and stuff like that, Bruce's Acusonic sound blows them off the floor. He took the art of recording to a new level and has defined the sound of recorded music in many ways.

Bruce wanted to record everything using stereo pairs of microphones, which meant we needed a lot more tracks. So he used SMPTE timecode to lock as many 24-track machines together as we needed. Bruce is a master engineer. The stereo tracks that he was able to capture were powerful, plus they had a distinct sonic personality that you just couldn't get in mono. That's why great engineers and artists today, 25 or 30 years later, still go to our music as a reference—that could be

Quincy Jones Collection

Bruce is absolutely fantastic—the best! No matter what they do today, with Pro Tools and stuff like that, Bruce's Acusonic sound blows them off the floor.

Kanye or Jay-Z, or anybody! We also had learned to limit each side of the album to 18 or 19 minutes to keep the grooves as big as possible on the vinyl.

Bruce and I met in Chicago at Universal Studios in 1954, where I recorded Dinah Washington and then Count Basie a little later in 1959. We locked right away. When I was in New York, I worked with Phil most of the time, but when I moved to Los Angeles Bruce and I connected. It's been great. We've had a lot of fun, man.

## On Q
# Bruce Swedien

Quincy is the most honorable man you'll ever meet, and he's the most genuine individual that you'll ever come across in life. Quincy is one of a kind, and what you see is what you get. He's the greatest. There's nobody like him.

The first time I worked with Quincy was on "What a Difference a Day Makes" and four other songs for Dinah Washington in May, 1954. He came to Universal in Chicago and we hit it off right away. Jack Tracey actually produced those Dinah Washington records, but in those days the producer was different than today. Quincy was the musical driving force that supported those incredible pieces of music.

Whether Quincy was working with Dinah, or Michael, or really anybody, he would always put the artist at ease in whatever the situation. For instance, Quincy always had Michael learn the lyrics from memory—he would never record Michael until he didn't need the lyric sheet in front of him. I think that Quincy did that with a bunch of other people, too. If the artist knows the lyrics from memory and interprets them from memory, their instincts are going to be different. They're going to be better, perhaps more real. It changes everything.

Quincy almost never uses musical terms to describe what he wants out of the musicians. He uses food-related terms. Personally, I think that if Quincy hadn't been one of the real musical big wheels of the century, he would have been a world-famous chef. Quincy can make the best lemon meringue pie you've ever had in your life. He does salmon and chicken salad and all sorts of things that you wouldn't expect. Food and music—they're both sensory related. I think that's basically where they're related.

*Off the Wall* was the first truly solo album that Michael Jackson had done. I think that it's definitely Michael's coming-of-age masterpiece. And Quincy executed Michael's musical desires to a "T." I think that's why that worked so well. There's no way to tell in advance if a record will be a hit or, especially something like *Thriller,* the biggest-selling record of all time. You can't know those things. However, we did know with Michael that we had some pretty special material and pretty special performances by him on these albums.

On different projects Quincy frequently threw out the

weakest songs for the vision of the album, and then tried to replace them with tunes that were better than the rest. The only thing about working with Quincy and Michael is that it's done at a different level. I mean, most of Michael's scratch tracks, his demos—people would give anything to have those as finished tracks. But Michael, Quincy, and I had a desire to do something *really* different, *really* special, and I think that's the way it worked out.

Quincy was great at bringing in a lot of talented musicians from a lot of different genres, but I don't recall anyone ever questioning Quincy's musical motives in any of the productions that we did. Quincy was so obviously head and shoulders above anyone else in music. And people don't usually know that Quincy's musical background is so legitimate. With Quincy, we're talking about someone who studied in Paris for years with the same teacher that taught Stravinsky and Steven Reich! It's really phenomenal when you realize that you're working with someone at that level.

Even though Quincy has always operated on the highest musical plane, his sessions were always smooth and effortless. It was easy to be creative working with him. His sessions would never be complicated at all. Quincy knows how to make people feel comfortable in the studio, and he knows what it takes to be prepared for a session. It might all come together at the last minute, but it comes together.

I remember doing a session for *The Wiz* where we were recording the main titles. We entertained some friends in our suite at the Drake Hotel on Sunday night, and the first big session, with all of the musicians, was booked for the next morning; Quincy didn't have a note on paper. Quincy has figured out that a deadline staring you in the face will coerce the best that you have to offer the music. I remember waking up at 4 o'clock in the morning, looking out my hotel door, and seeing all the lights on in the dining room and there was manuscript paper everywhere. Quincy was up, literally up the whole night the night before the orchestra came to the studio, orchestrating the opening titles. Now, that has happened on more than one occasion.

Even though Quincy can push hard to make a deadline, I think his real goal has always been to create the highest caliber music. Because he used to tell me every now and then that people don't care *when* the music came out, or when it was released, or if it was on time or if it was late. All they care about is how good it is. He used to say, "If you don't do the best, the people who are listening are apt to say, 'Gee, that's nice, but what else have you got?' And if anybody ever asks you that about the next piece of music, forget it, you've missed."

## The Acusonic Recording Process

When Quincy Jones, Michael Jackson, and I were recording *Off the Wall*, we wanted to coin a catchword phrase to represent my recording technique using multiple multitrack tape machines. So we came up with the phrase "The Acusonic Recording Process." To my continued amazement, I am frequently asked to explain. In fact on several occasions I have been offered impressive sums of money by recording studios and companies that wanted to purchase "The Acusonic Recording Process," thinking that it was a "black box"

Bill Gibson Collection

through which recorded sound could be processed.

I recollect one awkward circumstance when, several years ago, I got a phone call in the studio from someone's secretary who was saying that a photographer's team from a very respected, very important, foreign trade journal, was in an airplane on the way from somewhere overseas to shoot a cover photo of "The Acusonic Recording Process" machine! I don't remember exactly what I did, but I do recall mumbling something to the highly confused photographer about the machine being "away for repairs" indefinitely, and we'd have to reschedule the photo shoot! On my last lecture trip to Japan and Europe, I did admit to the press what the real deal with "The Acusonic Recording Process" was!

I had no idea when Quincy, Michael, and I came up with the name that there would be so much interest in it.

It was during the recording of the score for *The Wiz* that I came up with the basic system of organizing the tracks, the master tapes, and the slave tapes that I still use. I call it "multitrack multiplexing."

## The Real Deal on the
## Acusonic Recording Process

The following is from a talk I gave in October 1984 at a NARAS luncheon. It is an effort to answer questions about a subject that I am often asked to define.

The year is 1977. Quincy called me one night and said "Want to go to New York and do a musical movie?" I said, "Sure!" So off we went to do *The Wiz* for Universal Pictures. While we were working on *The Wiz*, we met this young 18-year-old kid by the name of Michael Jackson. [Michael played Scarecrow in *The Wiz*, the movie.]

It was on *The Wiz* that I began seriously using two or more multitrack tape machines together to realize the production values that Quincy and I were interested in.

It was during the recording of the score for *The Wiz* that I came up with the basic system of organizing the tracks, the master tapes, and the slave tapes that I still use. I call it "multitrack multiplexing." This is the basic concept that spawned the catchword phrase "Acusonic Recording Process."

The Acusonic Recording Process is, in reality, merely a name that Quincy and I came up with to describe my recording technique with multitrack recording machines. The phrase is essentially a combination of the words "accurate" and "sonic." I figured the "accurate" part of it referred to the accuracy of true stereophonic sound imagery; the "sonic" part of it referred to the fact that it is sound that we are trying to characterize.

More specifically, the name Acusonic Recording Process describes the way that I work with digital and analog multitrack tape machines and SMPTE timecode to generate a virtually unlimited number of recording tracks. Initially I designed the system specifically for the projects that Quincy and I have done together.

I think the most important feature of this technique, and my method of implementing it, is that I am able to use pairs of tracks, in abundance, to record true stereophonic images, and then retain them in discrete pairs until the final mix. This method also allows me (when I use analog recording in my work) to play the master tape only a few times during the initial stage of the project, and then put it away until the final mix. This feature retains much of the transient response of the analog master tape by not diminishing those fragile transients due to repeated playing during overdubbing and sweetening.

I frequently mix recording formats with my system of multiplexing multitrack tape machines. Now, of course, I use digital recording machines, in abundance, alongside my analog machines. I think that what the basic digital recording medium does, it does dramatically well. Once I have the character of the sound to my liking, I will use a digital recording device to preserve it. As a storage medium, digital recording is unparalleled.

When I am working in the analog format, I make several of what I call "work tapes," using the original master SMPTE track and regenerating it through a code restorer so that the timecode is always first-generation quality. I will then mix the rhythm tracks and make a stereo cue mix on the work tapes using as few tracks as possible.

Generally speaking, I will make a stereo mix of the bass, drums, and percussion on a pair of tracks. Then I will make a stereo mix of the keyboards and guitars on a separate pair of tracks. If there is a scratch vocal track, I will transfer a copy of that track across to the work tapes by itself.

Using this technique, in this manner, gives me a virtually unlimited number of tracks to work with. It was not obvious at first, but it soon became apparent to me that with this method, it is possible to do much more than merely obtain additional tracks for overdubbing.

Probably the most important advantage of this system is that I can record many more genuine stereophonic images by using pairs of tracks, instead of merely single monophonic tracks. These stereo sound-source tracks can be kept in discrete pairs until the final mix.

These true stereo images add much to the depth and clarity of the final production. I have a feeling that this one facet of my production technique contributes more to the overall sonic character of my work than any other single factor.

There's more to the story. My career actually began before stereophonic sound was of any interest to the industry, let alone the general public. This gave me the opportunity to do a great deal of experimentation in stereo microphone technique at my own pace. Consequently, I was able to learn about what true stereophonic sound reproduction really is, before the commercial pressures came to bear. This also gave me a chance to learn what the emotional value of stereo imagery in music can do to increase the emotional impact of recorded music.

When we first started to record in stereo, our goal was to create a natural sound field that had as its basis a real support of the music that we were trying to preserve. The big problem in modern music comes when we begin to overdub parts and layer the orchestrations.

The number of tracks necessary to realize the music can become astronomical in quantity, and thus becomes psychologically intimidating. This definitely need not be the case. I soon realized that this system makes it easily possible to have all the tracks I wanted to accomplish my musical objectives.

Another equally important value of this system is that I don't have to make balance decisions early in the production of a piece of music—decisions that end up being wrong because I couldn't make a good value judgment when I wasn't hearing all the parts of the music. In other words, I never finalize any premixes or balances in a piece of music until I have heard all its musical elements, and how those elements relate to each other to form the whole emotion of the music.

When overdubbing vocals, for instance, I can record all background vocals in stereo and not combine or premix anything permanently until all the parts in the song are complete, and I can hear how all the musical values relate. I guess I could say that with this method, I never have to erase a track!

That basically is the Acusonic Recording Process.
*Bruce Swedien, 10-12-84*

## On Q

# Bernie Grundman

Quincy and Bruce Swedien were always together during tracking and mixdown, and then Bruce would bring the mixes in here for the mastering. Quincy didn't come in often, because he trusted Bruce so much. I suppose that's one of his strengths—working with people who know what they're doing and trusting them to do it. Bruce was just trying to maintain Quincy's vision, and it was up to me to contribute what I could to the final product—to heighten the vision.

Bruce is one of the best mix engineers in the world—there are only a few that are really exceptional like that. Interestingly, his mixes sound fairly loud before I even touch them. On a lot of the other projects that we see, there are parts of the mix that are out of control, which causes us to use a lot of compression. In a Bruce Swedien mix, everything is very well controlled internally—there aren't many things that unintentionally stick out. Therefore, it's not as hard to make his stuff sound loud but still dynamic. The combination of great producing and great mixing is powerful. The music that Quincy and Bruce have done together is exceptional—it has a certain depth of space and, at the same time, a tremendous presence. That's almost a contradiction because it is very difficult to get everything to be in your face but still spacious.

Bernie Grundman shares his insight into the mastering world at AudioPro '93 in Seattle.

Both Quincy and Bruce are good at creating an atmosphere that feels safe for the artist. Quincy is always in control musically, and Bruce has a way of making you feel that you're going to be taken care of and everything's going to be okay. Artists have to put themselves in a vulnerable position to really perform well, so they want to work with people they really trust.

If anything goes wrong during a session, Swedien always has some kind of little joke or something. The place could blow up and you probably wouldn't care if you're working there with Swedien! You'd just think, "Well, Swedien is going to take care of us, we're safe!"

Bruce always brings in some of his old stuff that he knows is tried-and-true—he knows it's successful and that it sounds good wherever it plays. He'll also bring in some of the latest big-hit CDs, and then he'll reference himself by listening on my monitors. Then we play *his* mix. Then we pick a tune that's similar—maybe something from Michael or Quincy or even someone else. He just wants to make certain that what we're working on will sound as good or preferably better than the other stuff people are listening to. Mastering is all about that last common denominator. Even though the mixes might have sounded great in the studio, we need to make sure they'll compete in the marketplace.

## On Q
# Francis Buckley

When we're in the studio and all this craziness is going on, Quincy's focus is 100 percent on the music and the players and all that. Then there might be a phone call about a business issue, and he'll instantly narrow down his focus to that one issue. Then, when he hangs up the phone, he's all the way back into the music. It's an amazing, almost instantaneous transformation. He has an uncanny ability to turn all of his attention to the issue at hand, and then to tune right back into the music.

Q's *Jook Joint* was only supposed to take four days. It was going to be a semilive album, and I was going to track the band, which included a big-band horn section. The artists were going to come in and sing to the mixes of those tracks. At the end of four days we only had a few tracks cut, so I told the production coordinator that I'd clear my calendar and if Q needed me, I'd be there. Well, I worked on that album for seven and a half months, and it was the album of a lifetime. We worked with everybody from Ray Charles to Babyface to this new young girl, Tamia, he brought in. It was unbelievable.

When Q is in the room, everybody takes it up to the next level. There's something special about him. I've worked with producers who are far more hands-on, but with Q it's like the old saying, "The tide raises all ships." When he's in the room, the performance level raises—everybody's on their game.

QUINCY JONES
Q's JOOK JOINT

*Q's Jook Joint* was engineered by Francis Buckley and mixed by Bruce Swedien.

Quincy was always tuned in to what was going on with the artist, and each situation had its own set of challenges. When we had Tamia in the studio to do "Put a Move on My Heart," she was very nervous. We were trying to get a great take, but it just wasn't working. So Q said to Rod Temperton, "See if she can come back tomorrow. I won't be here, and maybe she won't be so nervous." He recognized that she was trying too hard and that she couldn't relax. So, he removed himself from the situation and gave her another chance. He had confidence in her abilities, and when she came back the next day, she was much more relaxed and did a great job. Then when she came back again with Q, she was just fine and they were able to finish the vocals.

With the session players that come in, even though Quincy commands their A-game, he has a way about him that gets everybody ready to go but having fun and being relaxed. He expects the most from you, but he doesn't interfere in any way whatsoever. He never questions if I'm using the right mic or if I'm doing the right thing with a certain piece of gear. He gives you respect. It's like, "You are the professional. You are here. Do your job." That's great and it works very well. I've been with a lot of producers that micromanage. That usually doesn't work out too well.

## On Q

# Peter Chaikin

I met Q when I was assisting on *Body Heat* at The Record Plant in 1973. I also assisted on *Mellow Madness* and on the first album he did with the Brothers Johnson, *Look Out for #1*.

The guy that I was assisting with on *Look Out for #1* had a lot of different projects going on and, as typically would happen, when he couldn't finish the project, as his assistant I ended up doing the dates. The Brothers Johnson was a great group, that was a great album, and it was great to work with Q.

When you work with Q, he'll eventually come up with his own name for you—he had names for everybody. Louis Johnson was Boot, George Johnson was Hen, Ed Eckstine was Bugs, Bruce Swedien was Svenk, and I was Jelly Roll. I never really knew why I was Jelly Roll, but that's who I was.

Q doesn't drive. At the time of the Brothers Johnson album, I was living in Beverly Glen and Quincy was living on Rockingham, so I'd go pick him up in the morning and drive him to the studio. In the car, he'd have horn charts or whatever we were cutting that day and he'd sit there for the whole ride, reading the charts and humming the parts. Sometimes he'd make changes and sometimes he'd be writing the parts in the car. It's like he's reading the charts, writing the chart, and playing them in his mind. Then, we'd go into the studio and cut the tracks. It was really very impressive.

I wound up doing a few projects with Q, including Lesley Gore and Barbra Streisand in addition to the Brothers Johnson. That was an amazing time for me. I was pretty new, a freelance engineer, and every day an unbelievable artist would come into the control room. One day Herbie Hancock comes in to play keys. The next day Harvey Mason comes in to cut drum tracks, and then Billy Cobham, and Toots Thielemans, and it goes on and on. For me, it was like lying on my back and having someone feed me seedless grapes: "Oh, have another grape," and you just push the fader up and hear another incredible performance. Some of the most enjoyable musical moments I've had in my life were sitting in the control room with Q and the people that he brought through playing these sessions.

Quincy is a musician's producer— he's an amazing musician and everybody knows it. He wouldn't really tell the musicians what to do. Instead, he'd lead them to their best performances. His power has always been in assembling the right people and creating the right environment for brilliance to happen.

Q is really into stacking different instruments together to create new colors. I remember one day he said, "Listen to this, Jelly Roll. That's an amazing sound. It's a flügelhorn and an alto flute. Together, they become a completely different sound. You ever hear a baritone and a piccolo together? They become another sound."

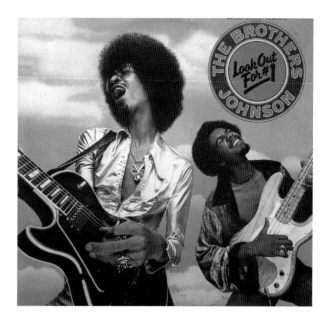

His whole way of painting colors is about layering sounds that add color to each other. If they are in tune, you get a new sound—you don't hear those single instruments anymore. He'd do things that had never been done before, and his records have always been so much fun to listen to.

When it really came down to it, it was always about feel. At the end of the day we'd make a cassette, and I'd drop it in his mailbox on the way home. He'd come in the next morning with a report: was it good or not good, was the mix good, was the performance good, and stuff like that. One of his barometers for a good-feeling tune was his new little daughter, Kidada, who was born while we were working together—Peggy Lipton was his wife. When Kidada became a toddler, Quincy would play a tune for her and if she'd just stand there, he'd say, "It's not happening." But if she started moving, he knew he had something.

## On Q
# Ed Cherney

It takes about two minutes, and you just fall in love with Q. He's the kind of guy that opens up his heart and brings out the best in people. *And* he gives you space to screw up, too, which is a lot of times where great art comes from. You can be courageous. If it's no good, it's all right—you just take it another direction.

## The Beginning

In 1978 I had just moved to L.A. from Chicago, and I was looking for a job. I went through the *Billboard* Directory backwards, and the first place I came to was Westlake Studios, so I applied for a job as an assistant and they hired me! It just happened that Quincy Jones and Bruce Swedien were working at Westlake, and it also just happened that they came in one day and I was assigned to their session. I ended up assisting them for the next six years.

## *Off the Wall*

When we were doing *Off the Wall,* we knew we were making something great, but it was still just another day at the office. But when you hear Michael doing "She's out of My Life" and the rest of the material on that record, you know you're working on something pretty special. Michael knew what he wanted vocally, and he always came in very well prepared—it never took many takes to get the right performance out of him.

We mixed *Off the Wall* in one of the studios at Westlake that everyone called the Mix Room. We'd print the mixes and send the cassettes to Michael, who was out on tour.

Michael's mixes were complicated, with two or three multitracks running in sync together. Bruce Swedien was one of the early adopters of multitrack synchronization, and at that time the technology was iffy at best. One of my duties during the mix sessions was to keep those machines running. Bruce was one of the first guys to make work tapes. Staying within 24 tracks was way too limiting for the way Quincy and Bruce liked to work, so we would record the basic tracks, sync up another machine, and then bounce the basics to a submix on that new reel. This became a work tape, to which we could add more tracks. There'd be a vocal work tape with just vocal stacks and stuff like that. Then, there'd also be separate work tapes for guitars, keys, percussion, and so on. We might have 10 to 15 work tapes that could all lock to the same master. When we were ready to mix, the separate tapes were all combined down to two or three reels that could run in sync during the mix. The vocal work tape might have 20 vocal tracks that were combined down to one or two stereo pairs on a mix master, or the lead vocal might have 10 tracks all compiled down to a single track. This made the actual mix a lot more manageable than if we had to synchronize 10 multitrack tape machines at once!

## The Dude

I was the assistant on *The Dude,* too. Quincy always came in, and he was absolutely prepared. At the tracking dates, he had charts out in front of him that he had written—I think he knew exactly what he wanted. He hired the greatest musicians, and those sessions were always fun. There was never a mean or nasty moment. We were making great music and Quincy was letting people play. His directions were very nonintrusive, but he was always getting the best out of people. In my opinion, I was just some dumb kid coming in there, but Q included everybody. You know, he was always inclusive and he genuinely cared about people, and if you were there working for him he just loved you and he was never afraid to show it. So you were always pulled in, always engaged, always a part of what was going on.

At some time during the process, Q would bring everybody from the label down to the studio for some refreshments and a review of the project. And everybody would come in and it would be a love-fest, and he would play stuff for everyone. Perhaps he would even solicit their opinions. He might not act on the opinions, but he made it inclusive, so that everyone there felt that they were somehow involved and contributing to the project. Whether he did anything they wanted or not wasn't the point. They left there feeling that they had a stake in the music and in the record and in their relationship with him. That definitely made an impression on me. He is a talented man and people just adore him. Women would fall down to get next to him, and he was just always humble and always inclusive and really giving. That was contagious. Everyone involved felt that they had a vested interested in his success and the success of the music.

James Ingram is another guy with all the heart in the world. When they brought him in to meet Q, everybody was just knocked out; it was instantly apparent that this guy was unbelievably talented. It's tough to get a performance out of some singers, but he would just go out there and sing his ass off—he'd just give it up! I don't remember it being any work doing vocals with him; it was always really exciting. He'd sing the song, and then everybody would be celebrating in the control room. And we didn't have to spend much time piecing his vocals together; the takes were all solid performances.

It's not frequently done this way anymore, but on *The Dude* we had a *lot* of different musicians there. We were tracking with bass, drums, and maybe two guitars and two keyboards all at once—the songs were actually played as a band. And, even though the arrangements were written out, Quincy could get the greatest feel out of his musicians.

In those sessions everybody had the freedom to suck. Quincy didn't put heavy pressure on people when they came in. The players he called were there for a reason— they were the finest musicians *and* they had the most heart of anybody around. He would just assemble the right guys, great songs, and great arrangements, then he'd let these guys go to town and play. He'd get a performance out of people that they wouldn't normally give anybody else.

## The Magic

There's a point at the beginning of a session, even with the best players, when everybody's playing the notes and the time and the changes, and it's just accurate. But there's another moment when the musicians are passing the plate between each other and moving together—it's a magical musical thing, and who knows how it really happens. I've been involved in sessions where we stop before we get to that point, and I've been in sessions where we pass right by it. But there's that little window there where the music is just right—Quincy is the master at finding that point. He gets it; he *feels* it. And everybody knows when he feels it, "That's it, man. That's it! We've got it, man! Beautiful. F---ing beautiful!"

## Chapter 6

# MICHAEL JACKSON

Q produced three of Michael Jackson's solo albums: *Off the Wall, Thriller,* and *Bad.* He also produced Michael's tracks on *The Wiz* and *E.T. The Extra-Terrestrial. Off the Wall,* released in 1979, was the first album to generate four U.S. Top 10 hits, including the chart-topping singles "Don't Stop 'til You Get Enough" and "Rock with You." It reached No. 3 on the *Billboard* 200 and eventually sold more than 20 million copies worldwide.

*Thriller,* released in 1982, was certified by the RIAA for shipments of at least 29 million copies in the United States alone, giving it Double Diamond status and making it the all-time best selling album in the States. In addition, it sold millions and millions around the world. It was, and currently remains, the best-selling album of all time, with more than 110 million copies sold worldwide.

*Bad,* released in 1987, had lower sales than *Thriller,* but was still a substantial commercial success, with seven hit singles in the United States, five of which reached No. 1 on the *Billboard* Hot 100 charts: "I Just Can't Stop Loving You," "Bad," "The Way You Make Me Feel," "Man in the Mirror," and "Dirty Diana." *Bad* has sold more than 30 million copies worldwide.

A lot of jazz guys were attacking me when I first produced Michael Jackson. They'd say I was lowering my standards or selling out, or that I was too jazzy. I didn't have to sell out for that. We had played *everything* growing up. I said, "Man, I'm not following a trend. I'm stretching out. We've been doing that all our lives." Ray was the same way. He was heavily influenced by Charlie Parker, and he sang like Charles Brown and Nat Cole. Then he brought gospel influence into pop music. He met a lot of resistance over that, but he was a revolutionary. Did they really think I would be following fads? There was nobody to copy to do *Off the Wall* or *Thriller*. That's nonsense. We didn't follow a fad—we *started* a fad!

## THE WIZ

Even though I had met Michael when he was 12 years old, the first time we worked together was in 1978 doing *The Wiz*, with Sidney Lumet directing. I didn't want to do the picture at first—I really didn't—but Sidney said, "You owe me," and I said, "You're right, you've got me." I loved working with Sidney. He and Richard Brooks were the only guys who'd call me before they called the actors. When they do that, you'll do anything for them. You'll do ten times the amount of work you need to do because they trust you so much.

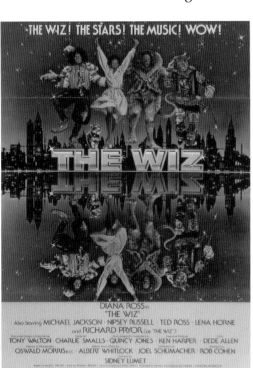

When we started *The Wiz*, Michael was getting ready to do his own album on Epic. He asked me to help him find a producer and I said, "Michael, I don't want to talk about that now. We've got to prerecord first. You don't even have the song in the movie yet." Prerecording is the most vital part of a musical, because that's what the actors sing to on film! Whatever sound you get, better be right. It's very delicate stuff, so you've got to really concentrate on that step in the process of filmmaking. We finally came up with "You Can't Win" for Michael (Scarecrow) to sing with the crows; the only other song he was singing was "Ease On Down the Road," with Diana Ross.

After we got the prerecords finished, we were at the Brooklyn Hotel and Sidney Lumet was blocking the four principals: Michael, the Tin Man, the Lion, and Diana. They'd mark off everywhere where the actors had to be during the scenes, and then they'd walk them through it. I was starting to watch Michael. He knew everybody's songs and all the dialogue. Plus, he'd have to get up very early in the morning to get the prosthetics put on. That took *five hours*, man, to get all that muddy stuff put on his face to turn into Scarecrow.

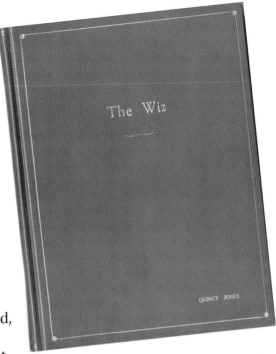

One of the things Michael's character did was pull little pieces of paper out of his chest and quote great philosophers. He'd say the quote and then the philosopher's name, "Blah, blah, blah…Confucius," or "Blah, blah, blah…Kierkegaard," or whatever. When he got to Socrates, he pronounced it "So-KRAY-teeze." I said, "Who?" and he said, "So-KRAY-teeze" I didn't correct him in front of everyone, because that's not the right way to handle those kinds of things. Never embarrass someone in front of a group of people. He kept pronouncing it the same way, over and over.

The second day I took him aside and said, "Michael, it's 'SOCK-ra-teeze,' not 'So-KRAY-teeze.'" He said, "Really!" and he had the sweetest look, you know, like a deer in the headlights. I saw something in him I'd never seen before: a special kind of innocence and sensitivity. It was in that Socrates moment that I felt inside that there was a lot of potential in Michael. Everybody said, "You can't make Michael any bigger than he was in the Jackson 5."

I said, "We'll see."

I heard things in Michael I hadn't heard before in the Jackson 5. I was very interested in hearing him sing in a lower register. I'd seen Michael on the Oscars singing "Ben," a love story about a *rat*, and I knew he had more to offer than just dance music, but I was interested in seeing how he'd handle a song about an actual emotional relationship between a man and a woman. I'd been hanging on to a song called "She's Out of My Life" that I was going to give to Sinatra—Tommy Bähler wrote it when his marriage with Karen Carpenter broke up. I was thinking I'd love to hear what Michael could do with that song.

# OFF THE WALL

Once things settled down with *The Wiz*, I told Michael that I'd like to do the album—that I'd like to take a shot at it. He went and told Epic and they said, "No *way*, Quincy's too jazzy. He's only done the Brothers Johnson. He's a jazz arranger and compos-

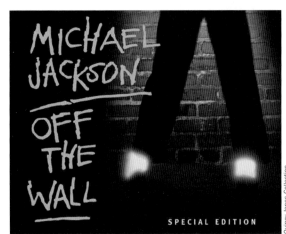

SPECIAL EDITION

*Quincy Jones Collection*

er." They didn't know about my background—they just didn't know. And they said, "No, Kenny Gamble and Leon Huff should do it." Michael came back and he was crying, but I said, "Don't worry about it. We're gonna be fine. If it's meant for us to work together, God will work it out."

Michael and his managers, Freddie DeMann and Ron Weisner, insisted, and said, "Quincy's doing the album." And we did. *Off the Wall* was the biggest-selling black record in history at the time. Epic was getting ready to fire their executives, but *Off the Wall* saved the jobs of all the executives (even all the black executives) who were saying, "Quincy was the wrong guy, he's too jazzy." We didn't have any more nonsense after that.

Michael's father did the contracts, and he would only give me a $30,000 advance! That's *nothing*! Absolutley nothing! And he tried to pay me through Jackson 5, Inc., which he controlled. I said, "No way! Not a chance!" I refused and insisted that I get paid straight from Epic Records. The contract also said that if I didn't get two Top 30 records, they'd get somebody else to do the next record. Man, please! We had *four* Top 5 records. *Two* of them, "Don't Stop 'til You Get Enough" and "Rock with You," were No. 1—they sold 2 million apiece! Even though the advance was nothing for an album like this, the real money is in the royalties. So, it's okay, I made it up on the back end. Despite the objections by my best friend [music executive and producer] Clarence Avant, Joe Jackson refused to pay me more than a $30,000 advance for *Thriller*. During the entire '80s, which we literally *owned*, this man never offered one kind or appreciative word, and I couldn't care less. Not even a little bit.

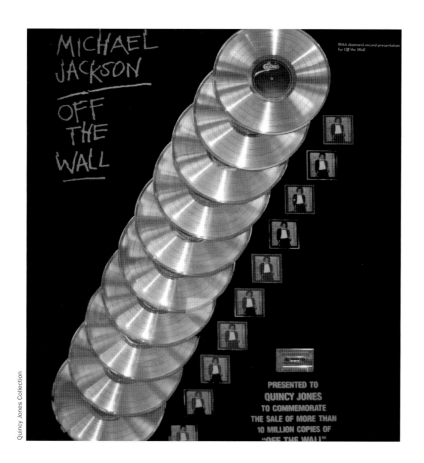

Quincy Jones Collection

## Grammy Nominations for *Off the Wall*

1979    **Producer of the Year**

**Best Disco Recording**: "Don't Stop 'Til You Get
Enough" (Michael Jackson); single from
*Off the Wall* (Epic).

# THE KILLER Q POSSE

Building a solid project, with a chance of succeeding, is
about having all the bases covered. If you want to produce
great music, you need to develop your core skills—you
must get good at what you do. You also need to understand
the importance of working with the best people you can
find at every step. Anything else is counterproductive!

    Michael Jackson had more talent than I had ever
seen: dancing, singing, and performing. In addition,

he'd been developing his musical passion and experiences since he was a little kid. I had years of experience producing, arranging, and composing for so many

Quincy Jones Collection

fantastic artists and for film, and I'd developed my craft. I was mentored by all the jazz guys growing up, and I studied with one of the best composition teachers of all time. We had Bruce Swedien with his Acusonic Recording Process, using SMPTE timecode to synchronize up to 15 24-track recorders, plus all the depth and experience that he contributed. It was a powerful team with everyone operating in their strengths. We just put everything together and were ready to change the world.

I've been blessed to work with the best musicians on the planet! I had what I called the Killer Q Posse, which consisted of Bruce, Rod Temperton, Jerry Hey, Greg Phillinganes, Louis Johnson, John Robinson, Paulinho Da Costa, and Ndugu Chancler. We've also had Paul Jackson, Nate East, Steve Porcaro, David Paich, Steve Ferrone, Michael Boddicker, Jeff Porcaro, Steve Lukather, and the list goes on. That's an amazing group of musicians, and we attacked each album with a vengeance.

## ROD TEMPERTON

Rod Temperton came out from the U.K. to visit me six months before we did *Off the Wall.* He wanted me to manage their band, Heatwave, who had a hit with "Boogie Nights" in 1976. I heard their music and just fell in love with it. I told Rod that I didn't want to be a manager, and that I had only managed the Brothers Johnson because we couldn't find the right person. But we really connected. He knew his stuff. He had an excellent compositional instinct and wrote great music. We just became brothers right away.

I called him three or four months later to write a couple of songs for Michael, and also a couple for Rufus and Chaka, who I was also producing at that time. Thinking we'd probably pick one of the songs he was submitting for Michael, he sent us "Off the Wall," "Rock with You," and "Burn This Disco Out"—we ended up using all three! Then he also wrote "Masterjam" and "Live in Me" for Rufus and Chaka. We've been working together for 36 years. Rod is a masterpiece of a human being, and I love him from the deepest part of my heart. He doesn't stop. Seriously, his creativity never stops! He's the best friend and brother you could ever work with. He doesn't stop— he just doesn't stop! "Baby, Come to Me," "Give Me the Night," and on and on.

Rod played lateral thinking games. He'd go on all night long with these mental puzzles, and he'd never give us any clues. He was disciplined enough to hold out all night long, or longer if he had to, and make us figure them out. Sometimes in the studio you start to burn out or just get bored, so it's necessary to find something to keep the mood up. Rod's games helped keep us sharp and alert. For instance, Rod would say something like, "A guy goes into a bar and he asks the bartender for a glass of water. The bartender reaches under the bar, picks up a gun, and just holds it up to his head and puts it back. And the guy says, 'Thank you very much,' and gets up and leaves. So what happened?" The stuff is very literal, so it has a logical ending. What happened? So think, he asked for a glass of water, and the gun to his head did the same thing—so what could that be?

Hiccups! The remedy for hiccups is fear and drinking a glass of water. But he had a hundred of those, man. I'd say "Goddammit, *tell* me man!" He wouldn't let us know; he'd hold it for three or four days. But you get really silly in the studio sometimes, especially on the big projects. But as long as you bring it home, that's all that's important.

Like junkies we made a lots and lots of good music together in the studio. We also made an art out of staying up for five days and nights in the studio. It was all joy and no pain.

## On Q
# Rod Temperton

I've always thought of Quincy as one of the last great record producers. First of all, before he became a producer, he'd been through all facets of the music business. He had all of his musical background and his time on the road with big bands in the United States and Europe, plus he had worked as an executive for Mercury Records. He learned how the music business worked from the label's perspective, he knew what it was like to play in a band, he knew what it was like to take a band on the road, and he knew music through and through. That insight is really what a producer should bring to any project. Quincy knows everything about the big picture. He finds the vision for the whole project and puts all of the pieces in place.

In the studio, because of his great background knowledge, he's got a finger in every pie. His fingerprint is on every part, but he gives his musicians a lot of respect and makes them feel completely at home in the studio. He provides them with the atmosphere and freedom to do what they do best, and then he tweaks it a little to make it even better. It's different with a lot of the young producers today, because many of them don't have that much musical knowledge—they don't necessarily know how to work with a band or vocalists. They're computer guys and they have their own talents but, for them, it's not an all-encompassing thing like it is for Quincy.

Quincy is the boss of the project, and everything comes down to him—it's a very big job! Every musician just loves playing for him because they know he'll bring out their best performance. It's not like he just hires great players and gets out of the way. He conducts the process. You wouldn't say about a bandleader or orchestra conductor that he just stands there and waves his hands around in front of all these great musicians—that's rubbish! He's controlling the whole thing. He gets the energy out of them. He makes them work together.

The first time I worked with Quincy was on *Off the Wall.* At the time, my band, Heatwave, was in New York recording with Phil Ramone, and Quincy called one night and said that he wanted me to write some stuff for Michael Jack-

Quincy Jones Collection

son's new album and also something for Rufus and Chaka Khan. Obviously, I was very flattered and wanted to do it desperately, but he was on a tight time schedule and I was in the studio day and night with Heatwave in New York. After a lot of discussion, and a very long phone conversation, I agreed to do one song each for Michael and Rufus.

To cut a long story short, I flew in on the next weekend with three tracks in hand. Those first three songs were written in the middle of the night, because my band would go into the studio in the morning and come out at midnight. I had a Fender Rhodes in my hotel room, so when I'd get back from the recording session, I would spend two or three hours writing. I had done my homework and figured out what kind of things I thought would be good for Michael based on the sound of his voice and how he sang on the Jackson 5 records. All I could do was bring those tracks and let Quincy decide what he felt was suitable—I didn't even know what else was on the record at that point. I wrote "Off the Wall" and "Burn This Disco Out" directly for

Michael. "Rock With You" was an idea that I had already started, but I then finished it off for Michael. I arrived at the studio and we cut them all on that Saturday afternoon, and I said to Quincy, "Well, which one do you want for Michael?" He said he wanted all three!

So, I hauled myself back to New York to continue recording and to finish the songs for Michael. I had arrived with those three songs, but I didn't have any of the lyrics. I always write the music and all of the arrangement first, and then I add the melody on top of that. I don't really write the final lyrics until I know we are going to record the song. I actually hate writing lyrics, so I always leave that part until as late as I possibly can. When we cut the initial tracks for Michael, I sang the songs so he could learn the melodies, but I didn't see the need to write lyrics until I knew which songs Quincy wanted to use. I flew back to Los Angeles to do the vocals with Michael the following weekend.

That was the beginning of our relationship. Once you work with Quincy and everything works out well, you become a member of his family one way or another. Quincy and I became like long lost brothers, even though we were from different sides of the world. We finished *Off the Wall* and went on to do about 20 different albums from then on. Also, don't forget Bruce Swedien, Quincy's engineer. The three of us caught on like a house on fire and decided to work together as a team, and that was the way it was from then on.

When we were in the studio, we enjoyed our time together and we worked long hours. It was exciting and we were very into what we were doing. We would work all the way through the night, and then we'd have to mix down the following morning. It was an amazing time. We didn't really have a clock in the studio, so when we would get on to something and it was happening, we would just keep going. A lot of the musicians would laugh and say, "Hey, you guys. When are we going to stop to eat?" And we'd give in and send some of them out for food, but we just went on and on.

We were always looking for the right way to present the music. I write songs very specifically; but then when we get in the studio, everything depends on the artist's approach. If there are words they can't get their head around—that sound awkward while they're singing them—I'll make a change! Or, maybe there's a phrase that they sing in one of the verses that sounds amazing. I'll write a new lyric on top of it to accommodate that, because it's always about that artist's interpretation of the song. You've got to be flexible enough to bend with anything that might come up. That's the way I approach it. But there's always a rigid structure in the first place—there needs to be a solid starting point. We always try to get the artist to learn the song as is before we start bending it to their particular talents.

A lot of what Quincy does with vocalists is about his charisma. He can drag a fantastic performance out of a singer because of who he is and how he treats them—he's quite unique in that regard. From a technical standpoint, I can go in the studio with a vocalist and get some good stuff out of them. However, Quincy has an uncanny ability to make singers feel totally at ease so they open their subconscious and give all of their best stuff. That's really it. I've witnessed it many, many times. It's not really something you learn. It needs to be something that's absorbed into a person's psyche.

When things aren't going well with the artist, you always have to make out like it's *your* fault or that they're not hearing something in their headphone mix correctly or that there's something not balanced properly. Or, you might just have to make the call that it's just the wrong day. We just needed to do whatever it took to help the artists get their best take on tape. Most of the people we worked with were amazing in the first place, so we'd just help them to focus their efforts to get that little bit extra into their performance. One of the biggest things we used to say with singers was, "If you go wrong, do not stop." It seems normal for a singer to stop and apologize when they've made a mistake. But we'd encourage them to just let it go wrong, because they might end up with a phrase that sounds absolutely amazing. We told them that we could always fix a mistake later, but on every take they should just be loose with it and do their thing.

I studied Michael Jackson a lot, so I knew his voice pretty well and I knew his style. Therefore, most of the stuff I did for him worked quite well. However, one of the hardest things we had to approach was getting him to sing the word "thriller." I tend to write words that fit the melody perfectly—words that sing easily on the notes of the melody. The notes are the things that are locked in place—it's the lyrics that need to adjust in order to flow well with the melody.

When I came to "Thriller" the title was set, and then I realized "thriller" was a terrible word to sing. People obviously know it so well now that it wouldn't seem terrible anymore, but if you think about it, the "thri" of "thriller" is very difficult for a singer. When I first took the song to Michael,

I told him he was going to have to spend some time to get his mouth around that lyric, and that he'd need to figure out how to pronounce it so it sang well. And, of course, Michael worked on it until he got it perfectly right.

Working with Quincy in the studio always turned out very nicely because our egos never really got in the way. Quincy was always the producer—always the boss—so in the end, what he said went. But, you know I worked with him every day. I was kind of his sounding board. He'd throw ideas at me, and I'd throw them back. Our styles actually complemented one another quite nicely. I am a songwriter who comes from the concept of doing whole arrangements for the song. In other words, I don't just put hooks in the melody and on the lead vocal track. I might put an important hook in the bass line or anywhere else in the arrangement. I try to write in an all-encompassing way. Quincy comes at producing in the same way, so we found that we work very well together.

The world needs to know that Quincy Jones is a very passionate man. There's something to be learned from people like Quincy that is often missed, especially by young people. The most important thing is finding your passion. Find what turns you on, and then really go for it! A lot of young people get out of school and think they'll just go about making money straight away. But money is not passion. You've got to have something that drives you— something that comes from deep inside you. Quincy found it at a very early age, and the man's been amazingly successful.

Quincy is somebody I love dearly and we've gone to the ends of world for each other, time and time again over the years. That's what great friends are all about. I'd go the distance for him anytime and he knows that—I'm sure he'd do the same for me. What more of a friendship could you ask for than that?

# THE PERFECT BALANCE

We had the perfect balance of soul and science—it's always about that. There's always a science behind the passion and fire in music—it's what enables the artist to fully unleash his or her creativity. People think it's all just about natural innate talent. No way! Herbie Hancock could not be who he is if he had to think about whether or not to cross his thumb under between the third and fourth intervals. It has to be second nature; it has to be so ingrained in you that the music flows freely out. Whether you're a producer, musician, or technician, you have to get past the point where you're wondering what to do or play or sing next. People think Aretha Franklin was just a natural. Granted, she had natural talent, but I've been with her when she'd sing a lick over and over and over again, exploring her sound and developing it. That's what it takes. This stuff doesn't happen automatically if you don't work really hard for it. It really doesn't.

## PRODUCTION

Michael was on the road with the Jackson 5 during a lot of the production for *Off the Wall*. He wrote two songs on the album: "Working Day and Night" and "Don't Stop 'til You Get Enough"; plus I had him write lyrics to "Get on the Floor" that the Brothers Johnson wrote.

When we recorded "She's Out of My Life," Michael *really* felt it. He cried on every take. I left the tears in because it was so real. The songwriter, Tommy Bähler, was really going through some pain when he wrote the song after going through a painful divorce. Michael felt that pain and he reflected it in his performance. Johnny Mandel wrote a beautiful string opening, and we kept the production simple to highlight the emotion in the song. I *knew* that Michael had more to offer than he'd given in previous records.

Michael was an extremely hard worker. He always came to the studio well prepared and well rehearsed. He would stay up all night learning lyrics or practicing a song if that's what it was going to take to get it right.

## AMBIANCE

Bruce was a big help when it came to setting the mood and capturing the best parts of the Michael's performances. He is seriously into microphones. We had all kind of microphones to use for different things, but Bruce also put a platform in the studio for Michael so he could dance while he was singing. And we turned off all the lights except for a narrow pin spot aimed straight down on the microphone. Michael was turning and doing all his dance moves while he was singing. He was able to perform. It was funny, because the room would be black while Michael was dancing between lyrics, and then, just in time for the next lyric, Michael's face would appear at the microphone.

It was very important that we let Michael do what made him most comfortable, which was performing. He came prepared, he was comfortable, and we recorded some amazing performances. Bruce was great at capturing the moment and at listening for anything that would enhance the music. On a lot of the master vocal takes, we left the sound of Michael dancing on the platform turned up during the final mix because it was so in the pocket. Many engineers would automatically take the dancing away between lyric or try to minimize it through EQ or filtering, but Bruce saw it as something that added to the feel and emotion, so we left it in.

## *THRILLER*

People didn't get it when we put *Thriller* out. They had no *idea* what it was about, with Vincent Price narrating the beautiful Edgar Allen Poe–inspired text that Rod Temperton had written, talking about 40,000 years of funk and so on. They'd never heard anything like that before, and they really didn't get it until we released it with the video, directed by John Landis, on MTV a year and a half later. Now, every Halloween there are 4,100 *Thriller* contests in 72 countries, even in the Asian prisons. All over the world there are people getting together to do the *Thriller* dance— regular folks as well as prisoners in their orange suits doing the *Thriller* dance. And this is almost 30 years later! It's crazy.

*Thriller* was released on vinyl before the CD really became the standard. CDs and DVDs changed everything because, all of a sudden, everyone had a digital master that could be copied and shared. You couldn't do that with vinyl. People were buying *three* records apiece because they would wear them out. They'd have to go back and buy another one, and they'd buy another one when they wore that one out. That's why it's going to be very hard for anyone to ever match the sales we had.

## Grammys for *Thriller* (1983)

**Record of the Year** "Beat It" (Michael Jackson)
(Epic/CBS); Producer: Quincy Jones
[cowinner: Michael Jackson]
**Album of the Year** *Thriller* (Michael Jackson)
(Epic/CBS); Producer: Quincy Jones
[cowinner: Michael Jackson]
**Producer of the Year** Best Producer of 1983:
Quincy Jones
[cowinner: Michael Jackson]

## Nominations

**Record of the Year** "Beat It" (Michael Jackson)
(Epic/CBS); Producer: Quincy Jones
[cowinner: Michael Jackson]
**Album of the Year** *Thriller* (Michael Jackson)
(Epic/CBS); Producer: Quincy Jones
[cowinner: Michael Jackson]
**Best Recording for Children** E. T. The Extra-Terrestrial
album (MCA); Producer: Quincy Jones [cowinner: Michael
Jackson, Narrator/Vocals]
**Producer of the Year** Best Producer of 1983: Quincy Jones
[cowinner: Michael Jackson]
**Best R&B Instrumental Performance** "Billie Jean" (Instru-
mental version) [Michael Jackson]; track from *Thriller* (Epic)
**Best New R&B Song** "P.Y.T. (Pretty Young Thing)"
[Michael Jackson]; track from *Thriller* (Epic)

# SONGS

Getting the right songs is *so* important! I learned 40 years ago that a great song will make stars out of the worst singers in the world, but even Sinatra or Streisand can't save a bad song. That's the truth. When we wrote "The Secret Garden," I had Stevie, Michael, and Lionel Richie in mind. We didn't get them, so we used Al B. Sure!, James Ingram, and El DeBarge. It was written for Barry White, really, because he *was* the secret with that low, sexy voice. My point is that the song would have worked with either group of singers. It didn't need to be defined by a single star—it stood on its own merit. But we had a great song and four fantastic singers.

We went through 800 songs to get the 9 we used on *Thriller.* And, these were some great songs by some great writers, too. Once we had the nine songs done, I listened to all nine very objectively to determine which four songs were the weakest. I'd be as discriminating and honest as I possibly could. Then I took those four out, and was determined to replace them with four songs that were stronger than anything else on the album. And it worked. The songs we took out weren't bad; they just didn't work together with the other songs as well. In fact, a couple of them went on to be hits with other people.

We replaced the four songs that we removed from *Thriller* with "Lady in My Life," "P.Y.T," "Human Nature," and "Beat It." Pleeze! It was over, man. It was over! We already had "The Girl Is Mine" with Paul McCartney, "Billie Jean," "Thriller," and "Wanna Be Startin' Somethin.'" It's unbelievable. It went straight through the roof! It was definitely worth it, cause I'll tell you, my three least favorite numbers are 2, 6, and 11. You never heard nobody bragging, "I've got a Top 6 record," right? And, if you're No. 2, you want to be No. 1.

Of our initial nine songs, Michael wrote three: "The Girl Is Mine," "Billie Jean," and "Wanna Be Startin' Somethin.'" When we cut the weakest four songs, I told Michael I wanted to put something on that felt like "My Sharona"—something more rock 'n' roll. The third generation of white kids think that rock 'n' roll started in Idaho! In reality, Rock 'n' roll was what the black neighborhood was playing all the time! Michael came up with "Beat It," and the rest is history. That was an emotional revolution for young white Americans, in the same way that the Beatles in 1964 were the emotional revolution for the English. The British at that time didn't have anything but tea—they barely laughed, you know. It was a big emotional change in England when the Beatles and the Stones started to influence the young kids. Michael was creating something new in the world that really started in black music and that led to him through Chuck Berry, Little Richard, and Tina Turner.

# CREATING DRAMA

It's funny, because we started the trend in using multiple producers on one album with some of the stuff I did with Patti Austin, but there's something you lose when there's more than one producer. You tend to lose the overriding vision for the album as a whole. With *Thriller*, everything worked together to create one album that gave the listener a dramatic experience in nine scenes. Take a song like "Billie Jean," which is almost like a mantra, and follow it up with "Human Nature," which has a kaleidoscopic collage of chord changes and textures moving all over the place. That's what drama is about—that's what sequencing the songs in an entire album is about.

Each song on an album should have its own thing that it contributes to the whole. That way the listener wants to come back for more. There are no formats to follow. Each case is unique, and you need to put some thought into how each song flows into the next and what part each song plays. It's really very important. What's also important is giving the ear six choices for things to listen to so that each time they listen they hear something new. It's like the listener can't experience the entire song with just one ticket. They need to come back for more. The six parts might consist of a unique bass line, or drum lick, background vocals, horn part, string line, or any other musical ingredient.

# DILIGENCE

We only had very few months to record *Thriller*. That was a huge task, but we had the right people in place, and everyone knew what they were doing. The entire

Roscoe's #4:
*one-half chix, smoth-*
*ered with gravy and*
*onions, two waffles,*
*their own mix.*

Bill Gibson Collection

album cost $569,000, which is not much money in the scope of what its return was.

We worked long, hard hours, and for much of the time we had three studios going 24/7. And we would *eat* during those sessions. Wooh! Every day we'd go through four cans of Planter's Red Spanish Peanuts and four huge Mr. Good-bars—that's real healthy, right? Then we'd each order a #4 from Roscoe's House of Chicken 'n' Waffles. That's the one with all the gravy and onions! In the studio all you do is just destroy yourself. You don't get *any* exercise, and you just eat all the bad food.

Rod and Bruce and I could out hang anybody, though, when we were working. They were taking our second engineers out on stretchers because they couldn't handle it. We would stay up for five days and five nights without a drop of sleep. I was smoking then. I would go through four packs of Marlboros a day! And so would Rod!

## EVEN IF IT'S A
## Distraction, Do It Right

While we were doing *Thriller,* Steven Spielberg was doing *E.T.* Steven and I were introduced by my guru Steve Ross at his Malibu home. While we were fast becoming great friends during that time, we used to visit each other—he was at Laird Studios, and I was at Westlake. I gave him a synthesizer, and he gave me a viewfinder and a director's chair. It was just a beautiful time. And then in the middle of everything, Steven came to me and said, "Would you guys do a song with Michael for the *E.T.* soundtrack?" I said we would, and I got Alan and Marilyn Bergman to write the lyrics and Rod Temperton to write the melody for "Someone in the Dark." When we were through I told Steven that we were glad we got a chance to do the song, but that we were running out of time on *Thriller* and we needed to get right back on it. But he said, "Man, this is so great, you've got to do the whole album!" I said, "Oh my God!" I love Steven with all my heart; I love him like my brother. Before I could respond, I look up, and here comes Steven's mixer/editor, Bruce Canon, carrying a whole box of *E.T.*'s footsteps, all the dialogue, and all of Johnny Williams's music. We've got to take the biggest movie in all history, which is two hours long, and condense it down to a 40-minute soundtrack. We had to do all the narration and restructure *E.T.*'s footsteps, and mix the dialogue and everything. And Michael did the narration. Jesus Christ, man! We were really scampering to try to make this movie and get back to *Thriller*. But we got it. Then Bruce got upset because he couldn't mix it—he wanted to make sure it was done right. We decided it was important for everyone's sake to make sure we did it right, so we let Bruce take the time to finish the job.

## TOO MUCH MUSIC FOR VINYL

When we first mixed *Thriller*, Rod's song was too long, and "Billie Jean" was 11 minutes! It had an intro you could get married on! I called Michael "Smelly," or "Smelly Jelly," and I said, "Smelly, we've got to cut it down." Michael came back at me in his sweet high voice with, "But it makes me want to dance!" Well, who were Rod and Bruce and I to tell him not to dance, as great as he was at dancing? That's how he shut us up, you know. But, we were coming back the next day.

We were finishing the album with an all-night session, recording "Beat It," that ended at 9 o'clock in the morning. I had three studios going, with Van Halen in one studio, Bruce in another studio where the speakers were on fire for some reason, and Michael was in another studio doing his thing. We finished at 9 a.m.

and Bruce took the tapes to Bernie Grundman to start mastering the final product.

I took Michael to my house and put him on the couch, put a blanket on him, and let him sleep until noon, but we had to go back to the studio to hear how the record sounded. What we would hear was what was coming out—what the public would hear. This counted.

It sounded like doo doo. Man oh man! It was pitiful! We had 27 minutes on each side and, as we knew when Bruce left the studio for Grundman Mastering, it was just too much music. With that much music the grooves on the vinyl were too close together and not deep enough—there was just too much to fit. You need big grooves for a big sound! And to be competitive on the radio, you want your record to blow everything else away! We listened to the record and Michael started to cry. A top Epic Records executive, Larkin Arnold, was there breaking open the champagne to celebrate, saying, "You guys are finished!" I said, "Man, *forget* about it! This album is not even thinking about coming out like this. No way!"

The first single with Paul McCartney and Michael, "The Girl Is Mine," was already out and at No. 2 on the charts—that's really the one that schedules the album. If that first single hits No. 1 and you don't have the album done, the record company starts screaming, and they already were. It was going up and up and up and up and everybody was getting very nervous. But it was important that we got it right—very important!

At 27 minutes a side, we couldn't win. I said, "Okay, guys, this is what we've been talking about. We've got to cut some of that stuff out, whether it makes you dance or not. We've got to cut it down, or we'll have to take it off the record. We need to get this down to 18 or 19 minutes per side, so we'll need to work on everything." We went in the other room with Freddie DeMann, and we all figured out our plan. We decided to go home and get some rest and then come back and remix one song per day, so we'd be done in eight days. And that's what we did.

# MTV

Michael was the first black artist ever played on MTV. Rick James tried to get "Superfreak" played, but they were only playing white records and he couldn't break through the barrier.

Steve Ross [CEO of Time Warner] owned and started MTV. Bobby Pittman wrote the business plan for $39 million. He said, "I think people want to see rock 'n' roll as much as they want to listen to it." He was right. Nobody had seen anything like that before. All of the content was free because it was looked on as promotional material for album sales. So they got their content for nothing! Please! Now that company is worth nearly $40 billion.

I was with Steve Ross down in Acapulco at the Warner Records villa. He asked me, "What is the next record you're putting out, Q?" and I said, "We're gonna double-clutch, with 'Billie Jean' and 'Beat It.'" So he told Pittman and all the rest of the executives that "Billie Jean" would be the next video that went on MTV. And he was right. It was astounding.

As it turned out, MTV was only part of what kicked off "Billie Jean." What really made it turn the corner was the 25th anniversary of Motown on TV, produced by Suzanne DePasse. Michael sang with his brothers, and then he said, "I love singing with my brothers, but I like my new stuff, too." He did the moonwalk on that thing, and it was *over*. Over!

# *BAD*

When I'm producing, I'm listening for everything at the same time. If it's not right, it just jumps out at me—that takes a lot of concentration and attention, and not everybody always understands what's really going on. However, it was undeniable that our musical family had grown very close through the

'80s, and when *Bad* came along in 1987, we were efficient and tight. Through everything that was going on with Michael and his father, and anything else, Michael and I always remained cordial. We were professional, we had a strong team, and we had a job to do.

## SONGS

Michael just had an amazing imagination. He was very good with unique imagery in his songs. His songs always had an autobiographical tendency. Knowing him as well as I did, I could see that these songs were about his life and his passions and experiences, along with the complexities that were always part of his life. A lot of his stuff was so different because his life was such an incredible fantasy.

I think he was very lucky to have that ability, as such a great songwriter and singer, to get the fantasy out—it was cathartic. I loved it that Michael had that theatrical, cinematic tendency. We had a good thing going. It was really a very blessed team of people.

Michael wrote some great songs for the album. He wrote "Dirty Diana" and "Bad" (which was written to be a duet with Prince), and he wrote "Speed Demon," "Another Part of Me," and "I Just Can't Stop Loving You," which Siedah Garrett was on with him. And then Siedah and Glenn Ballard wrote "Man in the Mirror," and we got Terry Britten and Graham Lyle, who wrote "What's Love Got to Do with It?" to write "Just Good Friends" for Stevie Wonder and Michael.

## PRINCE

We had a meeting with Prince out at Michael's place to ask him if he wanted to be involved in *Bad.* It's not like they were kissing cousins, you know. Prince was in the middle of starring in *Under the Cherry Moon,* which he took over as director.

After the meeting, Prince came to me and said, "This is going to be a hit with or without me, man." I said, "You're probably right," and he was.

# SALES

Coming off *Thriller* and over 120 million albums sold, Michael expected to sell 100 million with *Bad,* but that's just not how it works. It's tough when you're being compared to the biggest-selling album of all time. That's some crazy stuff. You really just never know about these things. You just have to do what you love and believe in, go with your instincts, and then hope for the best. But nobody's ever going to talk me into feeling that selling 25 or 30 million records is a bomb!

### Grammy Nominations for *Bad* (1987–88)

1987 **Album of the Year**: *Bad* [Michael Jackson] (Epic)
**Producer of the Year**
1988 **Record of the Year**: "Man in the Mirror" [Michael Jackson]; single from *Bad* (Epic)

# RAP IS DEAD

When we were finishing up *Bad,* Michael said a couple of times that he felt I wasn't in touch with what was happening currently in the market and so forth. And that was after I even had Run DMC in the studio ready to collaborate with him on an anticrack song. He said, "Quincy doesn't get it. He doesn't know rap is dead." In 1987! Man, you know I don't miss a thing! I had heard the Last Poets, and I recorded the Watts Prophets in 1975 doing Beautiful Black Girl. I saw every inch of that revolution coming like it had a red suit on. I *knew* rap was going to be huge!

I just said, "Okay, we'll see!" Then I did *Back on the Block,* and we had Big Daddy Kane, Ice-T, Melle Mel, Kool Mo Dee, and QD3—all great rappers. In 1990 we won the Grammy for Album of the Year and Best Rap Record and helped to usher rap into the mainstream.

## Chapter 7

# THE PRODUCER AND THE ARTISTS

As Quincy talks about each artist, we get a feel for how he works, how he gets the best out of them, and how his approach leaves room for their individual talents and creativity to shine through. We see a common thread of love, care, respect, and understanding, but it's also clear that each artist is unique and Quincy's techniques vary depending on the person. We also see sidebars from the artists in which they share insights about their interactions with Q. Note how they talk about him and how effective his approach to production really is.

The worst thing that can happen in any collaborative environment is that you have people around who just tell you what they think you want to hear. That's a waste of time and it's the most dangerous thing there is. I don't need any yes-men/women around me—I want the people I work with to tell me exactly what they feel all the time. With that being said, it's also extremely important to always deliver the truth in love. I've been more than well trained by people, with whom I've always shared deep affection and mutual respect, including Ray Charles, Stevie Wonder, Frank Sinatra, Dinah Washington, Billy Eckstine, and Miles Davis.

The love between a performer and a producer has to be so absolute and unquestioned. That's where the power is—that's the key to getting top results. When that love is established and understood, the producer can be very honest and sincere about everything it takes to record the best possible performance. It also works the other way. The artist and the producer have to share mutual respect and love to make the best possible music. As the producer, you have to read when it's time to push for another take, or say, "Let's take a break and forget all about this for a while." I always like to have food around the session. It helps keep everyone going and it makes the studio feel more like home. We might have fruit or cake or whatever. I used to make stuff and bring it in, too—I make a mean chicken sandwich! A lot of times, just giving the artist a few minutes to relax, hang out, and maybe have a little something to eat will make all the difference—they'll go back in and nail the track on the first take.

You also need to know when to stop. When there's a real struggle to get the right performance, it's okay to take the pressure off the artist and ask them to come back another day. You have to be a psychiatrist, almost as well as a brother, mother, musician, orchestrator, everything. You can't think about it too much—you have to feel it. It's a very, very amazing process.

The process is the same whether you're with a seasoned professional or with a young artist that's new to the studio. Once the trust is there, it's like a man and a wife, you know. It's powerful. The producer's love for the artist has to really be deep. That love provides the genuine platform for the producer to be able to examine the minute details of an artist's musical performance, as well as the creative concept behind the material. It's love that removes the threat to the artist. If they know that you truly care about them, they can trust their instincts and explore new musical and creative ways to express themselves. I'm always there for them and always on their side.

You have to find different ways to take each project on its own journey. There are no rules or system or format. No way! I don't even believe in that. You just assess the situation. No matter what artist it is that you're producing, you figure out how to make the best possible music. I've worked with so many artists and they're all good—

they're all different and they're all good. Frank Sinatra, Ray Charles, Stevie Wonder, Sarah Vaughn, Ella, Tony Bennett, and Michael are each legendary in their own way. And Shirley Horn … *please!* There's nobody better than her. I love Shirley, and my goddawg-daughter Patti Austin, and Siedah Garrett, and Aretha Franklin, and Roberta Flack. Pleeze! There's nobody better at what they do!

You need to be open and flexible, and you need to react to the opportunities that come up. Aretha plays piano, too. On her record in '71, she did a version of "Somewhere" [from West Side Story]. It is so beautiful that I want to have it played at my funeral. Rather than hiring a session musician to cover the piano, we kept the honesty and vulnerability that Aretha gave us when she played the part—it was just a magic moment. That's the whole thing: you have to leave space for God to walk through the room. That's what you're doing when you're producing music. It's almost like a prayer when it's done right and in love.

Sometimes, the artist doesn't understand what's behind the producer's actions or reactions because they don't understand the basis for those actions. The producer's decisions and actions are guided by his or her understanding of the soul of music, the art and science of music, and the relationships between the artist, the band, the environment, the engineer, the mood, and everything else. And it's the producer that has to keep the big picture in mind—the final product. Someone might walk into a session and think, "Oh, there's something wrong with this or that," and they might be right until the next parts are added. I focus like a laser on the arrangement and the textures. The structure *has* to be right for the song, and the textures need to flow in a creative and musical way. The art of producing happens when the producer takes into consideration all of his or her instincts, knowledge, and musicality and matches that with the talents and capabilities of the artist, the band, the background singers, everybody. There are some musicians that need to be guided through the recording. I prefer to work with musicians who can take the structure of my ideas and add their own instincts and love and creativity to it. That can be a beautiful thing—it really can.

If you're paying attention and if you understand the value and talents of your musicians and if you've established a loving relationship with the artist, you'll know how to react and at a certain point you won't have to think about it a lot—you'll just know. A lot of times you'll know because you made a mistake on a previous song. When we did "She's Out of My Life," it just wasn't happening until we trimmed it down to just guitar with Fender Rhodes and a string pad—once we did, it was magical. That song wouldn't have been nearly as powerful if somebody wasn't listening for the right path— the path that was most creative and powerful.

Sir George Martin is definitely one of my all-time favorite producers. He had a vision and he took a group of very talented young guys and helped them realize their full potential. George brought new creativity to The Beatles. He was able to maintain their personality while providing just the right amount of depth and interest. You don't think Ringo came up with the idea for a string quartet on "Eleanor Rigby" or the symphony on "A Day In The Life" do you? That was George Martin blending his abilities, instinct, and intuition with the artists' creativity. That's what it's all about.

I like Timbaland and Dr. Dre, Take 6, Acon, RedOne, and a some of the other new guys. Timbaland has a vision and he's able to pull it off. The effects of music and production are so goddamn personal. It's all music and it all uses the same notes, but the essence of music relies on the fact that each person adds their emotional component and each listener filters through their unique emotional state. When the producer is able to blend his or her creativity with the artist's creativity and the result is music that is more powerful than it could have been without that collaboration, you really have something.

## JAMES INGRAM

When you're looking for great songs, you don't go to amateurs—you go to the best writers and singers— people like Barry Mann and Cynthia Weil. Russ Titelman sent me a song one day when I was doing *The Dude*. He thought that "Just Once" might be just right for me. I called back and said, "I love the song, but who's the singer?" They told me they really didn't know but he was just the piano player with The Coasters and Ray Charles. I said, "That's BS! He's more than that, he is a

great singer." So I called James and he said, "No, man, I'm just the piano player, man, I've got a whisky sound in my voice." And I said, "The whisky sound is what I love." He's one of the best singers in America, man. He really is.

The first two songs he did were "Just Once" and "One Hundred Ways." I had originally gotten "One Hundred Ways" for George Benson's album *Give Me the Night*. It's a great song, but it needed a strong bridge, which Rod Temperton wrote in short order without even claiming songwriting credit! That song resulted in a Grammy for James on his first record! We opened the Grammy telecast that year, with James singing "Just Once" along with me conducting the orchestra. It was a cold opening. I don't think I've ever seen that before, especially with a brand-new singer nobody even knows! Even after 30 years, there are still people all over the world that play our music on the radio every day. Every day! James is still going all over the world singing those songs.

When we recorded "Just Once" and "One Hundred Ways," I made sure we had the right guys in the band. We got Louis Johnson, David Foster, Greg Phillinganes, Steve Lukather, John Robinson, Jerry Hey, Johnny Mandel, Abe Laboriel, and on and on. It was a great group of musicians. David was just starting back then, but he was already a monster player. On his first session with the Brothers Johnson, we did five to seven songs a night—he's just amazing! When recording the tracks in a production, you're dealing with intuition and instinct. There are no real secrets. It's about judgment that's based on your heart, your experience, and your musical understanding. You've really got to open up your soul to let nature take its course.

## On Q

# James Ingram

Quincy Jones is not from this planet. He's really an extraterrestrial—he just doesn't want anybody to know. He knew stuff about me that I never even knew! He discovered that I was a singer. I didn't know that—I thought I was just a piano player.

At the time I met Quincy, I was a musician who was playing on Ray Charles's record "I Can See Clearly." I also co-wrote "You 20th Century Fox" with Ray. And I was playing on Carl Carlton's album *She's a Bad Mama Jama*. I couldn't read a note of music, but I was playing on hit records for world-renowned artists. I was a successful musician, but I didn't consider myself a singer.

Buzzy Feiten and I were writing songs together, and he got me a job singing demos for $50 a piece at Sony/ATV Music Publishing. The first demo I did was "Just Once." I studied it for an hour and then came in and sang it in the studio. They gave me a copy and $50. I went down to Leon Haywood's house because he was producing Carl Carlton on *She's a Bad Mama Jama*, and told him I had just done a demo of a song he might like. When he heard it, he liked it but didn't think it was right for Carl.

Through ATV's contacts, they got the demo of "Just Once" to Quincy, who asked right away who was singing it. They said, "He's just a piano player for Ray Charles; he's just a demo singer."

Quincy called me and said, "Are you signed with anybody?"

I said, "No. What are you talking about?"

He asked, "Did you sing the demo of 'Just Once'?"

When I said yes, Quincy asked me to come and sing it on his album!

I said, "You want me to come play?"

He said, "No. I want you to come sing."

I thought it was a joke, but I went along with it. When I was in the studio, I started singing but I kept stopping the tape. When Quincy asked me why I kept stopping, I said, "Well, I'm trying to clean the gruff up out of my voice."

He came right back with, "No! That's why you're in here. That's your sound!"

Quincy Jones Collection

Quincy didn't just discover me *as* a singer, he actually discovered that I *was* a singer! He literally *found* me! I'm still amazed that he produced records for me. Quincy Jones changed my life! He transformed my whole life with that one song.

Quincy talked the people at the Grammys into opening up their telecast with "Just Once" instead of an uptempo dance number. So, there I was, scared as hell; I am trembling as I'm singing. This was in 1981, and in that same telecast I won a Grammy for Best R&B Vocal Performance on *The Dude*. I was up for three Grammys for "One Hundred Ways," [Best R&B Male Vocalist, Best Male Pop Vocalist, and Best New Artist].

Rick James performed just before James Brown and Tina Turner came out to announce the winner of the Grammy. Rick James was nominated for the same Grammy, and he was off to the side licking his lips waiting because he had just performed and he thought he was going to win. All I heard when they announced the winner was "James," so I'm clapping because I'm thinking Rick James had won, but they had said my name! So I'm the first person in the history of the Grammys to win a Grammy without having a solo album out! *The Dude* album was the most nominated album in the history of the Grammys at the time. Man, it was like *Alice in*

*Wonderland* or *The Wizard of Oz*! I can't even explain how amazing it was.

## Alpha State

Sometimes, Quincy produces in an alpha state of mind. It almost seems like he's going to sleep, but then he'll just pop right up and tell the singers or the band to do this, or do that, or take that out and put this here—he works a lot like that. He's not going to sleep; he's just in another state of mental awareness that's much deeper than normal. I think that's part of why he doesn't drive a car. He goes so far into the music that he loses track of everything else.

*alpha state—a condition of relaxed, peaceful wakefulness devoid of concentration and sensory stimulation. It is characterized by alpha waves at a frequency of 8 to 13 Hz as recorded by an electroencephalograph and is accompanied by feelings of tranquility and a lack of tension and anxiety. Biofeedback training and meditation techniques are used to achieve this state.*
—Mosby's Medical Dictionary, 8th edition.

## Producing Vocals

When Quincy's producing my vocal tracks, I'll do a take, and he'll say, okay, we've got that, but I want you to emphasize this or that idea, word, note—or whatever he sees that can make it better. We record multiple takes all the way through the song, and then he combines different parts of those takes together until and he has what he wants.

When I came in to sing "One Hundred Ways," I sang it through two times and he said, "No, no. Today is not the day. We'll do this later." I wasn't offended, because he was right and I trusted him—I was in *awe* of him, period. When I came back later, and I had studied it long enough to make it my own as opposed to just coming in and singing the melody, everything went great. I had it done in just a few takes.

## Decisive Production Style

Quincy came home one day and read an article in *W* magazine that talked about P.Y.T.s—Pretty Young Things. He immediately thought it would be the perfect title for a song on Michael's album, *Thriller*. Quincy had the hook and he got us all on the phone right away—his musicians and songwriters—and told us he wanted this song to go on Michael's new album. He wanted to hear our ideas as soon as possible.

I recorded a demo on my 4-track. The drum track was just me pounding the kick and snare on my wooden floor on one track, with two spoons on the floor for a hi-hat on another track. When he heard it, his reaction was immediate, "We're cuttin' it tomorrow." He started making calls right away to get the details together. The thing is, he listens to everybody's stuff, but when it hits him, there's nothing to talk about. It's not a "kinda-sorta" thing. It's a decisive, "That's it! I don't need to hear any more."

Even though Quincy would hand things off to be done, he always had something in mind. When it was time to orchestrate "One Hundred Ways," Quincy told Johnny Mandel, "I want a string line. I don't want to have an arrangement. I just want a string line to glide over the top of this." I was right there in the studio while Quincy was telling Johnny exactly what he wanted. I don't know of anybody that he just let go off and do a part of anything on his record without some instruction. It might be as simple as telling Jerry Hey, "I need some stabs right here," but he'd already have a vision of what he wanted next. Also, he knows just the right people to get to do what he has in mind. He'll let you show him what you have, though. He would usually let me go through the song three or four times before he would say anything. Then he might give me some direction on specific things he wanted to hear.

## "Baby, Come to Me"

When Warner Bros. released "Baby, Come to Me," it didn't do anything on the charts. Several months later, it was introduced on the soap opera *General Hospital* as "Luke and Laura's Theme," and America went out and bought it in a New York minute. That television show turned "Baby, Come to Me" into a No. 1 pop hit record. You never know what's gonna happen! My father, Henry Ingram, taught me that, with faith in God and confidence in myself, there was nothing that I couldn't do. I believed him. The musical gift that I had gotten from God was nurtured through Quincy Jones. Quincy saw something in me that I didn't know existed. He opened up that door and *made* me walk through it!

And that sent me all the way around the world. That would never have happened. That's why I'm saying, this dude ain't from here. Quincy Jones just isn't from this planet! I mean it; he's extraterrestrial for real!

# QD3 (SNOOPY)

Oprah called me the other day, and said, "I didn't know your son was a film producer!" I said, "No, he's a music producer *and* he owns a video production company." Snoopy is a monster—he has such a high-tech mind. Oprah had seen Tupac's film documentaries, *Beef, Thug Angel,* and *Letter to the President* and found out that Snoopy had produced them. In addition to Tupac, Snoopy has produced Ice Cube and L.L. Cool J. He's in his 40s now, but he's been into producing since he was 17—he's been around the block.

I had both Snoopy and Martina with Ulla Andersson. They grew up with her in Sweden. In the beginning we said, "We're not gonna have this father/daddy stuff." He needed his own identity and he needed to make it on his own. His mother named him Quincy Delight Jones, III—I wouldn't have done that. We wanted to make sure he could develop his own image and his own sense of independence, so we came up with QD3. It's great and it has worked—he has been able to maintain his own personality.

I love Snoopy to death! We're very close. He has always been extremely talented. Even at 14 he was in a big hit breakdance group, called Berzerk, in Sweden. He is a stone pro, totally self-educated and motivated—his mind absorbs everything. He even speaks and writes correspondence like a college graduate. It's astounding!

## On Q

# QD3

I spent a lot of time in Sweden with my mother, but when I was here for summer break I would go to recording sessions with my dad. I met Michael Jackson when they were working on *The Wiz*, and then I also went to the sessions for *Thriller* and *Off the Wall*. In Sweden, we lived in a regular working-class area. I would bring my dad's records to school and I would tell people what he did, but they thought I was lying! And when I would go away for the summer and come back with all these stories about hanging out with Michael Jackson, Spielberg, or seeing something like the VCR before the rest of the world had it, they thought I was just making it up. So I didn't really have an opportunity to *wear* that so much. I just lived a cool, normal life.

One of the things I learned from my dad was the importance of not confining yourself to one area or category in the industry. He had a publishing company, he would score movies, he would do hit songs, and he would produce movies—he was ambidextrous within the creative community. He was also one of the first musicians to become an entrepreneur on multiple platforms. Seeing him bring in African singers and Brazilian percussionists, and merging all these different cultures seamlessly and making commercial music out of that, gave me a really broad palette. So when I started doing music, I automatically assumed that I'm supposed to be scoring movies also and scoring TV and doing all these different things and being entrepreneurial and creative at the same time. Growing up, seeing him do so many different things, from the outset, I thought that was what you were *supposed* to do. I thought it was natural to venture out—to work in a lot of different areas within the entertainment industry.

When I got my first Platinum record with Ice Cube, I asked my dad, "What do you think I should be thinking about doing next?" and he said, "The first thing you should do when you get that record is do something *totally* different, so people can't peg you." So I got into filmmaking and all kinds of other things based on that.

When I told my father I wanted to do music, he immediately broke out Stravinsky and Coltrane. There was no half-stepping. He said, "Whatever you do, go for *the best*, and you've gotta be the baddest mofo out there doing what you do. Once you can master one thing, you can master anything." He also said, "Just focus on one thing that you really want to do really well." So for me it was music production within the hip-hop field. I studied technology, engineering, music, and hip-hop as it was emerging in real time. I don't know if you can truly master any one musical genre, but I got as far as I could, then I started venturing out into other things. I understood the concept of mastering something, knowing everything from top to bottom about the thing you have a passion for. Sometimes people do just enough to get by, or they'll get a certain amount of success and then develop a huge ego. When I got my first Platinum record, or my first four or five, I'd go to my dad's house and look at *one* plaque with 50 Platinum records on it. I was like, "Dang, I've got a long way to go!" So I never was able to get an ego or feel like I had accomplished as much as maybe some of my peers thought I had—I knew there was a whole other level, which has helped keep my paradigm pretty realistic.

My dad has always stressed the importance of having a spiritual base, an underlying mission, for why you're doing what you're doing. If somewhere in your rationale for doing a record or a film is that you're trying to help a certain part of the world or a certain demographic, then when things get tough, you'll always have energy to keep pushing through. Whereas if you're *just* doing it for the money or the fame, eventually either people will get tired of you or you'll get tired of pushing. He always has a sense of purpose in everything he does. His work in almost all cases has helped somebody. And I have to think that he influenced Michael Jackson along those lines, too. Whenever I make a film now, I try to think about, "What's my underlying mission?" and that underlying mission helps to guide me through the trials and tribulations that occur during any project.

My father is universal. He's able to bring together cultures and classes. He's got a warmth about him that people can relate to no matter who they are or what kind of disposition they have; when they're around him they change and they become more open. It's unparalleled, in my opinion. I think that's a huge part of why he's so great in the studio, too. In the recent *We Are the World 2* session, you see him in there with a hundred egos—a hundred of those super-accomplished artists and producers—and he just brings them together seamlessly. I think that's a talent in itself. I think that's why a lot of his records are so great, because he'll gather 30 great minds in the studio and get them all to harmonize.

I think that the records that he makes are timeless. Just listen to *Off the Wall*, and sonically, even 30 years later, it's like, *"Damn, this is good!"* His focus on excellence is something that crosses his personal life and his musicianship. He appreciates art and excellence to the extent that it's like watching a movie where every single frame is like a beautiful still photo. That's how I think he approaches his music. And he's always been able to merge things that people wouldn't imagine being merged, bringing in all these different influences from all over the world and making it sound good. He's the best at that.

My dad didn't a have very strong template for what a parent was supposed to be. And he was busy with a lot of things on a lot of different planes when we were growing up, but he loved us and he made sure we stayed on the right track when we were growing up. He would always say, "You've got to respect your mind and reach for the top." Some kids just get pushed to get good grades, but for him it was always looking way, way, way up. I always kept that in the back of my mind, and I've never reached for anything lower than the highest level. That's not to say that I've reached that yet, but at least that's where I'm aiming. If I get halfway or even a quarter of the way there, I'll be better off than most people. I think almost everybody in our family is like my dad in our energy and hustle and our quest for excellence. I think that's pretty rare.

My father is like a sponge for knowledge, and he's always learning new things. That's definitely something I got from him, too. No matter how old I get, I'm not afraid to ask questions or become passionate about something new. That's the best lesson you can get from a parent in the world—a passion for life and knowledge.

## QD3 Timeline

1968   Born Quincy Delight Jones III in London to Quincy Delight Jones, Jr., and Ulla Andersson. Subsequently raised in Stockholm, Sweden, where he got his start in hip-hop as a touring breakdancer with the group Apoptygma Berzerk

1979    Attended recording sessions for Michael Jackson's *Off the Wall*, produced by his father, Quincy Jones, Jr.

1982    Got his first drum machine and started producing demos for local hip-hop acts in Stockholm.

1982    Attended recording sessions for Michael Jackson's *Thriller*, produced by his father, Quincy Jones, Jr.

1986    Produced (with Karl Dyall) his first hip-hop hit, "Next Time." Earned first Gold record at age 16.

1986    Attended Berklee College of Music.

1987    Moved to New York and spent a year and a half working with old-school legends such as T La Rock (first artist signed to Def Jam) and Special K (of the group Treacherous 3 featuring Kool Moe Dee).

1987    Connected with Dr. Dre and Ruthless Records. Began producing alongside Ice Cube, Tupac, Warren G, Snoop Dogg, and many others.

1992    Composed the theme song for *Out All Night* featuring Patti Labelle.

1993    Won ASCAP Composers Award for his work on *Fresh Prince of Bel Air*, starring Will Smith.

1995    Composed theme song for the *In the House* comedy series starring L.L. Cool J.

1999    Composed the theme song for *Grown Ups*, starring Jaleel Erkel White, and for *The PJs*, Eddie Murphy's animated comedy series.

1999    Started a documentary production company focused on chronicling the many dimensions of urban culture.

2000    Received Emmy nomination for *Grown Ups*.

2002    Began working on the critically acclaimed *Beef* trilogy, which provides a definitive look at hip-hop's most notorious conflicts and resolutions between artists.

2002    Produced the multi-Platinum-selling DVD, *Thug Angel*.

2003    Won *Vibe* magazine's Best Music DVD Award.

2006    *Beef* TV series premiered on the BET network.

2010    Continued production work; list of credits includes albums and singles with artists such as Tupac, Ice Cube, and LL Cool J., and remixes of records by Prince, Ronald Isley, Queen Latifah, Coolio, Naughty By Nature, Everlast, and Morcheeba.

# Q: THE HEART

Quincy Jones is as passionate about people and their needs as he is about music. He spends much of his time travelling the globe, working on humanitarian projects, and devoting time and energy to promoting global understanding. His music has provided a unique platform from which to affect change among peoples of the world.

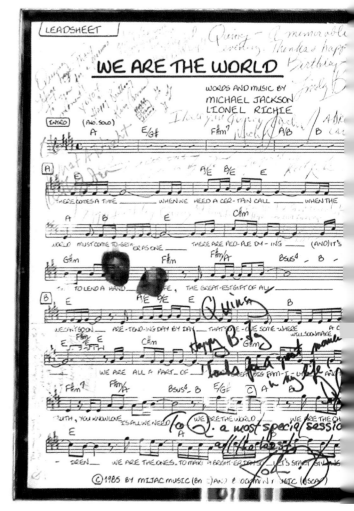

▲"We Are the World" was the biggest-selling single of all time, raising over $63 million for humanitarian aid in Africa and the US. The participating stars were asked to check their egos at the door during the recording of this song, which inspired this book by Doonesbury creator Gary Trudeau.

◀ Q: The overriding survival cry and mantra for South Africa is *ubuntu*, which means the collective is always stronger than the individual. It's true. That's what music is all about—many people working together, sharing a common creativegoal. It's deep and it's ancient.

▲This piece of music was signed by the participants of the original We Are the World project. It is displayed in Quincy's home. We Are the World and its 2010 sequel, recorded to benefit Haitian earthquake victims, are only two of Quincy's many humanitarian efforts, which include benefit concerts around the world.

# THE INSPIRATION

On September 26, 2008, the Quincy Jones Performance Center was dedicated in a ceremony at Seattle's Garfield High School. At the ceremony, Seattle school superintendent Maria L. Goodloe-Johnson, PhD, said, "We are proud and honored to have Garfield's performance center named after a musical visionary that *Time* magazine named as one of the most influential jazz musicians of the 20th century. Quincy Jones is not only a musical luminary whose award-winning career encompasses so many roles and accolades, but he is also a graduate of Garfield High School and of Seattle public schools. This performance center will stand as testament to both Mr. Jones's many prestigious accomplishments and to Garfield High School's long-standing commitment to the arts."

The Quincy Jones Performance Center encompasses a brand-new auditorium that seats 592, state-of-the-art sound, and lighting and rigging systems. The performance center also includes a new gymnasium, which features bleacher capacity for 1,800 people, three regulation basketball or volleyball courts, a built-in sound system, and the ability to accommodate gymnastics competitions.

Quincy has been a loyal alumnus and an ardent supporter of Garfield since he graduated in 1950. He has continued friendships, musical associations, and business dealings with many of his fellow Garfield graduates. These photos include the performance center and scenes from the dedication ceremony.

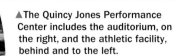

▲ The Quincy Jones Performance Center includes the auditorium, on the right, and the athletic facility, behind and to the left.

iv

▲Quincy with Garfield High principal, Ted Howard.

▶Song written by Quincy, Rod Temperton, and Lionel Richie for Garfield High School, based on "Miss Celie's Blues" from *The Color Purple.*

Lorie McKloskey and Beaux Arts Studio

◀ "We Are the World" session with (L-R) Quincy, Stevie Wonder, Michael Jackson, and Lionel Richie.

**Quincy Jones**

Over his illustrious career in music, television and film, Quincy Jones has won over 25 Grammy Awards, composed 30-plus major motion picture scores and launched the careers of countless performers. He produced the historic recording *We Are The World*, Michael Jackson's album *Thriller*, and co-produced the movie *The Color Purple*.

vi

With Pope John Paul II

With Michael Jackson

▲ With Ray Charles

▼ With
Sarah Vaughan

◄ With Count Basie
and Frank Sinatra

# 2010 WORLD Expo Sessions

Quincy composed and produced the theme for the 2010 World Expo in Shanghai along with China's premiere composer, Tan Dun. Quincy also included Siedah Garrett and Alfredo Rodriguez as co-writers and performers on the recording with other members of Quincy's musical family, sometimes referred to as "the usual suspects." The line-up of musicians included: Greg Phillinganes (keys), Alfredo Rodriguez (piano), Paul Jackson, Jr. (guitars), Nathan East (bass), John Robinson (drums), Siedah Garrett (vocals), and Antonio Sol (vocals). Quincy's good friend (and Chinese media icon in her own right) Yue-Sai Kan guided the vocalists in the correct pronunciation and diction of the Shanghainese lyrics. Francis Buckley engineered the session. Members of Quincy's team Adam Fell (vice president of Quincy Jones Productions), JoAnn Tominaga, and Rebecca Sahim, were there to manage innumerous details related to the sessions. There was also a cast of studio assistants, photographers, videographers, and a steady stream of Quincy's friends and other members of his musical family.

The song being recorded was called, "Better City, Better Life." The session was held at Westlake Studios' Studio D in Los Angeles. This room was built to Bruce Swedien's technical specifications for Michael Jackson before the *Bad* album started production. The room is large comfortable, and sounds excellent. Included in the construction is a stage at the far end of the studio, built so that Michael could dance and perform his songs while he was recording.

A Quincy Jones recording session is an event. When Quincy walks in, the picture is complete and the love starts flowing. The members of his musical family interact with genuine care and affection for Quincy and each other.

▲Quincy at the console getting into the track. He talks about working in the alpha state of mind, in a place where your instincts are finely tuned and accessible.

▲Nathan East on bass guitar.

▼John "JR" Robinson on the drums.

▼ Page 1 of the Master Rhythm chart for "Better City, Better Life"

ix

▲(L – R) Nathan East, John Robinson, and Alfredo Rodriguez pay close attention to Q. Siedah Garrett and Greg Phillinganes are in the background.

# The Mentor

Quincy has repeatedly given a hand up to talented musicians around the world. He has mentored and influenced countless young musicians.

After Quincy discovered Alfredo Rodriguez at the Montreux Jazz Festival in 2006, Alfredo made his way from Cuba to Los Angeles to take Quincy up on his offer to work with him. Alfredo has been rehearsing and focusing on his career. With Quincy's guidance, Alfredo is getting his shot at building a successful music career. He has had engagements across the United States, at The Playboy Jazz Festival in Los Angeles, at various jazz clubs, and on an extensive tour of China. The photos (near right) were taken at a session produced by Quincy at Capitol Records in Los Angeles. Alfredo was recording his rendition of "Bare Necessities," from the animated Disney feature film, *The Jungle Book*.

▲ Back row (L – R): Peter Chaikin, Rebecca Sahim, JoAnn Tominaga, Paula Salvatore. Front row (L – R): Adam Fell, Steve Genewick, Quincy, and Alfredo Rodriguez.

▲ Quincy talking with Peter Chaikin. Peter, now with Harmon Kardon (JBL), was one of Quincy's engineers in the '70s, assisting on *Body Heat* and *Mellow Madness* as well as engineering the Brothers Johnson's *Look Out for #1*, and other projects for Gore and Streisand.

# The Archives

A walk through Quincy's six well-secured and climate-controlled vaults is an immersion in some of the world's most important jazz and pop music history. The original charts from Quincy's earliest arrangements are neatly organized and catalogued. Charts for his band that travelled Europe are near his arrangements for Count Basie and his charts and master tapes from Michael Jackson, the Brothers Johnson, Quincy's albums, and many other projects. Here are some photos of materials in Quincy's archives.

▲Lesley Gore LP notes

▼Ellington tapes

▲The archives

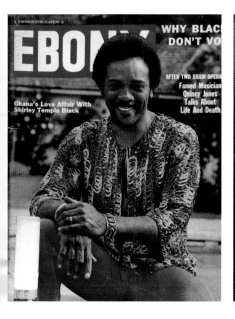

▲Examples of practice music notation in Quincy's hand.

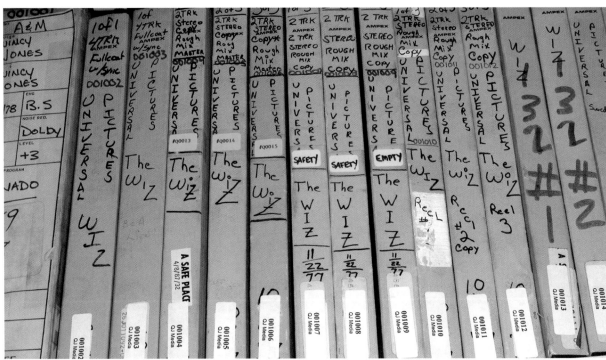

▲*The Wiz* tapes

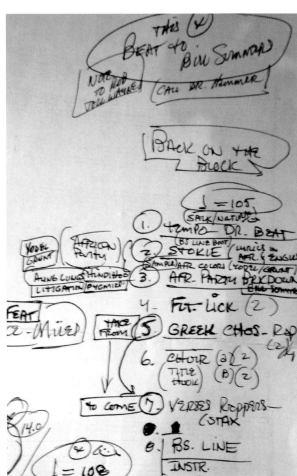

▲*Back on the Block* notes

▶*Jook Joint*
outtake sheet

Out takes from Final Mixes
1. TONE LOC-                    "Killer Joe"
2. CHARLIE WILSON-        "It's got me movin my feet...."
                                        "It sha feels good to me..."
                                        ".....Moan..." (2)
3. CHARLIE WILSON-        ".....Another big helpin'"
4. BRANDY-                       "All of a sudden..."
5. WAH WAH-                    Laugh
6. WAH WAH-                    "Baby" 1
                                        "Baby" 2
7. RAY CHARLES-            Lick
    WAH WAH-                    "Whooh, I Like it myself"
8. TAMIA-                         "Stuff like that"
                                        "I wanna feel you close to me"
                                        "Come closer"
                                        "That's right, right there"

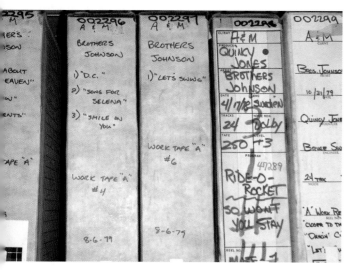

▲The Brothers Johnson tapes

▼The 1st Trombone part from Quincy's first composition, "From the Four Winds."

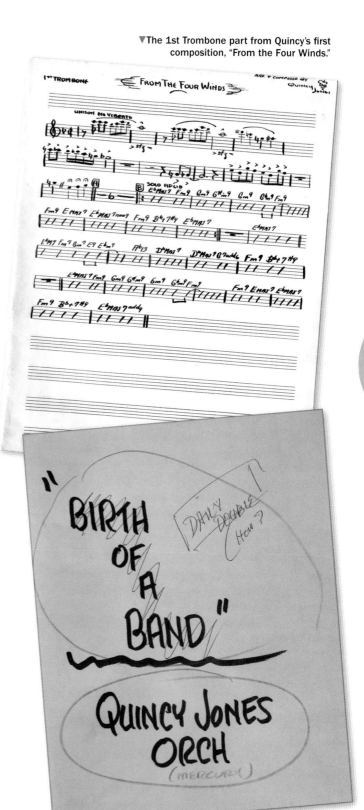

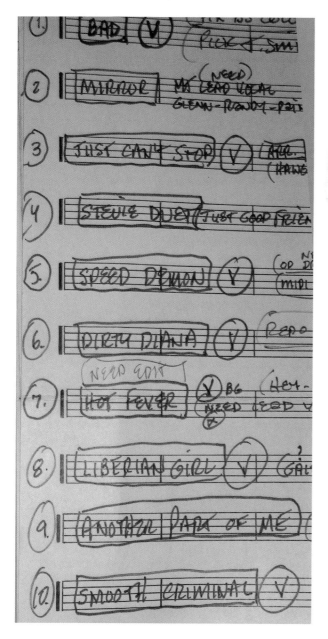

◄*Bad* notes

▲*Birth of a Band* note

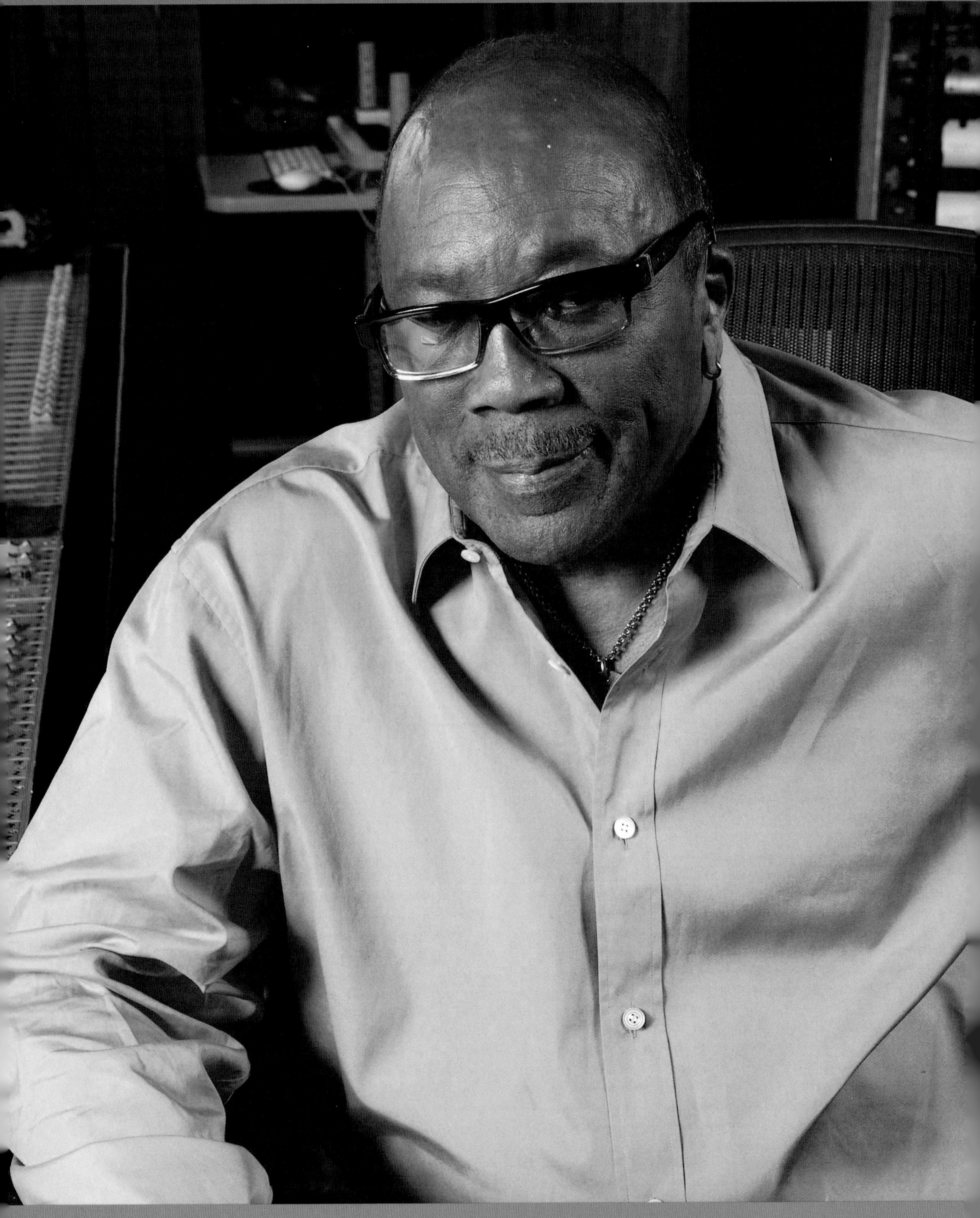

# PATTI AUSTIN

In 1954 Dinah Washington introduced me to this little four-year-old girl who, Dinah told me, was her god-daughter, Patti. Patti Austin has been a part of my soul ever since. She was a great singer, even at four years old! She had a photographic memory for music. She could remember anything she heard. She's always been a monster vocalist—she's not normal.

Patti would be at a recording session with Dinah, and later you could ask her to sing any take of a song and she would nail it. Any *take*! I could say, "Sing take 8 of ..." whatever song and she'd know exactly what it was! I knew right away that she would be something special.

Every time we worked together over the last 40-plus years, it has been incredible. In fact, with Patti, I expect more out of her than anybody, because she's so capable. She can do anything and she can phrase like any instrument: trumpet, sax, or anything. And she has incredible ears—she'll catch everything! She kind of spoiled me. After having worked with Billie Holiday at 14, Ella, Sarah Vaughn, Sinatra, and Ray Charles, you get a sense for when something is special—Patti Austin is special.

## On Q

# Patti Austin

Quincy and I worked together the first time when I was nine, doing *Free and Easy*. I was kind of like his little spy. There was a lot of drama and backbiting going on with the producer and the director. Some people wanted to sabotage Quincy; they'd make changes and wait until the last minute to tell him. But when I'd hear anything, I'd run down and tell Quincy so when they'd spring a last-minute change on him he would have already adjusted accordingly. He'd just say, "Oh, I've got that done already." He never asked me to be his spy, but when you're a kid and you're in the business and you're precocious, you keep track of everything that's going on, because you are interested.

A session with Quincy always has an environment of great silliness and fun, complete with hysterical laughing and telling stories and goofing around. And of course there's twice as much of that when I'm around. He calls me the "budget buster," but I learned it from him—it's a lot of fun! There is always great music, and he just creates a wonderful Petri dish for creativity.

Quincy has always worked on a lot of projects at once. There have always been business negotiations or meetings or conference calls going on during and around the sessions. I've very rarely known him to do just one project at a time. He's always worked on a lot of different stuff and a lot of different mediums: films, TV shows, magazines, and a bunch of other stuff.

Quincy tells the story about me memorizing the takes from a Dinah Washington session. That had a lot to do with my dad, who played trombone with Fletcher Henderson and Lucky Millinder and Father Hines and Billy Eckstine. He was always practicing his instrument, sitting me next to him, and showing me everything about music. And he listened to music all day long. Around my house, you'd hear Stravinsky and then Stan Kenton, and Basie, some Big Mama Thornton, or Tito Puente, some blues, some hillbilly music, or some Patsy Cline. He listened to absolutely everything. He loved marching bands; you'd hear some of that. So it was a big mix of all kinds of music, and he was always quizzing me about everything I heard. So he'd very often have me echo something I had just heard to see if it was penetrating, and it worked.

Q is really the same person in every aspect of his life. He doesn't compartmentalize his life, his music, and his relationships. It all comes from the same place, and it all functions in the same way. He is tremendously generous, whether he's working with you, or he's your friend, or whatever. It's always going to be the height of ecstasy with Quincy. And if, personally, you ever hit the depths of despair, there is no better friend to help you get through it. He's a very precious person. He really is.

One thing that astonishes me most about Quincy now is that he continues to grow and correct his flaws—he's

Quincy Jones Collection

Patti Austin, age 4, with Dinah Washington.

always working on himself. He's always getting better and he's the first one to apologize if he screws up; that doesn't usually happen, as you get older. You tend to go the other way. You tend to get a little more locked into whatever your drama is. Usually, if you're an idiot, you become an even more "staunched" idiot as you get older. He seems to get more flexible with age. I haven't figured that one out yet, but I told him I'm going to try to steal whatever it is. When I was a kid, he always used to say, "If somebody I haven't seen for a long time tells me I haven't changed a bit, I find it to be an insult." So he's definitely ever changing, and always for the better. That's pretty tough to do at any age, but I think even tougher as you get older.

Quincy is the master of adapting and adjusting to pull things together. That's one of the things a performer is required to do. There's nothing worse than playing to a crowd that's not giving anything back—it's your job to be able to fix a situation like that very quickly. So you tend to function that way in your entire life, which can serve you very well. For example, when we did the 25th anniversary version of *We Are the World*, Quincy had to step in and get the rappers to do their parts the way he had envisioned. Before he stepped in, just as the train was getting ready to hit the wall, people were looking to me, wondering if I was going to handle it. I just said, "You've got Quincy Jones upstairs. Go get him. Everyone will shut up and listen to him." All he has to do is say two sentences and they'll all go, "Oh, okay."

Quincy refuses to compartmentalize things, and I agree with his approach. You're not supposed to just listen to classical music; you're not supposed to just hang out with white folks; you're not supposed to just go to the Catholic Church. You're supposed to explore the world and embrace as much of it as you possibly can. Don't judge the stuff that you can't figure out. Factor it *in*, don't factor it *out*. That's the way he lives his life—he's able to roll and flow, with anybody anywhere anytime in any situation.

Music is music. You hinder your own progress if you're constantly saying you can't do something. It's like me saying, "Hmm, they want me to sing opera—I can't sing an opera. Well, I can sing music! I might have to train differently, but I'm sure as hell not going to shy away from something because it's in a different genre. As long as it has notes and rhythm, it's music.

## Selecting Songs

In the days when Quincy had Qwest Records, he was cranking it out. There were a lot of songs submitted to him from a lot of different writers. I would often sit with him as he was going through piles and piles of cassettes looking for good material. He really literally used to listen to everything. If you had a tape that got to Quincy, you could guarantee one thing: he listened to it and either accepted it or rejected it. Some of the stuff was really bad. You'd find one great song in the middle of about 50, but he'd listen to all 50. He wouldn't listen to stuff very long, because he didn't have to. It's like when you work in a factory and you have one thing you do over and over. You get to the point where you just know whether something is right or wrong. So Quincy could usually listen to eight bars and the intro and know whether the song had something to offer. Even though it was a very quick process on each song, it still took hours and hours.

Usually he would have the lyric sheet in his hand when he would listen—they would need to be sufficiently intriguing for him to invest extra time. If you're already bored at the beginning of the song, do you think somebody's going to sit through it to get to the bridge where it really kicks in? No way. There's no time for that.

I was with him the first time he heard "Just Once," with James Ingram singing. When he heard the demo he was like, "Damn! Who's singing that?" He immediately got on the phone and tracked James down. But he figured the song was going to be good, because it was written by Barry Mann and Cynthia Weil—one of the best songwriting teams ever.

# LOUIS AND
# George Johnson

Louis (Thunder Thumbs) and George (Lightnin' Licks) instantly became part of my rhythm section and went on the first tour I did after I had my two brain aneurysms in August and October of 1974. I had committed to 15 dates in Europe and 15 dates in Japan, but I was

147

Quincy Jones Collection

convinced I could never make it because I had amnesia—I couldn't remember my kids' names or anything else—and my whole left side was paralyzed.

My second operation had been in October and the tour was in February, but Elsie Giorgi, one of the doctors that helped me through everything and wouldn't give up on me said, "If you don't get your ass out on the road, you'll be a vegetable the rest of your life. You get a stool or whatever it takes, and go do it!" And I went out and did it. I could barely stand up so I got a stool, five horns, and a big rhythm section. By the time we were finished in Japan, my paralysis and amnesia were gone! I was so thankful to God.

When we were putting the show together, I already had Louis Johnson and Wah Wah Watson on guitar. Then Louis introduced me to his brother, George, and I heard him play. *Please!* Louis is a monster—one of the best bassists ever! And the two of them had such a great thing going as a team.

They were so much fun and I immediately felt their originality. George and Louis both played on *Mellow Madness* as the Brothers Johnson. I had changed their name from The Johnson Brothers to the Brothers Johnson, and they were featured on four songs to launch their upcoming album, *Look Out for #1*. They were still learning how to write songs, but we fixed their tunes up and look out, man, they had four double-Platinum albums!

## Aneurysm Chronology

### August 1974

*Body Heat* has been released and nearly has gone Platinum, selling 800,000 copies. Quincy is living large at 42 years old with actress Peggy Lipton and their daughter, Kidada.

On a hot August afternoon, Quincy suffers his first aneurysm after working three straight days and nights on *Mellow Madness* at his home in Brentwood.

Eight days later, Quincy's doctor, Elsie Giorgi, instructs Peggy to take Quincy to Cedars-Sinai Medical Center immediately, saying "I hope it's not too late." Quincy is diagnosed with a berry aneurysm, in which the main artery to the right side of the brain ruptures—the equivalent of having 16 strokes. Quincy is given a 1-in-100 chance of survival. At the suggestion of Giorgi, two tubes are inserted through incisions in the throat to freeze Quincy's brain at 32 degrees so that the operation can be completed while keeping the brain intact.

With Peggy Lipton, Phil Ramone, a couple of other relatives, and his brother, Lloyd, at his side, Quincy is taken into surgery. Quincy sees his life pass before his eyes. In his words, "It's like you're on a computer and you hold the Arrow key down and scroll through your life. All the people I hadn't taken time to tell how I felt about them flew past my eyes so fast I could barely see them. Everything I'd ever known and felt and would never feel again flowed past my eyeballs, and I could feel myself going toward that tunnel of white and gold light. I couldn't believe that leaving this world could be so beautiful; it's hanging in there that's the hard part."

Dr. Marshall Grode and Dr. Milton Heifitz tell Quincy, "The good news is, you are the 1 out of 100 who lived. The bad news is, we found another one on the other side that could be ready to explode at any minute. In two months we have to go back in again."

Friends in the artistic community who were told Quincy wasn't going to make it started planning a memorial concert at the Shrine Auditorium.

**September 1974**

Quincy attends his own memorial, where he is honored by just about everyone he's ever known, including Cannonball Adderley, Freddie Hubbard, Sarah Vaughn, Minnie Ripperton, The Main Ingredient, Cuba Gooding, Sr., Ray Charles, Billy Eckstine, the Watts Prophets, Marvin Gaye, Roscoe Lee Brown, Brock Peters, Sidney Poitier, and Richard Pryor.

**October 1974**

Quincy survives the second aneurysm surgery, suffering from paralysis of his left side and amnesia.

**February 1975**

Quincy does a tour of 15 cities in the United States and 15 cities in Japan. Even though he started the tour with anemia and paralysis, he returns from Japan with neither!

*"Q is the ultimate role model for positive thinking. When facing the most delicate surgery for an aneurism, we were wheeling him down into surgery. He was heavily sedated. He looked up at the doctor and said, 'When you get in there, don't steal any songs!'"*
—Phil Ramone in *Billboard* magazine, December 9, 1989.

## SIEDAH GARRETT

Siedah is a beautiful, wild lady! She's one of my favorite people. We've worked so many times together, and it's always a complete joy. And she was relentless in the beginning. I had been hearing her on a lot of demos and eventually ended up working with her on several projects. When we were recording *Bad*, she wrote "Man in the Mirror" with her writing partner, Glenn Ballard, and she made *sure* that I heard it and gave it a shot—the rest is history. That's a great song, and it was a great fit for Michael.

Siedah also wrote the lyrics for "Tomorrow (A Better You, Better Me)." We had recorded it on *Looking Out for #1* with The Brothers Johnson, but it was an instrumental. We wanted to use the song with Tevin Campbell, and Siedah was able to capture just what we wanted for the song.

## On Q
# Siedah Garrett

He's a sage. There aren't too many things that he hasn't "been there and done," and he's the first person to lend a hand, to lend support, to talk you through whatever the issue is. He makes you feel like a member of his family. He knows that I don't really see my immediate family much, so every year on Christmas and Thanksgiving I'm cordially invited to spend the day with Q and his family and friends. That really makes a difference in my life and it makes me feel so warm.

Q has had a lot of hardship in his life, and he nearly died from his aneurysm. I believe that when you come that close to the end of your life, you have a huge appreciation for every day. Each day is something you didn't think you were gonna have. So Q says, "Life is like rain, and when it rains, get wet!" So, that's what I'm busy doing. I just want to eat life up, and enjoy every opportunity that's presented to me. Enjoy every friendship that I'm offered. Entertain every invitation to experience joy, or to learn something, or to meet somebody new, or to create something. I don't want to sit at the table of life with a little napkin and a dainty little teacup. I want ladles and a huge salad fork, and I just want to eat it all up.

I first met Quincy when I auditioned for a cattle call. A friend called and said, "Quincy Jones is doing auditions. You've got to be there!" He didn't know what time they started, so I got there at 7 a.m.—there were just two others in line. The auditions didn't start till noon, but by then the line was around the block, down the street, and around the corner. Quincy told me later that 800 people showed up for those auditions! I was one of the first people to audition and Quincy told me that I set the bar right away, so the others had to be better than me to be considered.

Q was trying to put together a group with guys and girls kind of like Manhattan Transfer or the Fifth Dimension. Over the course of the next nine months, I would get these letters: "Congratulations, you are one of the 500 people Quincy Jones has chosen," and then, "…one of the 250," then 150, 100, 50, 25, 10, 5, and finally 4! It was three gentlemen and myself making up a group called Deco. We released one record, the movie soundtrack from Sidney Poitier's directorial debut, *Fast Forward*. It was out for about 20 minutes. From that soundtrack, there was one song that played in the movie that I sang. When it played in the movie, they only used the guitar solo, so you don't even hear me sing! But that song went on to become a No. 1 dance record.

I wasn't a songwriter before I met Quincy. I had won an

151

eighth-grade poetry contest for Los Angeles County; other than that, I hadn't written squat! When Q signed the four of us for Deco, the guys asked Quincy for a publishing deal and he said okay. Well, they were great musicians that played and wrote. I don't play anything other than a CD! In the deal, we had to write 12 songs a year, but in a co-writing situation with two writers, that would be 24 songs—or with three writers, it would be 36 songs a year!

They started cashing their publishing checks, and I started writing songs. After a year, they were let go and I was signed on as a songwriter under my own contract. Two years into my writing deal with Quincy, I hadn't written anything that anybody could use; I hadn't written a song that had ever been recorded; I hadn't done anything. However, because I was signed with Quincy's publishing company, I was invited to the publishing meeting with his other *real* songwriters to come up with a song to finish out the *Bad* album. I sat in the corner and got out my little notepad and took notes about what he wanted for this song.

I took my notes to my writing partner, Glen Ballard, and filled him in on what Quincy had said. Two years before that day, I was writing with a famous jazz keyboard player, a dear friend of mine, John Beasley. While I was waiting for him to finish his conversation, I heard him say, "Yea, the man. What man? Oh, the man in the mirror." I wrote "Man in the mirror" down in my notebook and didn't think much about it. Two years later, I'm flipping through my notebook and I see the phrase "Man in the mirror." It kinda pops out at me while Glen was playing the piano. I could not write the lyrics fast enough. I just remember scribbling the ideas as quickly as I could get 'em out of my head and onto the page. They were the lyrics for the first verse and chorus of "Man in the Mirror," and they took about 20 minutes to write while I was laying on the floor in Glenn's living room. That was on Wednesday. On that Friday night we demoed the song. When it was done, I *had* to get it to Quincy. The Qwest publishing office was closed Friday afternoon, so I called Quincy and said, "Quincy, I've got the song. I've got it! I've got the song for you. Glen and I wrote this, and you've gotta hear it!"

A few days after I got the song to Quincy, he called and said, "Sid, we're in the studio recording your song. Michael has a problem with the bridge. He wants it to be twice as long and we need more lyrics." This was all about the second part of the bridge. On the demo we had, "If you want to make the world a better place, take a look at yourself and then make a change." Glen and I gave them several options for the additional lyrics and Michael chose, "You gotta get it right while you've got the time, cuz when you close your heart then you close your mind."

So this single from the album sold very well, and then 25 years later it comes out again and this time it's tenfold! It was Michael's final gift to me. He told me that "Man in the Mirror" was one of his favorite songs, along with John Lennon's "Imagine." Quincy Jones and Michael Jackson introduced me to the world. One day I'm just this little demo singer, and the next I'm a hit songwriter for Michael Jackson. That song has changed my life!

I didn't discover the true magic of Quincy Jones until we went into the studio to record *Back on the Block*. That's when I really started to get to know him. We were spending days and days in the studio, and I co-wrote several of songs on that album. It was so much fun just hanging out and getting to know him, because up till then he was just this mystical, magical producer guy. Q taught me everything I know about writing a song. The most valuable lesson was something that he just threw out one day when we were writing for *Back on the Block*. I would turn in some lyrics and he'd say, "Yea, this is good, but I think you can do better," and I'd be frustrated, but then he said, "The best songwriters are rewriters." That was the most important lesson he ever taught me about writing a song! And he's right. A lyric and melody are like a chunk of wood, and you're carving off the extra stuff that you don't need. Inside that piece of wood is everything you need to make a beautiful song.

Hanging out with Quincy and the people he works with has been an incredible experience. It's so beautiful to hang out with people who are at the top of their game. I've learned that, to be at the top level, you have to have an amazing amount of passion for what you do. It doesn't really matter what that is, whether it's writing songs or collating papers or cooking. Whatever it is, do it with all your heart and always try to be the best at your task. I have a great amount of respect for *anyone* who is at the top of their game. And, I admire and respect the energy and passion it takes to maintain it.

Quincy is able to create an environment where everyone *wants* to do their best! Every musician who comes in to play for Q is gonna give him the best they have to offer. He just has something about him that motivates people to perform at their peak level. I don't know what that is or why he has it. I don't know how to bottle it or market it. But he's got it!

# LL COOL J

LL is like a razor! He is as sharp as it gets. All of the hip-hoppers are, man. These cats are incredible! And they're smart!

I met LL when he was 15 at Def Jam, in the very early days of the label's beginnings. My son had been a star breakdancer in Sweden, and I wanted to take him over to Def Jam to meet everyone. The jury was still out on hip-hop at that time. But LL was the first rapper that showed curiosity about where hip-hop fit into the history of black music.

The first time we met, LL asked me, "Mr. Jones, what do the musicians and the singers think of us?" thereby acknowledging that [rappers] were a third, separate category of performer. To be only 15 and have that type of awareness really knocked me out. LL is way beyond his years, and his career is still thriving more than 25 years later.

My passion is for young musicians to understand their roots, and for rappers to learn about the imbongi (the praise shouters from South Africa that Nelson Mandela used in his inauguration) and the griots (the oral historians that Alex Haley focused on in Roots). LL has that type of self-awareness, it's why I chose him to write the rap bridge on the new "We Are the World: 25 for Haiti." I was out with [Henry] Mancini one day, and we went down to an exhibit of a lot of South African stuff. I saw this carved statue and this little sucker says, "I wanna go home with *you*." It was like, "I'm yours and you're mine." So that was it. He was instantly "The Dude." Business had gotten bad for a South African farmer, so he got all of his workers into sculpture. One of his workers, named Josiah, was the one who created "The Dude." And it just *stuck*.

That was in 1980, the year we recorded the album, *The Dude*. Ten years later, I'm on the floor of Record One telling the rappers this story and explaining that "The Dude" is a metaphor for the black wisdom of the street and the history of black knowledge and all that stuff—that he's very symbolic. And they got it, man. They really did. I didn't tell any of them that they couldn't use profanity or talk about bitches, and hos, and all that. I didn't say a word about it. They just said, "Let's get together tomorrow at 3:00." I said, "What are you gonna do, talk?" And they come right back with, "No, to record." And they did, man. They didn't play. They came and *knocked it out.*

## On Q

# LL Cool J

First time I worked with Mr. Jones, interestingly enough, wasn't on music. It was on *In The House*, a sitcom that aired in the late '90s. Mr. Jones was the executive producer along with David Salzman, and he actually gave me my first television show.

Mr. Jones taught me a lot about class and how to conduct myself as a businessman. He also reinforced the importance of music as an art form. I'm very grateful for what I've been able to accomplish in music, but when I look at what Quincy Jones has accomplished, it makes me want to dig deeper. When you see his collection of 27 Grammys and the *Thriller* plaque with 50 Platinum records and all of the accolades that he has throughout his home, it's *really* inspiring.

When I did "It's Time for War" on my *Exit 13* album, I used a lot of classical instrumentation. I got composers to help, and live strings, and musicians and stuff—I was reaching a little higher and was definitely trying to create something that was a little bigger and more sophisticated. That's inspired by the ways I've seen Mr. Jones produce records.

I think of Quincy Jones as the best and most accomplished producer in the world. He is someone who transcends the whole idea that your relevancy as an artist is based on your last hit record. He has been involved in a lot of other things for the past few years, but when it came time to do the second *We Are the World*, to benefit Haitian relief, it was only Mr. Jones who could pull that off. Who else could come back and raise $100 million for something like that. He just operates at another level. It was amazing, and I was superhonored to be part of it. Mr.

155

Jones asked me to write the rap bridge, so I tried to write something that was really "high road." He agreed with the direction and wanted it a certain way. He came up with this idea to do a Greek chorus, so we stacked the vocals a *lot* of times—even many more than the dozen or so that usually make up the Greek chorus. He was a joy to work with, and I was humbled to be part of it. I just kept my mouth shut, wrote my lyrics, delivered my performance, and let him do the rest.

He let me go for it, but one thing is for sure about Mr. Jones: he's going to be totally honest. What he didn't want was for me to be so focused on trying to make it "street" that I missed the message. It was about really speaking from the heart and saying something that was relevant to *We Are the World*. Once I had his approval, I went with it. I'm very happy I did, because the song has obviously done extremely well and raised a lot of money *and* awareness for the people of Haiti. I always like to be involved in anything he's doing, and when he calls on me I'll always try to be there for him. He's a real good guy; I have a *lot* of respect for him.

I recently did the remake of "Secret Garden" for his new album, *Soul Bossa Nostra*. He wasn't there when I recorded my part, but he called in on the speakerphone and told me exactly what he wanted and how he wanted it. He was very clear in his communication about what he was looking for—that's an executive producer's job. When the track was done, it was great.

Mr. Jones's son, QD3, has produced quite a few songs for me. One song we did together in the '90s was called "Back Seat of My Jeep." It did really well and was a big underground song. He's a very talented producer, too.

To me, Quincy Jones is "Mr. Jones" because I respect him so much. It's funny, because he's all, "Call me Quincy, man!" I'm not trying to make him feel old; I'm just trying to figure it out. So whenever I'm not around him I call him Mr. Jones, and then when I'm around him I'll call him Quincy if he insists. I spent a lot of time around him when I was coming up, and I learned a lot from him just by how he carries himself and how he lives his life.

I think the most important thing I've learned from him is to keep my attitude right. He has a free spirit and good energy. He is an excellent model of how to treat people with kindness and respect. He's just a good guy. I also learned from him that dreams don't have deadlines. One thing about

Mr. Jones is that, no matter what, he always seems to come up with something really interesting to work on, whether it's a global cause or a project that people care about. I find that very encouraging because I'm in the hip-hop industry where your relevance is based on whether or not you're on the radio. But Quincy's relevance is based on his body of work; he has definitely encouraged me. He has made me believe that, with the right focus, it's still possible for me to go on and do more great albums in the future.

Mr. Jones taught me to always make sure there's room for the vocal track. The vocal needs to have its own place where other frequencies aren't encroaching on it—it needs to have space to *live*. And, I learned about creating an exposed line that's the foundation of the song. Everything else hangs off that line, musically *and* sonically.

Another great thing that Mr. Jones taught me was about goose bumps in the studio and how they're God's divining rod. When you hear your music and it gives you goose bumps, you know the track is right; you know that it's time to leave it alone. Any time I've had that happen to me, it's worked out to be accurate. I did a song called "No Crew Is Superior" that's used on *NCIS: Los Angeles*. When I recorded it, I got that feeling. When it was released, it was received well on the Internet, but download sales weren't that great. But when the show came out, it did *really* well. No one can predict the future, but thus far, those goose bumps have turned out to be accurate for me. It almost gives you a prescient type of power.

Quincy Jones is eternally youthful. *Young* is a chronological condition, but *youthful* is a psychological, psycho-emotional condition. He's always youthful and always open. I have a lot of love for Mr. Jones.

# FRANK SINATRA and Lena Horne: The One That Got Away

When you like to push the envelope, you learn the importance of giving everything your best effort, trusting that, if your plans are meant to be, everything will work out. You also have to realize that, even when you've given your best effort, if it's not meant to be,

Quincy Jones Collection

there's nothing you can do to force the issue.

Frank was very excited about an idea I had for an album featuring Lena Horne and him in 1983. I [had] produced an album for Lena called *The Lady and Her Music* in 1981. It was on my label, Qwest Records, and was one of the biggest albums she ever did. We had recorded her show on Broadway, and that record was on fire—it won two Grammys! So, we already had her audience's attention, and they would have been very interested in this new project!

It was an amazingly ambitious plan that would have resulted in a wonderful 3-disc album full of solos and duets, starring two of the all-time greatest singers, along with many of the best musicians and stars the industry has ever seen—it was going to be spectacular! A lot of heart and soul went into the planning of this project, which would have resulted in an ultra-deluxe album. [It was my] vision to record an extravagant collection of music with an amazing all-star band, including Miles Davis, Dizzy Gillespie, Benny Carter, Jerry Mulligan, Ray Brown, Toots Thielemans, George Benson, Herbie Hancock, Michael Jackson, and more!

I had scheduled day and night recording sessions at A&M studios, in Hollywood, during the week of the Grammy Telecast. The studio was booked for two days before the Grammys and three days after. It was a plan you cannot believe; it would have been a dream album! We had selected the songs, scheduled the musicians, booked the studio, the arrangements were being written, and everything was in motion. We were swapping some of the all-time best songs back and forth between Frank and Lena to get just the right ones for each of them. If I had Lena slated to sing "Stormy Weather," but she didn't feel as comfortable with that song, I'd just say, "Well then, we'll let Frank sing that and you can sing "One for the Road."

I worked so hard on that plan! To me, this was the ultimate canvas for these two fantastic vocalists. All I had left to do was to get Frank and Lena together to talk through the material before we started tracking in the studio.

That's where the project got caught up in the swell of bad timing ... First, Don Costa, Sinatra's good friend and conductor, died, delaying the meeting. Then Horne had vocal problems. Then Sinatra had back-to-back gigs in Atlantic City and Vegas. And by the time the two next found time in their schedules to talk, they'd both lost the momentum they needed to carry them through the week's worth of sessions the album would've taken. Still, setting aside that album was a great personal disappointment to everyone involved and, indeed, to the music world as a whole.

**HANK CATTANEO:** "Frank never got involved in choosing his partners for the Duets recordings except with Ella Fitzgerald; that was the only recommendation he made. He did say it would be great to get Ella. We tried, but unfortunately she was too ill by that time." ...

**FRANK SINATRA:** "We were ready to do the album, and she [Lena] had a vocal problem—a nodule on her vocal cord. Quincy Jones tried several times to get it back on track, but consequently we didn't do the project. It was quite an undertaking—it was gonna be three albums."

—*from* The Sinatra Treasures *by Charles Pignone (Bulfinch Press, 2004)*

159

We were very excited about this project and it was definitely one of the biggest disappointments of my life that we couldn't get it together. Shortly thereafter, I produced *L.A. Is My Lady* for Frank, which was great, but I always regretted letting Frank and Lena's album get away. The important conclusion to this entire event, though, is that we all remained great friends through everything! As far back as 1961, Lena, along with Lenny Hayton, graciously wrote the liner notes for *Quintessence*, not to mention that it was also thanks to Lena that I got my first scoring job for *The Pawnbroker* in 1963. That was something I'd dreamed about since I was 15! And, Frank and I remained as close as brothers for the duration.

## The Plan

February 2. 1983

**PROJECT: FRANK SINATRA, LENA HORNE, QUINCY JONES PROJECT, '83**
RECORDING DATES: FEBRUARY 21, 22, 24, 25, 26, 1983

LOCATION: A&M RECORDING STUDIOS, STUDIO 'A'
1416 North LaBrea Avenue (At Sunset and LaBrea)
Hollywood, California 90028

PACKAGING: DOUBLE RECORD SET/ULTRA DELUXE PACKAGE

**1. SESSIONS AND SONGS**
 A. Session 1. (With the Jazz All-Stars) Monday, February 21st, 1983
 3:00 pm to 6:00 pm - Pre-rehearse with band only
 7:00 pm until - Lena Horne and Frank Sinatra with band
  1. "MACK THE KNIFE" (Duet)
   Musicians
   1. Jimmy Smith
   2. Steve Gadd
   3. George Benson
   4. Ray Brown
   5. Eddie "Lockjaw" Davis - solo
  2. "'ROUND MIDNIGHT" (Frank Sinatra)
  3. "THE LADY IS A TRAMP" (Duet)
  4. "IT'S ALL RIGHT WITH ME" (Duet)
  5. "GIRL TALK" (Duet)
  6. "BLUES .IN THE NIGHT" (Duet)


 B. Session 2. (With Big Orchestra) Tuesday, February 22nd, 1983
 3:00 pm to 6:00 pm - Pre-rehearse orchestra only
 7:00 pm until - Lena Horne and Frank Sinatra with orchestra
  1. "QVERTURE" (Orchestra)
  2. "TWO FOR THE ROAD" (Duet)
  3. "I'VE GOT YOU UNDER MY SKIN" (Frank Sinatra)
  4. "BELIEVE IN SELF" (Lena Horne)
  5. "LET ME LOVE YOU" (Frank Sinatra)
  6. "STRANGERS IN THE NIGHT" (Lena Horne)
  7. "SOMETHlN' STUPID" (Duet)

C. Session 3. (With the Jazz All-Stars) Thursday,
February 24th, 1983
3:00 pm to 6:00 pm - Pre-rehearse with band only
7:00 pm until - Lena Horne and Frank Sinatra with band
      1. "EYES OF LOVE" (Frank Sinatra)
      2. "WATCH WHAT HAPPENS" (Frank Si natra)
      3. "SOMEWHERE" (Lena Horne)
      4. "FOGGY DAY" (Lena Horne)
      5. "AIN'T MISBEHAVIN'" (Duet)
      6 . "I'VE GOT THE WORLD ON A STRING" (Duet)

D. Session 4. (With Big Orchestra) Friday, February 25th, 1983
3:00 pm t o 6:00 pm - Pre-rehearse with orchestra only
7:00 pm until - Lena Horne and Frank Sinatra with orchestra
      1. Ken and Mitzi Welch Medley (Duet)
      2. "STORMY WEATHER" (Frank Sinatra) *
      3. "MY WAY" (Lena Horne) *
      4. "YOU MAKE ME FEEL SO YOUNG" (Duet) *
      5. "FROM THIS MOMENT ON" (Frank Sinatra) *
      6. "IT WAS A VERY GOOD YEAR" (Lena Horne) *
      7. "L.A. IS MY LADY" (Frank Sinatra)
      * These songs may be incorporated into the Ken and
      Mitzi Welch medley. Will advise.

E. Session 5. (Lena Horne and Frank Sinatra only)
February 26, 1983
3:00 pm until - vocal overdubs on orchestra tracks to be recorded at Westlake
Studios February 14th - February 19th, 1983.
Following songs to be submitted no later than
February 10th, 1983
      1. "THE ENTERTAINER"
      (Duet - Lyrics by Alan and Marilyn Bergman)
      2. "WHATEVER (X-RATED KID STUFF)" (Lena Horne and
      Frank Sinatra with guest artist Michael Jackson)
      3. NEW, ORIGINAL SONG BY DAVID PAICH AND TOTO
      4. NEW, ORIGINAL SONG BY ASHFORD AND SIMPSON
      5. "WE'RE DANGEROUS" - ORIGINAL SONG BY BARRY
      MANN AND CYNTHIA WElL
      6. NEW, ORIGINAL SONG BY THE BERGMANS AND
      MICHEL LEGRAND
      7. NEW, ORIGINAL SONG BY ROD TEMPERTON
      8. "FUNNY" - ORIGINAL SONG BY LIONEL RICHIE
      9. NEW, ORIGINAL SHOW SONG
      BY MARVIN HAMLISCH (Duet)
      10. NEW, ORIGINAL SONG BY CAROLE BAYER SAGER
      AND BURT BACHARACH

## II. SONG TITLES IN THEIR KEYS
A. Title

| | | Lena | Frank |
|---|---|---|---|
| 1. | "AIN'T MISBEHAVIN'" (Duet) | A | Bb |
| 2. | "AND I LOVE HER" | Ab-A(R) | C |
| 3. | "ANGEL EYES" | Abm | Bbm R) |
| 4. | "BLUES IN THE NIGHT" (Duet) | Gb | G(R) |
| 5. | "DO NOTHIN' TILL YOU HEAR FROM ME" (Duet) | D | E or (F?) |
| 6. | "EYES OF LOVE" | B/Bb | Bb/B |
| 7. | "A FOGGY DAY" | C | Db |
| 8. | "FROM THIS MOMENT ON" | Cm/Ebf (R) | |
| 9. | "GIRL TALK" (Duet) | D/Eb | F |
| 10. | "IF YOU BELIEVE" | B (R) | Db |
| 11. | "IN THE WEE SMALL HOURS" | Ab | Bb(R) |
| 12. | "IT'S ALL RIGHT WITH ME" (Duet) | Gm/Bb(R) | C(R)/Am |
| 13. | "IT WAS A VERY GOOD YEAR" | Cm | Dm |
| 14. | "I WANNA BE AROUND" | | |
| 15. | "I'VE GOT THE WORLD ON A STRING" | C(R) | D(R)* |
| 16. | "THE LADY IS A TRAMP" (Duet) | Ab-A(R) | Bb-B(R) |
| 17. | LET ME LOVE YOU" | E(R) | F or Gb |
| 18. | "LOVE ME OR LEAVE ME" | Cm/Eb(R) | Dm/F |
| 19. | "MAC THE KNIFE" (Duet) | Gb to Bb | Gb to C |
| 20. | "I'VE GOT YOU UNDER MY SKIN" | B or C | Db(R)* |
| 21. | "MISTY" | C | Db(R) |
| 22. | "MOOD INDIGO" | Db(R) | Eb(F-orig?) |
| 23. | "MY WAY" | Bb | C* |
| 24. | "ONE FOR MY BABY" | A | C(R) |
| 25. | "'ROUND MIDNIGHT" | Bm | Bm |
| 26. | "SOMETHIN' STUPID" (Duet) | C | E(R) |
| 27. | "STORMY WEATHER" | Eb-E(R) | F(R) |
| 28. | "STRANGERS IN THE NIGHT" | D,Eb,E | F-G(R)E* |
| 29. | "WATCH WHAT HAPPENS" | Db(R) | Eb-E(R) |
| 30. | "YESTERDAY" | A or Bb | C(R) |
| 31. | "YOU MAKE ME FEEL SO YOUNG" (Duet) | F | G-Ab(R)Bb |
| 32. | "L.A. IS MY LADY" | Bb | |
| 33. | "NICE 'N EASY" | G or Ab | C(R)*Bb |
| 34. | "BELIEVE IN YOURSELF" | Bb | |
| 35. | "TWO FOR THE ROAD" (Duet) | Eb | G or Gb |
| 36. | "THE ENTERTAINER" (Duet) | F/C/E | Gb/Db/E |

Code
  * Current Key
  (R) Record Key

### III. JAZZ ALL-STARS
 A. Guitar/George Benson
 B. Bass/Ray Brown
 C. Alto Sax/Benny Carter
 D. Tenor Sax/Eddie "Lockjaw" Davis
 E. Drums/Steve Gadd
 F. Trumpet/Dizzy Gillespie
 G. Vibes/Milt Jackson
 H. Trombone/J.J. Johnson
 I. Baritone Sax/Gerry Mulligan
 J. Organ/Jimmy Smith
 K. Harmonica/Toots Thielemans
 L. Tenor Sax/Ernie Watts
 M. Keyboards/Herbie Hancock
 N. Trumpet, Flügelhorn/Jerry Hey
 O. Trumpet/Snookie Young
 P. Trumpet/Clark Terry
 Q. Jazz All-Stars Coordinators
 1. Pam Crocetti
 2. Wilbert Terrell
 R. Contact/J.J. Johnson

### IV. BIG ORCHESTRA
 A. Trumpets
  1. Harry "Sweets" Edison
  2. Chuck Findley
  3. Snookie Young
  4. Jerry Hey
  5. Gary Grant

 B. Trombones
  1. Charlie Loper
  2. Bill Watrous
  3. George Bohanon
  4. Bill Reichenbach

 C. French Horns
  1. Vince da Rosa
  2. Brad Warnaar
  3. Marni Robinson

 D. Tuba
  1. Tommy Johnson
  2. James Self
 E. Saxes/Woodwinds
  1. Ernie Watts
  2. Larry Williams
  3. Tom Scott
  4. Jerome Richardson
  5. Jack Nimitz

 F. Keyboards
  1. Dave Grusin
  2. Greg Phillinganes

 G. Basses
  1. Ray Brown (Acoustic)
  2. Neil Stubenhaus

 H. Guitars
  1. Lee Ritenour

 I. Percussion
  1. Harvey Mason (Mallets)
  2. Paulinho do Costa

 J. Harp
  1. Gail LeVant

 K. Strings – Concertmaster – Gerry Vinci
  1. Twelve (12) violins
  2. Four (4) violas
  3. Four (4) cellos

 L. Contractor for Big Orchestra
  1. Trevor Veitch

 M. Contact
  1. Jerry Hey

### V. ARRANGERS

 A. Orchestra
  1. Billy May
  2. Dave Grusin
  3. Jeremy Lubock
  4. Marty Paich
  5. Quincy Jones
  6. Jerry Hey
  7. Gerry Mulligan
  8. Joe Sample
  9. Tom Scott
  10. David Paich
  11. David Foster

 B. Vocal
  1. Ken and Mitzi Welch
  2. Ray Charles

## Chapter 8

# THE BAND

Throughout his career, Quincy has worked with the most legendary and iconic musicians. If a musician is considered fantastic, then he or she has probably worked with Quincy. From Nadia Boulanger to Ludacris, from Miles Davis to Wyclef Jean, or from Lionel Hampton to Lionel Richie, Quincy has shared the personal and intimate process of performing, producing, composing, arranging, and conducting music.

Through it all, he has developed a core of musicians and performers—a trusted group of exceptionally talented, genuine, caring, and loving people. They are as much a family as any blood family in any neighborhood, anywhere. There's a lesson to be learned here: care for the people with whom you work! Listen to Quincy talk about these musicians, and then listen to them share how they feel about him. You'll see Quincy's production style and the methods he uses to get the best performances out of these musicians. Quincy likes to analogize music through painting. In every way, he paints his music—starting with charcoal sketches, to watercolors, to oil—before notes come. The musicians are his colors, his shading, and his depth. It's very amazing, incredibly enlightening, and inspirational.

## GREG PHILLINGANES

I was on the road in 1972 promoting *You've Got It Bad, Girl,* when I met Greg Phillinganes. He was 17 years old, and had played hooky to come to a signing that I was doing to promote the album at a record store in Detroit. When he made it to the front of the line, we had a nice talk about the Fender Rhodes and a lot of different stuff. We had a great conversation and formed a good bond, even just from that meeting. A few years later, he played with me on a Billy Eckstine date, and he's played with me on everything I've done since then. He's a great player. It's amazing—like I knew it in that first meeting that something was going to happen with Greg. Malcolm Gladwell called it "blink." It's your first instinct. You don't think about it, you just feel it.

## On Q

# Greg Phillinganes

The first project I did with Quincy was in 1976. I was 20 years old and I played a Rhodes part on a single release, called "The Best Thing," for Billy Eckstine. Q was producing it with Herb Alpert at A&M. Before I knew it, I was on a 45 produced by Quincy Jones that said, "You are the best thing that ever happened to my life."

Quincy is a loving, giving, caring human being who makes you feel like you're the only person in a room full of thousands. He has an innate ability to bring out the best in people. He treats his human relationships the way he handles his food. He likes to mix it all up. He excels at making gumbo—at combining things. You can tell a lot about a person by the way they eat. He likes to do different combinations and he's very methodical about it, never just slapping stuff together. He'll take one thing and neatly place it on another and then wait for the taste. And that's how he is with relationships.

"You're no greater of a musician than you are a person." Quincy learned that from Nadia Boulanger. I believe it; I've seen it work. He lives by that edict. You hear musicians say, "Music is my life." It's really the other way around; it's not that music is your life, it's that your life is in your music. That really does reflect the way Quincy operates.

Quincy is often very subtle in his production style. He knows the right thing to say in any musical situation to give you just enough of a boost to take you to the level. It could be something as simple as, "This needs more grease." He's never a taskmaster. People are always intrigued by producers. They're especially intrigued by Quincy, because whenever you see pictures of him, he's just sitting down. He looks like he could be reading a crossword puzzle, or you might see him intensely looking down at a chart or just sitting there in thought or maybe he's on the phone. You're thinking, Shoot, I could do that! But, he's not just on the phone; he's not just reading a chart; he's searching for the ultimate effect in the grand picture. And he's piecing things. He already knows what's going on, and he's piecing things together in his mind. His process is very well defined, and yet he knows how to get out of the way enough to let his musicians be inspired, too. He has a saying, "Leave enough space for God to walk in the room." In other words, leave room for the inspiration to hit. He makes it work. Most of his effectiveness is in how he treats people.

Producing never works through intimidation. People think it does, but it doesn't. Some producers think they have to be all hard-nosed and scare the hell out of you. That absolutely never works for me. I don't need it. So, after hanging with Q for so long, I've seen the effects of the way he works. I know how his methodology affects me, and I've seen how it affects other people. I've also seen what happens when I use a similar approach. It's an extremely effective way to work.

There's a very cool energy level in a session with Quincy, whether with Michael or whoever. It's exciting and it makes you want to come to work. In the Michael Jackson sessions, there was always a cast of very strong, larger than life, characters. Bruce Swedien was Quincy's engineer.

Quincy Jones Collection

Greg is a great player. He played with me on a Billy Eckstine date, and he's played with me on everything I've done since then. It's amazing.

167

Bruce is this big Swedish guy with a handlebar mustache and a very deep, commanding voice. And then there was Rod Temperton and all the guys in the rhythm section: JR on drums, Paul Jackson on guitar, Nathan East or Neil Stubenhaus on bass, and me. It was always fun!

I am constantly learning from Quincy. Even as recently as the new *We Are the World* project, I saw how Quincy is the master of keeping the big picture in mind. At first, this version was going to be produced in celebration of the 25th anniversary of the original *We Are the World,* which I also played on. When the earthquake hit in Haiti, the focus shifted to aid the Haitian people. Someone else was originally commissioned to produce the song, but it turned out to be a little too much, considering the massive amount of vocals that needed to be layered on top. Q brought a different producer on board to lay a new foundation; it included much of the original recording, but opened up more space to accommodate those vocals. I respect the original producer and what he did—he's an excellent musician and producer—but when you break it all down, you have to feature the vocals. It was a learning experience for everyone to see the difference Quincy made.

## JOHN ROBINSON

JR is the best, man, really the best. If it's possible, I get him to play drums whenever I'm doing anything. And he's usually there, too, wherever we go, all over the world. Maybe we bonded because JR went to my alma matter, the Berklee School of Music."

He was with Rufus and Chaka when I worked with them on *Masterjam* in 1979, the same year I did *Off the Wall.* That's also how I got together with Rod Temperton. JR is rock solid!

## On Q
# John Robinson

Knowing that we're in a session with Quincy Jones, we already know that we're making history in the present. It's really quite extraordinary and abstract. It's like you know you're working with Einstein, and it's like that every time! Q models all the best attributes of a producer: leader, mentor, father, friend, and soul mate. You're sharing everything. Playing with other people, you don't necessarily feel like that. You don't feel like a history maker or soul mate. Thanks to Quincy, I'm the most recorded drummer in history. I have a lot to be thankful for in my relationship with him.

A great producer brings out the best in an artist. Quincy is the greatest producer of all time. He has the ability to cast a musical project the way a director casts a motion picture. He puts all the right ingredients together and follows everything through to the end, and there's nobody better than him at building toward the final product. God broke the mold when He made Quincy Jones!

He's as genuine today as he was when I first met him in 1978. He started as a trumpet player, so he understands the musician mentality. With Quincy's qualifications and background, it's easy to put him on a pedestal, but in reality he puts us on pedestals. At the same time he keeps it all very real. There's no BS; it's camaraderie and everyone's equal. It's nice. You don't always get that on records.

We had probably already done five records when we got to *The Dude*. I remember coming in on day 2; Steve Lukather was playing guitar, Greg Phillinganes was on keys, and I think it was Abraham Laboriel on bass. I walked in probably ten minutes after Lukather, and he's laughing. I can tell he's laughing at my drums, which were surrounded by baffles. I peeked over the barrier and everything was gone except a kick drum, a snare drum, and a hi-hat. Then all of a sudden I see Bruce and I go, "What's up Bruce?" He responded in a classic Bruce Swedien deadpan, "Q doesn't want any tom fills on this record," and he turned around and walked away. I'm thinking, "Well, okay; yes, sir." Quincy had the vision to leave more space in the production and knew in advance that he wanted to build the drum parts without toms. Four Grammys later and who's to argue? He did let me overdub a whole bunch of stuff on "Ai No Corrida," though, because it was such an energetic vibe. He had a vision for the drum parts on the record, but he was willing to bend when the music demanded a little different approach.

Quincy is great at giving suggestions. He has a way with describing what he wants that gets you into the right space very quickly. He might walk from the control room into the studio and say something like, "JR, you're dancin' too much," meaning I'm playing too much stuff. It's stuff like that has helped me realize what it takes to make a *hit* record. Q would also gather the group together and say, "Guys, we're making a record of 12 tunes, and I want 12 hits. We're not making a record of 2 hits; we want 12 hits." That's a completely different mind-set. It doesn't leave room for slack or lag time. It's good and it kept us on our toes, all the time.

Q is great at getting the best out of singers. I remember him working with Chaka Khan back in the early days. She was one of the greatest singers of all time, but she could easily take a melody and bend it into something completely different. A song is made up of melody, lyrics, and groove—melody is first, melded with the lyrics. Quincy knows the importance of sticking to the melody, and he could always guide her back into the right balance, keeping it close enough to the melody but still personal.

When Q works with the rhythm section, he'll sometimes give us specific directions, but a lot of times he'll let us make decisions as a rhythm section. If we're off course, he'll steer us back in the direction that he wants the tune to go. The rhythm section tends to head in the same direction together, so if one of us is off, we are all off. It's usually most efficient to direct us as a unit, and he is secure enough to make room for what we have to offer. It's very symbiotic.

Quincy gets an amazing amount of respect in this business. He's a great record producer and everybody knows it. When he says, "Leave your ego at the door" and all these stars with huge egos listen, that's remarkable! He also hangs with a legendary crowd—people that reflect his standards for music. We were rehearsing for Quincy's 50th birthday, and Q enters the room and says, "JR, Ray's coming in. He's probably going to put you through some stuff." Ray Charles comes in and we start the first tune. Ray stops everything and says, "Drummer! Man, what's your hurry, man?" I swear to God I wasn't rushing—I don't rush. The whole band looked at me and left;

this was a full big band along with Quincy, and they all left. Ray has me play the groove and it was like, *Booooom ... Bat!* He stopped me and said, "No man! I want you to go ... *Booooooooooooooom ... ... ... ... BAT!* And that's just one bar so I exaggerated, and he goes "Nooooo, man, you're rushing! What? Are you in a hurry?" And then finally, he's like, "Ah, that's it, drummer. That's it." I know I'm not the only guy he's done that to, because everyone else who had worked with him knew exactly what was coming when he walked into that first rehearsal.

JR is the best, man, really the best. If it's possible, I get him to play drums whenever I'm doing anything.

171

I've seen Quincy get frustrated with outside sources that have affected the flow in a session, but he's never a tyrant like some producers. After the Rufus album, when we were doing *Off the Wall*, he always had a yellow legal pad with him. Every time somebody showed up late he'd write down a number, the excuse, and the name on that pad. So, if somebody missed a session or was late, for whatever bad reason it was in those days, he'd just be able to say, "Oh, that's number 14, you know." You could only say there was a parade going by your front driveway and you couldn't get your car out once, because it was always noted and numbered on that pad. It was light and fun, but everyone knew exactly what he was saying. No amount of ranting would have been any more effective.

His track record speaks for itself. His use of harmony makes him stand out above everybody else. When you listen to his old stuff from the '60s, it's quite amazing. You can hear how that stuff has blended into a lot of the music we hear in popular culture today. And nobody has bigger ears than Quincy. If I'm having a little bit of a rough time on something, he'll always hear it. Usually he'll walk into the studio and notate just the right thing on the chart and then walk away. It's very cool and extremely effective.

# NDUGU CHANCLER

My brother, Ndugu Chancler, was the drummer on the *Thriller* album and many other records that I produced. On "Billie Jean," he spent a lot of time in the booth replacing the electronic drums with real drums. That drum track is a classic. Ndugu is a fantastic drummer and a wonderful human being!

We had the electronic drum track in place, but it wasn't even close to the sound and feel that is produced by a great drummer playing real drums. You can really tell the difference, you know. I love to combine synthesized or sampled instruments with the real thing, too—it can create momentum that's extremely powerful. When you start with electronic drums and then add real drums, it raises the bar because the real thing is so much more expressive. The listener might not know what happened, but they can sure *feel* it. This technique works the same way with strings. Start the track with synthesized strings and then, at just the right point, bring in a real string section. It's a fantastic effect because it's like "ear candy." Segue directly from one part to the other, matching the colors as closely as you can during the transition. There's a powerful metamorphosis as the electronic strings unfold into real strings—it's like breathing life into the music. It's not about saving money on the string parts, or the drums, or whatever you apply this to—it's about taking the listener on a joy-filled sonic journey!

## On Q

# Ndugu Chancler

I came up during that period where music was music. It wasn't so categorized and sectioned off as it is today. You just played everything and you enjoyed it—you had a passion for great *music*. And believe it or not, it was Quincy and Miles who were largely responsible for that passion we felt. They were always a step ahead. Most of the time, everyone else was just trying to catch up.

Quincy draws this calm, heavy, creative spirit out of you without really exerting a lot of energy. He comes in and he says, "I'm hearing this," or "This is what I want," or "This is the direction I want to go," and then we start doing it. He could draw stuff out of you that you never knew you had. He always has the A-team in the studio, so everyone is striving for excellence, but these are also some of the nicest people you'll ever meet.

Quincy has an incredible understanding of the music of the past and present, but he also has an amazing ability to see into the future. He's the master at combining various musicians who wouldn't normally work to-gether. There is an amazing chemistry when these musicians come together under Quincy's leadership. It's like he knows that if he takes a little of this player and combines it with a little of another player, he'll get something really special— something different, contemporary, edgy, and even futuristic.

In addition to being excellent players, a lot of the musicians he brings together are producers or songwriters, so they bring an unselfish discipline to the session. They surrender their egos to the music and to Quincy's vision. It's like going into a saloon in an old western movie where all the gunfighters put their guns at the bar and say, "Okay, now we're all on equal turf." When you go in the studio with Quincy, your ego stays at the door; everybody walks in on equal creative terms. It doesn't matter who's who out in the world. Once you get in the studio, you're in a world of greatness with Quincy Jones and all the people that sur-round him. Whenever he goes into the studio, he has a vi-sion that starts with him and the artist. That vision shines the way for everyone.

Most people associate my work with Quincy and Michael Jackson. They forget about Frank Sinatra, Donna Sum-mer, George Benson, James Ingram, Patti Austin, Michael McDonald, and so on. I've seen Quincy work with a *lot* of different artists, and with each one he has a slightly differ-ent approach. He makes adjustments in what he does to help the artists do their best—his approach isn't based on some set formula.

His work with Michael Jackson marks a major creative and innovative milestone in the history of pop music. On some of the songs, he wrote out the drum part and we work from there. "Billie Jean" was very disciplined and structured but also very straight ahead. On that song, he let me hear it and then we started recording.

It's a natural tendency for most drummers to overplay. However, on "Billie Jean" he went back to the way R&B records used to be made. When I'd worked with Ike Turner and Sly Stone and all those guys, they just wanted me to lay down a solid groove with kick, snare, and hi-hat, then they'd take it from there—that's the way they recorded. So, here's Quincy combining the history of recording and the history of music with new technology, new sounds, and new equipment to come up with a modern masterpiece that still sounds great today. So, when you're working with Quincy, you know he believes in what he's doing and you can bet he's on to something. Also, with Quincy you don't spend a lot of time in the studio fumbling and experimenting with a bunch of different parts. You spend your time experimenting with different ways to *play* the parts.

On "Billie Jean," I played along *with* the drum machine; both parts are in the mix throughout the tune. This was done before Pro Tools became a standard, so the drums had to actually be played precisely enough that there were no flams between the acoustic and electronic sounds. The reason it sounds the way it does is because both things are playing simultaneously and the listener hears the stability of the drum machine and the expression of the real kit. That was very innovative for the time. Quincy and his production team were on the leading edge of new technology—they pushed the envelope whenever they could. Even the fact that they were doing multiple tracks for the drum set was new. No one else was doing that.

It took about two and a half hours to record my track for "Billie Jean." After I heard the song and jotted down a few notes, Bruce Swedien started building the drum sound. Bruce and I had a history of working together on some jazz projects when he was back in Chicago. So he knew me, and knew what my drums sounded like, but we did spend a little time on some new mic techniques. He had the drums on a platform that he had specially built to enhance the room reverberation. It was a different sound than just setting up on the floor at Westlake. He had an SM57 on the snare drum, but it had a lead shield with foam on both sides of the mic to help guard leakage from the hi-hat. Then he had a special pad that zipped up over the front of the kick drum, with elastic around it to hold it onto the drum. The kick mic slipped in a hole in the front of the pad. We experimented with that, and then finally we took the toms off so we just had kick, snare, and hat for the original track.

In order to record with Quincy Jones, you have to be calm and relaxed. He brings that out of you through his own calm and relaxed demeanor. He never delivers his suggestions in anger or anything, even in the most trying situations. He's always calm and controlled and he prepares you mentally for whatever the job requires. That's the way he is, no matter how large or small the session.

I saw him in the most stressful situation with Frank Sinatra; the way he handled it taught me so much about production. Quincy handpicked an elite band for the session with Frank; he was conducting and was in complete control of every musical detail. We were in the middle of a take and Frank stopped us. Quincy wanted to just go on and do another take, but Frank wanted to do an inner cut. They discussed it and finally Quincy says, "Okay, we'll do an inner cut." I'd never seen him have to go through that with anyone, but this was Frank Sinatra jammin' up Quincy Jones. And he was very cool and said, "Okay, band we're going to do an inner cut." I'm not even sure if we did another take after that, because I was so floored by the way Quincy dealt with something that could have quickly blown up. He didn't raise his voice. He didn't say "Well, Frank, I said …" He just discussed it with Frank for a minute and made a decision. At that point I thought, "You know what, the music really is bigger than all of these egos." I'm sitting here watching the great Quincy Jones and the great Frank Sinatra, and somebody has to back down for the sake of the music. We're still trying to make a record here, right. That's what it's all about.

# LOUIS JOHNSON

Louis and George went on the tour to Japan with me after I had my aneurisms. During the course of that tour I heard this unique unity and sound between them, and that immediately inspired me to try to produce an album for them. So I introduced them on *Mellow Madness* on the first four songs. That was a good way to kick them off. We were just coming off *Body Heat,* which had done pretty well. I switched their name and made them the Brothers Johnson instead of the

Johnson Brothers. We chose all positive titles, like "Look Out for #1," and we just went with the flow. They had four double and triple Platinum records in a row! They went straight to number one—they did not play around!

It says a lot for their music that we just did a new release of "Strawberry Letter 23" with Akon and everybody says, "Nobody should ever try to redo the one that the Brothers Johnson did." I also produced their version. That's the tune that Johnny Otis's son, Shuggie Otis, wrote.

Louis and George are definitely family. Louis used to sit quietly on the floor when I was playing and writing songs so that when we got in the session he knew exactly what to do. But his intuition is unbelievable! He played on *Thriller*, everything! He played "Ai No Corrida" and "The Dude" and all that stuff—almost everything during our busiest years in the studio."

## On Q
# Louis Johnson

I met Quincy because I had been playing with Billy Preston and Joe Greene in The God Squad. We recorded a song for Taka Boom, Chaka Kahn's sister, and the next thing I knew they had taken that song to Quincy Jones. Billy and Joe knew him and they were trying to get Taka Boom a deal. Quincy liked the bass playing so he had them put us in contact with each other. Shortly after that, Quincy called and asked me to come over to his house and to bring some songs.

My brother George and I went over together because he had also played on the track. Quincy liked the songs, and he asked me to play with him on his tour to Japan, so I went. Ray Brown was also on the tour on upright bass, and he would stand off in the wings and watch when I was playing. He taught me how to play a walking bass part without repeating the same thing over and over—how to change the scale around and how to keep it interesting.

When we were in the middle of the tour, Quincy asked me if we wanted to do an album and I said, "Sure." He just told me that he'd help George and I put the album together, and that's really when we started working on *Look Out for #1*. We wrote the songs and showed them to him. He wrote some string parts for them, and I would hum some parts that I thought would work; if he liked them, he'd use them, and if he didn't like them, he wouldn't. It was a pretty simple process, but Quincy is a genius the way he puts everything together. He reminds me of a wise old owl when it comes to music. He would listen to our tunes and then hear all the parts in his head and just write them down on music paper. After that, we'd just go into the studio and record the tracks.

Quincy was already with A&M, but when we had the tunes together and took the album to them, they refused us. Then we took it to Motown, and they refused us. And we took it all over to different labels, but we were just ahead of our time. We were doing tunes like "Get the Funk Out Ma Face" and people had just never heard of that kind of stuff. It was pretty edgy for its time, and somebody had to take a chance on it. Quincy produced the album because he has always been able to see the future in young artists, and that's what he saw in us. He ended up telling A&M that he really wanted them to take a chance on us, so that's what they did. The next thing we knew, overnight we had a million seller. That's when everybody found out about the Brothers Johnson.

I had seen a lot of the groups that came before us reign for a few years but then fade away, so while we were doing the Brothers Johnson, I started doing session work, too. A band's career can be short; the only thing that's permanent is your skill and being unique and bringing something special to the song. That's what I've always tried to do. Quincy told Grover Washington about me, and I went to New York to play on his album *Feels So Good*. It was a success, too! From there, all my sessions started linking together. I was playing with Herbie Hancock and everybody—it was nonstop.

Quincy worked a lot with George and me to help us get our ideas out and to make sure we captured the spirit of the music. That's what I admire so much about Quincy. He really cared about capturing our spirit and storing it on vinyl. He produced the songs and helped put everything together, but it was important to him that George and I were on the record. We made suggestions about parts and everything, but Quincy had the final say on what made it on the songs. When it was time to mix, he and Bruce Swedien took over. It gets too complicated with a lot of people around during the mixing process.

When we went on the road, after Quincy's aneurisms, he made a great recovery. That was the point. We stood by him like warriors. We grew up during the time when you really had to be a player to survive and you had to stick together. I always saw Quincy as a warrior in the music business. At that time, there were a lot of great players around; it's like they were a dime a dozen. Quincy only worked with the best players and best people. If anybody came in with an ego trip or something, he'd always say, "There's a train leaving every ten minutes." If you showed up late for the session, there was a good chance Quincy would have called somebody else and they'd be there playing your part when you showed up.

At the time, I was studying martial arts and I was always very quiet and very respectful and just did what Quincy said. It's as simple as that. I added the parts I wanted but was always ready to do whatever he wanted me to do. But that's how I was with all my sessions, whether it was Quincy or Grover or Michael Jackson. I was peaceful and relaxed and showed up ready to learn—ready to devour the parts. I also brought something very unique with my slapping technique. I started out very young working those techniques out, and they really brought in a new dimension. I used the thumb slaps, slapping with my whole hand, hammer-ons, and pull-offs. I was using a lot of techniques to develop my parts, and I liked them all. Quincy told me I had a good ear for bass parts, and a lot of the time he'd just turn me loose and just tell me to come up with a part that followed the chord changes. It was great fun to come up with a part and just see him in the control room bobbin' his head and smiling.

Quincy has the most amazing musical mind. When we were starting out with him, he could write a symphony sitting at the breakfast table. He'd have his score paper out and be writing string parts, string bass parts, and horn parts right out of his head. There would be music paper all over the table filled with notes. His sessions were always fun. There were long hours, excitement, a lot of people around, and a lot of laughing and good times. We were like little kids in a candy store! In a lot of respects, it was the best time in my life. Quincy Jones is a kind and loving man and he's the best producer in the world. No one can do Quincy Jones like Quincy Jones. I've seen them try, and they can't do it. He's a genius!

# NATHAN EAST

Nathan East is an incredible, incredible, man—he's definitely part of the family. It still comes back to what Nadia always told me about a person's music never being more or less than they are as a human being. It's so true. Nathan is one of the nicest people I've ever met in my life. He's a very sweet man. I get postcards from him and Phillinganes all the time from cities around the world that I can't even pronounce. I love that, especially since I believe so strongly that you've got to go to know—you've got to get out and experience other cultures and ways of life for yourself.

## On Q
# Nathan East

He's a mastermind, a visionary, and a true creative genius. I can only explain his talent and the way he uses it as some kind of anointing—some kind of special spiritual gift. It's like God is being funneled through this person. Regardless of your spiritual belief, you can see the power in what's going on. It's fantastic. One of the things I've learned from Quincy is the importance of the spiritual power of music and the power that goes along with that. Also, that the power is magnified when the people you're working with realize the same thing.

The first album I worked on with Quincy was Michael Jackson's *Bad*. I was out of town a lot in the late '70s and early '80s, and I can remember missing a couple of calls. You know, as soon as I leave town, I get a call saying, "Can you come play for Quincy on Michael Jackson's new album?" And I'm thinking, "Man, I waited all my life to get a call from Quincy." It was frustrating, but you need to honor your commitments. We finally connected on *Bad* in 1987. It's unbelievable.

I used to hear JR and Greg and all the guys on Quincy's records, and I would literally dream about what it would be like to play with them. Then, once you get involved, you realize that every note that you strike on your instrument is going to go out to millions and millions of people—that it's going to be preserved and become

Rob Shanahan

part of history—you definitely feel that weight. It's a huge honor to be able to take part, though. I'm speechless when I think about it.

When Quincy is in the room, everybody's game goes up. It's like an unspoken rule or a spirit that enters the room. Also, whatever he does sounds like *him*. When you look back at all the kinds of music he's produced, there's a thing about each project that is definitely Quincy Jones; that's without him even playing one note.

I play bass for a living every day. I went to school, I studied, I got a degree, and I sharpened my skills the best I could. But when I'm in the studio with Quincy, I learn a little each time about music and how all the pieces fit together. I remember one session where he just came over, in a very subtle and unobtrusive manner, and said, "Put this note in right there." It was just a simple change, but I never would have thought of it. And it was the most brilliant way to get to the next note. I was thinking, "How does he know that?" He knew enough about my instrument and what he wanted to hear to just whisper a tiny little thing that I'd put to use for the rest of my life. In addition, it took something that was really good and made it into something really great. I've seen him do that with some of the finest musicians and singers in the world. It's as simple as, "You know, I tell you what, just relax, and do this," and the music instantly elevates to another level. It's no accident that he's the most successful producer of all time.

I think another of Quincy's big strengths is his ability to put the right people together for each project. I know he'd rather be around a bunch of good guys who feel like family than with the hot, smokin' guy that comes in and thinks he owns the place. But the players he brings in all want to be part of something very special *and* they're nice people. When you look around the room in a Quincy Jones session and you see Greg, JR, David Foster, Harvey Mason, or whoever—the very top guys—you realize that every single guy is there for one reason. Every one of them wants to take the standard as high as possible. The collective energy is just amazing. It's something very magical and I don't take it for granted—it's what we got into this for.

Everybody knows that Quincy has the Midas touch. Everything he has touched has turned to gold, but he has never stagnated. He always continues to push into new territory, and he's done that for his entire career. That's an important lesson for all of us. If you look at the vastness of the different types of music he's been involved in, Michael Jackson was almost just an afterthought. When you consider Ray Charles, Count Basie, Frank Sinatra, Ella, Sarah, and all of Quincy's film scores, and his Oscars and Grammys, it's just overwhelming. As a kid, I remember listening to the bass line on the *Bill Cosby Show*—that's what I cut my teeth on.

Nathan is one of the nicest people I've ever met in my life. He's a very sweet man. I get notes from him and Phillinganes all the time.

I've done one-nighters in London, Switzerland, South America, and all over the world with Quincy. Every event was produced to help someone in need. He demonstrates amazing kindness toward humanity. I also remember playing at the Seattle celebration for his 50th birthday. He had heard that they were going to close the music department at his high school in Seattle, and he wanted to help. Public school music programs are important. We wouldn't have a Quincy Jones if he didn't have a place to grow and learn as a kid. It's really the same with most of the guys I work with on a regular basis. Quincy had the Seattle Symphony and the full band and our rhythm section at this benefit concert. I think they raised about $250,000 that night to keep the Garfield High School music department going. For me, that's gold right there—it's an American treasure.

## NEIL STUBENHAUS

Neil Stubenhaus is a a great bassist, and he's a great person. He fit right into the family from the start. We've spent a lot of time in the studio and made a lot of music. We've also spent a lot of time just talking about life and people all over the world.

## On Q
# Neil Stubenhaus

I got turned on to Quincy when I'd been playing bass for a couple years. I was 17 years old and I discovered *Walking in Space* and then *Gula Matari*, both incredibly brilliant records. I really learned a lot from that music! "Killer Joe" really hit me. Just that one simple tune and the way Ray Brown approached the bass line completely turned into an institution of learning for me. It demonstrated how a bass part could be inventive and creative and fun, even when you're just walking through two chords! When I was on the road with Little Anthony and the Imperials, the drummer always told me that his ultimate goal in life was to play with Quincy Jones. Quincy's music was so powerful like that. A lot of the young players coming up were inspired to a new level of musicianship because of what Quincy brought to the table. The first project I worked on with Quincy was an Ernie Watts record in 1982 called *Chariots of Fire*. I got the call thanks to a recommendation made by Jerry Hey—I still remain indebted to Jerry for making that introduction!

Segueing ahead, I ended up playing on the 1994 version of "Killer Joe" with Quincy. That was a real knockout because we had to do a completely different version. I had to come up with something new, knowing of course that Ray Brown is really the king of that bass part. It was a wild experience and quite an honor to be playing on a new version of something that was so important in my development as a musician.

When I first met Quincy, he was already beyond iconic in my mind. But the big surprise was meeting him and seeing that he was the nicest guy. He had no pretense, and he was incredibly real and genuine. He's the most approachable person you could ever meet, especially at the highest level in the music industry.

Quincy is the most intuitive producer that I ever worked for. He's patient and he's willing to let the musicians find their way through the music. When everything is really coming together, he'll start to make comments that fine-tune the track into what he needs from the song. He's willing to open up his vision to include what the musicians bring to the session. It matches his personality—he's willing to share, and everything gets stronger because of it. He loves the players enough to let them help find the pocket, or to let the pocket find the musicians.

"Secret Garden" came from a jam that we did warming up for a James Ingram demo session. Quincy likes to let the band play before we get down to what we're supposed to do, and Bruce Swedien always has the tape rolling just in case we find something magical. This always gives the band a chance to loosen up and find each other. It also lets Bruce fine-tune his settings, and it gives Quincy a chance to see musically where everybody's senses are on a particular day. In that demo session, we landed on what became the core of "Secret Garden." About eight years later, Quincy called the same musicians back to the same recording studio to cut the tracks for the entire song. What we'd been jamming on in the original session turned into the verse, and they added a chorus and some other details—and that's what became "Secret Garden."

That's Quincy's style. He provides direction, he puts the right people together, he knows how to select songs, he knows everything about painting the whole picture, but he doesn't always tell you precisely what to do. He selected you because of what you bring to his production palette. Music evolves from a combination of musicians. Quincy is confident and insightful enough to give the music a chance to come through the players. That's very respectful to the musicians and an incredibly effective way to produce music.

In my experience, when producers are incredibly "hands-on," they don't get nearly as much life out of the music as Quincy does—they don't let the music breathe. And when you tell them how Quincy works, they don't believe it. They think that every single note and every single lyric must be his idea. That's the brilliance of how he works! He doesn't need every little idea to be his. He's painting the big picture, and we're all helping him put it together.

Quincy's musical insights are incredible. All of his musicians play on countless records year after year, but Quincy and just a few others have a certain amazing pop sensibility. He creates music that is so fresh and new in the moment—things like "Billie Jean" and so many of his other great productions that catch on fire around the entire globe!

I don't know that there's a better producer for pop or jazz in the world. He makes everybody feel like they are equal with him in the making of a great record. He gives you every reason in the world to do your best. He draws it out of you, often without particular words. And Quincy is the master at recognizing when the notes have become music. It's the biggest surprise when we run something down and maybe do it again and then look at each other like, okay, let's get ready to do it again, but we hear Quincy saying, "That's great! Let's start doing some overdubs!" And we look at each other like, "That's it?" A lot of producers will overfuss a song to death. They'll do 15 takes and

Quincy Jones Collection

go back and realize that take 2 was great. Well, Quincy knows take 2 is great right after take 2 is done, so nobody gets worn down by going over and over the same song for no reason. It really helps keep the creative level at a peak, and it makes the whole process very enjoyable!

Most people don't realize that, aside from his musical greatness, Quincy is doing everything he can to change the world—to make it a better place. He travels all over, he goes to the Middle East, he makes contacts, and he's behind the scenes trying to create world peace. That's who he is, and that's literally what he's been doing. The glass, to him, is 99 percent full at all times, and he's working on that remaining 1 percent. That's how he lives. There's no half empty; there's no half full. It's 99 percent, and he's doing whatever he can—taking advantage of his success and everything that he's already accomplished—to make the world a better place. He's not kicking back and relaxing. There's no doubt that Quincy Jones knows how to enjoy life and how to have a good time, but he's out there trying to rearrange the world, trying to make it right. He's just an incredible man.

## PAUL JACKSON, JR.

Paul Jackson, Jr., is the best. I was trying to remember when I first met him, but it just seems like he's been playing for me forever. He has excellent instincts, and he's able play the right part for the music. Plus, he's a very nice person.

### On Q
# Paul Jackson, Jr.

I played on a song for Michael Jackson called "PYT." Part of the song is done with a drum machine, and part of it uses real drums. There is some synth bass and some real bass. There are four different guitar parts on it that come in and out. On other songs there might be two different drummers: one for the intro and one for the middle. Jeff Porcaro played most of the drums on "Beat It," but the intro was someone else. The guitars on "Beat It" were Steve Lukather, Eddie Van Halen, and me. Lukather could have done the whole thing by himself, but that's not what Quincy wanted. He wanted three guys to do it; he wanted the musical personalities from three separate people.

He's like the master chef. He takes a piece of this and a piece of that and combines them for just the right flavor. He might take just two bars from one musician, but those two bars might make all the difference in the final production. It's like making a big pot of soup. The whole thing can't be made of pepper, but adding a teaspoon of pepper might be what makes the pot of soup taste fantastic. It's the same thing with choosing the right two bars from one musician, or choosing the right musician to play the two bars. Q does that better than anybody else.

When we recorded "How Do You Keep the Music Playing?" the rhythm section included Ndugu Chanceler (drums), Nathan East (bass), David Foster (piano), and me. Quincy would come from the control room to the studio and give us subtle encouragements and direction. He'd say, "We're just three inches away," and then he'd ask us to steer it this way or that. He always had the big picture in mind. David Foster came up with the intro and the outro. Quincy comes back with, "The intro is good David, but I need …" and then everything just falls into place. He pulls you along, but he does it in a very nonthreatening way.

I've worked for tons of people who say, "This is what I want. I've been singing this in my head for months, and this is what I want." So I play the part and they go, "I don't like it. Can you play something else?" Q never does that. He says, "Whaddya got?" Then you come up with something that takes advantage of your musical sense and experience. Sometimes it works right away, and sometimes Quincy will guide you in the right direction, but eventually you'll end up with something that's just right for the song. That's a very valuable lesson that I've learned from Quincy—call people who can take your idea to the next level, and you'll end up with something great. Let people do their job and hire qualified people.

For people who want to succeed in the music business—people who want to produce great music like

Bill Gibson Collection

Paul always adds just the right touch. We've done a lot of music together and had a lot of fun!

185

Quincy—I would tell them to first of all embrace musicality. There is no substitute for good technique, for knowledge about your instrument or voice, or for knowing how to read, compose, and arrange music. Really *learn* music. Also, embrace technology. In this generation, if you want to advertise something or if you want to be famous, you put it on YouTube; you don't try to get it on television anymore. And learn how to record yourself on Pro Tools, Logic, or some other digital workstation. Learn what a microphone does. Learn about doubling. Learn how to send files over the Internet. And don't use technology as a substitution for musicality. Use it to enhance your musicality.

Finally, in anything that you endeavor to do, work hard as if there was no God and no divine help. After you've done everything you could possibly do, trust God like you've never worked at all.

# JERRY HEY

Years ago, when I had the time to do master classes at universities and colleges around the country, Cannonball Adderley asked me to go with him to the University of Illinois in Champagne. That's where I met Jerry Hey, who has become like a blood brother since then. His group, Seawind, had been playing in Hawaii, but they had moved to Los Angeles and their horn section was playing on a lot of records. We started working together on "Midnight Soul Patrol" from *I Heard That!*, which was released in 1976, and we still work together to this day. Greatness runs in Jerry's blood. His son Andrew is like a genius; he can sing Charlie Parker and Coltrane solos note for note. He's amazing!

Jerry's an arranger and has done the horn charts for almost everything I've produced since our first time working together. He's one of a kind and, seriously, like a brother. This really is a team—it's a family. That's what's always made it so emotional and rewarding. That's why everybody always gives 150 percent, doing what they do better than they've ever done it before—every time!

Jerry is a fantastic person, too, and he's a real 360-degree musician who can do it all. We also did his first string arrangements together on *Give Me the Night*. He worked on *Thriller* and *Off the Wall*, and his spirit and talents have been present for almost everything we've done.

When we work together, we start with a lot of talking about attitudes and concepts; a lot of times Rod's in the discussion, too. Most of it comes down to intuition. I've always found it best to start by talking about a general direction. Then when he's alone and writing, he'll usually come up with something that's just right because he's been able to start at the right place and just open up, writing from the heart and following God's whispers.

## On Q

# Jerry Hey

All of a sudden I get a phone call, "This is Quincy Jones. I want you to play on my record, and I'd like you to do some arranging." Seriously, Quincy Jones called me personally out of the clear blue! And of course I said, "When do you want me there, and what do you need?" We did one instrumental song, "Midnight Soul Patrol" on his album *I Heard That*. I know that Cannonball Adderley had seen my band, Seawind, in Hawaii and told Quincy about us, but I don't know exactly how Quincy found me or how he got my number. But that's how Quincy operates. He seeks out young talent and gives them a chance—he can just tell who's ready to come up. Fortunately for me, that one session cemented our relationship, because a *lot* came out of that evening: a lot of work, a lot of great music, a lot of fun, and a lot of excellent associations with a lot of wonderful people. When you consider all the offshoots that have come from the sessions I've done with Quincy, my entire career can be traced right back to that one evening.

The first full album I did with Quincy was *Blam!* with the Brothers Johnson. Harvey Mason played drums on that album, and David Foster played piano. Harvey was producing Seawind, and I had worked with David a few times, so they recommended me when the opportunity arose. Unfortunately, I wasn't paid by the note, because I wrote a zillion notes for that album, but arrangers are paid by the project.

Quincy, especially since he'd been a trumpet player, always got his fingers in the arranging pie. I was still pretty new to the whole concept, and with *Blam!* being one of my first real jobs, I spent a lot of time on it. We'd play the stuff down and Quincy might say, "How 'bout trying this?" or "What about doing that?" I really listened to what he

Jerry Hey in the studio with Quincy and Arturo Sandivol.

said, and I learned a lot from his input. I've always had great respect for his background in arranging and playing and producing and everything. The arrangements that ended up on the album were usually pretty close to what I brought into the sessions, but they were fine-tuned by Quincy. It was a big learning experience for me.

When I was in the jazz program at Indiana University, I didn't really study arranging. I'd done the writing for Seawind, but that was just for a few horns and we always just played whatever I wrote. It wasn't like I was trying to please a producer or an artist. But when we first moved to L.A., about six months before Quincy called, a whole bunch of different artists asked our horn section to come in and play on their records. So, I had a lot of time to experiment with what I thought worked and didn't work—it was all on-the-job training and it helped a lot.

I did some serious listening, too. I paid close attention to the Brecker Brothers, Tower of Power, and Earth, Wind, and Fire. And I've always been a fan of big bands. My experiences and influences, along with Quincy's guidance, got me to the point where I sort of knew what I was doing. The great thing about music is that there's always room to learn more, but eventually I became confident that the arrangements I'd bring into a project would be pretty good.

One of the most important things I learned from Quincy was to stay away from the vocals. If the horns or strings are going to be at a decent level in the mix, then the arranger needs to make sure they're not stepping all over the vocals. If that happens, then they *will* be turned down in the mix—it doesn't matter how good your arrangements are if they can't be heard. Quincy also encouraged me to write horn parts in a chorus that connect to the melody. My best example of this is in the Beatles song "All You Need is Love." On the chorus, right after the vocals sing "All you need is love," the horns go, "Reet, te, de, de, de." The horn lick is joined to the melody. It's like the listener can't think of the vocal line without also hearing the horns answering in their head. That's a powerful thing.

Quincy and Bruce were always playing with textures and different ways to get unique sounds. We've done some crazy stuff with multiple layers. For example, on "Don't Stop Till

You Get Enough," there's a horn part about halfway through that consists of two trumpets layered six times. On every new track, we'd move back about 10 feet. On the first track, we were close to the mic; the second track was played from 10 feet away from the mic; the third track was played from 20 feet; and so on. On the sixth track, we ended up standing on some speakers way on the other side of the room from the microphone. So it's really 12 trumpets playing at once, but it sounds like one huge trumpet.

Through all the records I've done with Quincy, the process has essentially remained the same. Fairly recently, he asked me to arrange "The Good Bad, the Bad, and the Ugly" for a tribute CD called *We All Love Ennio Morricone*. That was with Herbie Hancock, Vinnie Colaiuta, Neil Stubenhaus, Paul Jackson, Patti Austin, and Matteo Laboriel. We wanted to do a funky version for Herbie, sort of like what he was doing when he first went into the funk era. I brought the chart in for Quincy to take a look at, and he was pretty happy with what I'd written. But he still adds his touch to everything, and somehow, no matter what, it ends up sounding like a Quincy Jones record. He always keeps the overall picture in mind from the very beginning. He hires the right person for each particular job because he knows what to expect, but he brings something extra into the equation. I mean, anyone can call Greg Phillinganes or John Robinson or me or anybody else for that matter, but they certainly haven't turned out *Thriller* or a whole host of the incredibly successful records that Quincy has. During the heyday with Michael Jackson, James Ingram, Patti Austin, George Benson, and so many artists, there were hundreds of millions of albums sold that were produced by Quincy Jones. And he produced those albums drawing from the same talent pool as everybody else.

Everyone loves Quincy—it's just that simple. There's an aura about him and he gets everyone to give their best, every time. And he's definitely one of the best, if not *the* best, producers I've worked for. He knows the overall vision better than anyone, and he puts the right people together to get the best results.

Hanging out with Quincy outside the studio reveals the depth of his world vision and how he treats people. He always shows such respect to somebody the first time they meet him and every time thereafter. I've especially tried to model my professional career with Quincy in mind; just the way he treats people in the studio and respects what they bring to the table is inspiring. He is an incredibly warm and loving being.

189

# JOANN TOMINAGA

JoAnn is fantastic! At one time she was the head of my record company, Qwest Records. We still work together, and she's a true professional. JoAnn just put together the benefit concert we did in Bermuda. It was a huge undertaking, and she pulled it together perfectly. She's the best.

## On Q
# JoAnn Tominaga

While I was taking classes at UCLA to finish my masters degree, I worked at Warner Records for Michael Ostin, who was head of A&R for Warner Brothers and also the liaison between Warner and Quincy's label, Qwest Records. That was in 1984, after *Thriller* and before *Bad*, so I was working with all of Quincy's artists, including Patti Austin, James Ingram, and Siedah Garrett. In 1990, I started working directly for Quincy and Qwest Records. It was a very exciting time because he was producing *Back on the Block* and Tevin Campbell and Tamia and all the rappers that were on that album. It was my job to find the studios, book the musicians, monitor the budget, make sure that the credits were correct, and essentially to just make sure the sessions went smoothly. I had a fantastic time working with Quincy and Rod Temperton and Jerry Hey and the whole team, plus I got to be in the studio with them all the time.

Quincy knows how to bring the best out of everyone. It's a gift. I've seen him in the studio and I've seen him on the business side with all of the record executives, and he's the same guy in either setting. He's able to speak with people and make them feel like they are the most important person in the room—it doesn't matter who they are, whether they're the president or someone on the promotion team. I'm in contact with a lot of the past executives from Warner Brothers, and they always ask about Quincy because they remember all the good times they've had with him over the years. Quincy makes people feel good about themselves—that's a powerful gift.

In the studio, it's important to Quincy that he is tuned in to the player's musicianship. He brings charts to his sessions, but he likes to refer to them as "road maps." In order for him to get the results he wants, which is to record the best possible music, he needs to know what the players have to offer. Only then can he guide everybody in the right direction. One day a couple years ago, Quincy was in the studio recording song demos for his publishing company and he was working with players that were new to him. Even though these were excellent players, they needed to loosen up and start to work together. So, Quincy asked them to just play the blues for a while. He'd call out solos here and there, but mostly he just let them play. By the end of that jam, everyone was really relaxed and they were tuned in to each other's musicianship. At that point, Quincy looked at me and said, "Okay, now I know what everybody can do." I remember thinking how smart that was—he learned what the players brought to the session; the players learned a little about their fellow musicians; and everybody was relaxed and ready to play. As a bonus for everyone, some of their jam actually ended up being part of a song that Quincy did later, so he shared songwriting credits with them.

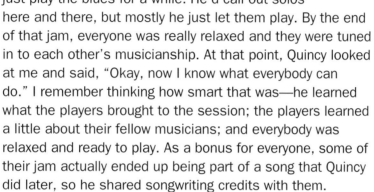

In his own way, Quincy is bringing beauty and harmony into the world with his music. He has a great gift of empowering people; you walk away from him feeling great, every time you're with him. I think that's why everyone wants to be around Quincy so much. Part of the magic, for me, is that he makes it okay to be yourself.

I've learned a lot from Quincy. I remember an extremely valuable point that Quincy made a while ago. When I was running his label for him, he used to say, "JoAnn, you're looking at all the little things just a little too much. You have to look at the big picture—look at what it is that you're trying to accomplish. If you keep getting snagged by the little thing, you'll never get to the bigger thing."

Quincy's music is timeless as is demonstrated by the release of his newest record, *Soul Bossa Nostra*. All those songs that he recorded long ago sound incredibly current in these new rereleased versions. He is music, through and through. And, he knows music, completely! Just recently, he said to me, "You know JoAnn, the last things that are going to be left on this earth are going to be music and water." I imagine he's right.

## Chapter 9

# THE POWER OF MENTORING: QUINCY'S MUSICAL FAMILY TREE

Undeniably, Quincy has produced many of the most powerful and profitable records in history, not to mention the most successful album, *Thriller*. Equally effective has been his ability to spot and cultivate young talent. In many ways he has repaid the kindness and generosity of his mentors: Count Basie, Clark Terry, Ben Webster, Frank Sinatra, Ray Charles, and all of the original big-band musicians who essentially raised him from boyhood to manhood and from musical neophyte to musical giant. The list of people he has discovered is staggering. He found Oprah Winfrey when he was in Chicago on business, spotting her as a newscaster on a local TV channel. He was looking for just the right actress to play Sofia in *The Color Purple*, and when he saw her, he knew instantly that she was the one. He relentlessly broke down doors to get Hollywood to give Will Smith a shot as *The Fresh Prince of Bel-Air*. Earlier, he was the only executive at Mercury Records who recognized what Lesley Gore had to offer the music world. Then there's Tevin Campbell, Tamia, Patti Austin, James Ingram, and even Michael Jackson—the list goes on and continues to grow.

# DISCOVERING TALENT

I don't know how the hell I got into a business like this—and at such a young age, too! My daddy used to say, "Oh, you've got to get a real job!" Nobody had any faith in music back in the '30s. Are you kidding— do music for a living for the rest of your life? In reality, you've got to decide when you're really young that you want to do music for the rest of your life; that's what it takes. I met Michael Jackson, Aretha Franklin, Stevie Wonder, and Tevin Campbell when they were 12 years old, and they were already great! It's amazing. If they've got it then, you know they've got it.

I can't drive a car, but I can see talent before anyone else. There's been James Ingram, the Brothers Johnson, Patti Austin, and Marvin Hamlisch, Arif Mardin, Siedah Garrett, Alfredo Rodriguez, Bianca, Karina Pasian, Lesley Gore, Tevin Campbell, and LL Cool J. We had Al Jarreau when nobody knew who he was; he was singing percussion on *Body Heat*. Minnie Riperton was singing "If I Ever Lose This Heaven" on *Body Heat* in 1974 before her first hit, "Loving You," in 1975. And then there's Valerie Simpson. Before she ever sang on Motown, she sang "Bridge Over Troubled Water" and "Walking in Space" for me. And then we go on from there to Michael Jackson, Oprah Winfrey, and Will Smith—it's ridiculous, man! Will is the biggest actor in the world, and Oprah ... we won't even discuss her. She got just $35,000 for *The Color Purple*, and look at her now!

When people ask how I find so much great young talent, I have to admit that we tend to find each other. Greg Phillinganes played hooky to come to a book signing I was doing and we connected—he has played keys on nearly everything I've produced since shortly after that initial meeting. I found Cannonball Adderly and recorded his first album in 1955. I got a call from Cannonball in the mid '70s and he told me about a group that he had seen in Hawaii called Seawind. He specifically mentioned their arranger/trumpet player, Jerry Hey. Jerry has been with me on almost everything I've done since, and it was really just an accident that I found him. That's how it works. However, I keep my eyes open. I'm always paying attention and I'm involved in what I do. Nobody is going to connect with you, or vice versa, if you're just locked up in your house all the time.

When I see a musician who has potential, I just feel it, deep down inside. It's very intuitive and I've come to trust what I feel inside about the potential of a developing musician. When I first heard James Ingram and he told me he just had a "whiskey" sound, I knew that sound was right for me. It's pure instinct—it's all about going with what your gut tells you.

And again, it's also about who the person is as a human being as much as how hot they are on their instrument or voice—they won't be a great musician if they're not a great human being. It was the same with Marvin Hamlisch. I knew he had potential, and I could tell he was a good kid. He was 15 years old when we met, and he had just graduated from Professional Children's School—my daughter was just going into PCS. I did his first record because his dentist called me up and said, "A friend of mine just wrote a song called 'Sunshine, Lollipops, and Rainbows.'" We recorded it on Lesley Gore's second album, and when the movie [*Ski Party*] came along, that song became a hit. Marvin went on to get a Pulitzer Prize for *A Chorus Line*. When I find a new talent, I can just tell that they have a lot to offer. I can feel it!

I give a hand up to young musicians all the time, because that's what Basie and the guys did to me. They adopted me. Clark Terry, Basie, Duke, and Ray Charles became my fathers. Ray was only two years older than me, but he was so much smarter because he'd been through so much. They put me on their shoulders. They could see my potential, and they knew where I was going. And they knew I wasn't gonna stop 'til I got there.

I'm always looking for that drive in young talent. Right now I'm keeping an eye on a little nine-year-old blonde girl from Anchorage, named Rosie. We were up there for an opening of a water factory, a ribbon cutting, and afterward they had some music. Rosie had on a little portable microphone and everything. She's just this cute little girl and she walks up and says, "Mr. Jones, can I sing a song for you?" This little girl put it in the pocket, man! Nine years old! Shaking her booty and everything. I love it when young kids are gutsy and just lay it all on the line! She reminds me of Tevin Campbell. He's ready, and I think he's right up there with Luther Vandross.

# ALL ABOUT THE BENJAMINS

A lot of the rappers are coming to me and asking for help. They have learned how to make money in the music business, but they're realizing that there is another musical level. I want to see them grow, because I love them. When they say, "Will you teach me how to be a real musician?" my response is, "Absolutely!"

Rappers, like all musicians, need to learn the language of music. Imagine needing to have someone read the newspaper to you every day because you don't spell, you can't read, and you don't know punctuation. That's exactly what a lot of people do with music. It's not as much about being a monster sight-reader as it is about being fluent in the musical language. How are you going to carry on a sophisticated conversation if you don't know the language? You have to feed the subconscious mind through repetition—practicing scales and technical exercises. You must get to the point where you stop thinking about what you're doing and start doing what you're thinking. There are only 12 notes, so you're not going to reinvent anything. Just get busy learning the core musical skills.

*You must get to the point where you stop thinking about what you're doing and start doing what you're thinking.*

Just do it! Just do it like I did with Basie and all the guys. If you look at all the pictures of me back in those days, I was always on my knees looking up to Louis Armstrong, Duke Ellington, Count Basie, Clark Terry, or any of them. And I *listened*! As I said before, I talk my booty off now, but I listened then. I shut up and listened because I didn't even know what they were talking about.

During that era, it was only about quality, craftsmanship, and creativity. We couldn't care less about fame or money! You wouldn't play bebop if you were into either of those things, because it was too advanced.

Charlie Parker took a leap that influenced and changed music all over the world, but it was very advanced—too advanced to receive the general acceptance of popular culture, especially in America.

To this day, I never run after money. I just keep doing what I love. I've had my own foundation for 20 years, and we've accomplished some amazing stuff. That's what I love. When you're doing what you love, for the right reasons, somewhere along the way something miraculous happens—I know that for a fact. I'm not the least bit interested in survey groups or focus groups. If I get those goose bumps, somebody else is going to love it, too. I'll never change from that, never. If you're passionate about something and truly believe in it, that's what you should be doing. That's why you should work with people you love, so you can give them everything you've got. Empty that cup, and it will come back twice as full every time.

# ALFREDO

I recently found Alfredo Rodriguez, a young Cuban pianist. He's 24 years old now—gives you the mumps! Cuba, Brazil, Africa, and America are the most musically developed countries on the planet. They have conservatory training, salsa, jazz, and real Yoruban influences from Africa. They play everything and they have fantastic rhythmic instincts. I've been to these places for 54 years, so I know what they're about. I go to the Carnival every year in Rio, and Baia, and São Paolo. They've got some of the greatest musicians on the planet.

Alfredo and I are tight. It's like we're walking around in each other's minds, man. When I was young, two of my favorite composers were Polish and relatively unknown: Witold Lutosławski and Krzystof Penderewski. When I mentioned them to Alfredo, he sat down and started playing their music. He wasn't just going through the motions; he was playing it!

I've been one of the biggest fans of Claude Nobs and the Montreux Jazz Festival in Switzerland for about 45 years. I call it the Rolls Royce of all the festivals. Claude's chalet in Montreux looks like God used to live there. It's breathtaking! There's nothing like it

198

Bill Gibson Collection

Alfredo rehearsing
"The Bare Necessities"
at Capitol Studios in
Hollywood.

on the planet. In 1991 I had the honor of being asked to coproduce the festival, which I did for three or four years with Claude, so it's now like home.

In 2006, we were up at Claude's chalet one day, eating and relaxing with close friends, having a great time, and just kicking back. Twenty-year-old Alfredo and another kid from Cuba sat at the piano and started playing music like I'd never heard in my life. Cuba has a big Yoruban influence from Africa, just like the Angolan influence on Brazil. It's huge, man. They are fully grown musicians with conservatory and street educations in jazz, classical, salsa, and African music. Their music is polyrhythmic and very sophisticated. They have it all!

Alfredo is bringing that entire rich heritage into modern-day popular culture. I've worked with so many Cubans! Tito Puente is from Puerto Rico, part of the Greater Antilles, which also includes Cuba, Hispaniola, and Jamaica. In the '60s, he said to me, "Q, I want you to go up to this event with me tonight. I just wrote this song for an 18-year-old kid." The event was Woodstock, the song was "Oye Como Va," and the kid was Carlos Santana. A lot of people don't know Tito wrote that song. We were very close buen amigos for almost 50 years and I miss him a lot.

As soon as I returned home from Montreux, after meeting Alfredo, I told my right-hand man and business partner, Adam Fell, "We have to get in touch with this pianist! He's one of the best I've ever heard; we have to work with him." I sent Adam, who speaks Spanish, to Merida, Mexico to meet with Alfredo and his family. Alfredo wanted to come to America to pursue his music career, and within about two and a half years, he was standing at the Mexico-U.S. border asking for asylum! We've got him at every festival in the country now—the Playboy Festival with Hefner, the Monterrey Jazz Festival, Newport Jazz, and everywhere we can get him in.

It's ridiculous. My dream now is to see him achieve his dreams. Johnnie Williams asked to work with him on a big reception at the Hollywood Bowl for Gustavo Dudamel, who's taking over for Esa-Pekka Salonen as conductor of the Los Angeles Philharmonic. Gustavo is the next Leonard Bernstein. Alfredo's composing and orchestrating a concerto and I can already see the two of them together: Alfredo playing piano and Gustavo conducting.

It's rewarding working with Alfredo and seeing him grow. That's how it should be—joy and positivity. His body language when he plays is just like the jazz guys I grew up with. He does things that remind me of Thelonius Monk, or Ray Charles, Herbie Hancock, or Oscar Peterson—a lot of the best guys. It's like he's a member of that same musical family. It feels like such a kinship with him; he's 24 years old and a full 360-degree musician.

## On Q

# Alfredo

As a Cuban you don't have the right to travel, so I had to get permission from the Cuban government just to *go* to Switzerland. I was one of two Cubans who were granted permission to play at the Montreux Jazz Festival in 2006. All of the musicians at Montreux were invited to Claude Nobs's home for a reception. [Nobs is founder and general manager of the Montreux Jazz Festival.] Coincidentally, Quincy Jones was there and Claude asked me to play. I wasn't completely prepared, but I played anyway because it was for Quincy! He was very complimentary and said, "I'd love to work with you one day." That was a huge honor for me because I've always been a fan of Quincy. We exchanged cards, but I didn't have any idea how it was all going to end up.

Quincy came home from the Montreux Festival with an email address. He just walked into my office, put the email address on my desk, and said, "You have to find this pianist! He's one of the best I've ever heard and we *have* to work with him." So when I sent that first email to Alfredo, I didn't really know anything about him. I quickly discovered that because he was a Cuban National and due to the embargo, it was a felony for us to work with him. We couldn't really do anything to move ahead, but we did seek counsel from an attorney who has dealt with similar situations in Major League Baseball.

—*Adam Fell (Vice President of Business Development, Quincy Jones Productions)*

As a musician, I was allowed to do a small amount of travel with my father to other countries to perform. Prior to one of those trips, I spoke with my parents and told them that Quincy Jones had offered to work with me, and that I wanted to pursue that opportunity. In January of 2009 I was able to get political asylum in the U.S. (For a more complete story of Alfredo's journey to the U.S., see the excerpt, below, from his Website.)

My father is one of the most famous singers in Cuba and I grew up in an extremely musical household, listening to all styles of music. Quincy's music has been very influential in my musical development, and I've had many chances to learn from Quincy since my arrival. I've been listening to his music for my entire life, and I appreciate the fact that he has a very open mind. He explores all types of music, and his work spans across many genres.

Within a few months of my arrival in the U.S., I was in Capitol Studios with Quincy Jones. He was producing my jazz interpretation of "The Bare Necessities," from the Disney catalog. It was a dream come true to finally be in the studio working with him. Within a short time of that session, I also had the pleasure of being presented by Quincy at one of the most important festivals in the country, South by Southwest, in Austin, Texas. It was an amazing feeling to hear Quincy say so many nice things about my music to such a large crowd of music fans, especially considering that just a few months earlier, I had been in Cuba.

Obviously, I'm here because I want the world to hear my music, but it's my first priority to keep studying and increase my abilities. I spend about six hours a day practicing but I'm always studying and contemplating music, even when I'm not seated at the piano. All of my life experiences trickle down into my music because music is everywhere. It comes from nature and all the sounds in the universe. The sounds of animals, birds, wind, rain, and so on, are the same to me as a metronome. Music is life and life is what comes from music.

## Alfredo Rodriguez

By the time he was ten years of age, piano was his life. At 14, he was the school's prize pianist and the student chosen to play at graduation. He also wound up graduating first in his class with the highest marks the conservatory had ever seen.

Alfredo quickly became a go-to producer and musical director for some of Havana's most famous musicians, including his father. He also scored a number of popular Cuban television shows, but his success and talent remained mostly local and barely known outside of Cuba.

In 2006, Alfredo heard about the Montreux Jazz Festival in Switzerland, which accepted applications from Cuban musicians ... He sent his application and to his amazement, he was accepted.

After meeting Quincy Jones at Montreux, Alfredo secretly made plans to defect from Cuba on his next government-sanctioned trip to Mexico. But in October 2008, Cuban Foreign Minister Felipe Perez Roque and Mexican Foreign Secretary Patricia Espinosa complicated things. They announced the signing of a new agreement, which mandated that all Cubans found traveling across Mexican territory to the southern U.S. border would be deported back to Cuba.

Despite the huge risk, on his next trip to Merida, Mexico, to play a show with his father, Alfredo walked into the Rejon Airport and purchased a ticket in cash from Merida to a small town just across from the U.S. southern border. But as soon as his flight landed, Mexican federales arrested him and threatened to deport him back to Cuba.

After two hours of questioning, Alfredo finally came clean: he described his love of music and how it changed his life; he wanted to be a musician who performed on the world stage. The officer was shocked to hear the truth. He had never encountered anyone in Alfredo's predicament who told the truth. They talked about music for a while and before he knew it, the officer inexplicably put him in a taxi and asked the driver to take him to the border.

On the night of January 15, 2009, Alfredo arrived at the U.S. southern border. He presented his Cuban passport and asked for political asylum. He was questioned and forced to sleep on the floor of the border station. Then, at 7 o'clock the following morning, Alfredo Rodriguez was paroled into the United States.

—*from Alfredo Rodriguez's bio at* www.alfredomusic.com

# HIGH STANDARDS

It is extremely exciting to see these young talented people coming up. I see little Jurnee Smollett. I met her and her big beautiful family when she was five years old. She is growing and she's gonna be a big, big, big star. And then there's Tatiana Ali, who I met in New York City when she was 10 years old. She was the cute little girl on the *Fresh Prince of Bel-Air*. And Karina Pasian from the Dominican Republic—watch out for her. She's a major singer in ten languages and a classical pianist. It even goes back to finding Arif Mardin in Ankara, Turkey, when he was 24 years old, and now there's Alfredo, and they just keep coming! That's the best.

Anyone who is coming up just *has* to remember to keep their standards *high*. That's the thing: extremely high standards. You can tell the kids who really go for the top—they want to be the best at what they do. That's what really gets my attention.

# PRODUCING YOUNG TALENT

You have to build a truly honest relationship so you love each other enough that you can sit and talk and share ideas. You have to be able to say, "What do you think about that?" Then each of you, the artist and the producer, has to trust the other enough to feel comfortable responding with what you really think. It's exactly the same whether it's Alfredo, or Karina, or Tevin, or Michael, or Sinatra, or Ray Charles, or with a brand-new young artist.

Be sensitive in your delivery. If there's a group of people around—in the studio, at a performance, or wherever—make your suggestions privately. Don't confront the artist in public about anything that might make them feel uncomfortable. Just care about them. It's about love. If you love the artist, you understand their demeanor, and you know when they're pushing too hard or when they need to be pushed more. You can see everything about how to get them to do their best. Your senses open up and it's not an adversarial kind of a thing—it's total love, and you're working together. When everything is functioning as it should, you creatively become one. Then you can really help; you can be the artist's other set of eyes and ears.

# LOYALTY

The people that I've worked with over the years have become family. You have to make a real serious choice when you're coming up, because you run into a lot of people and they run into you, too. God's given me the help to see many of the real big ones before they really made it, but a lot of other people see them, too. Lesley Gore and Brenda Lee were the first rock 'n' roll girls—the female versions of Presley and Bill Haley. It goes all the way up to the young kids that I can see will make it, soon.

I've worked with a lot of the guys and gals over and over: Jerry Hey, Greg, JR, Nathan East, Paul Jackson, Louis Johnson, Siedah, Patti, James, Phil Woods, Neil Stubenhaus, Ernie Watts, Rod, Bruce, Phil Ramone, and a lot of others. I work with them because they're the best at what they do, but I keep working with them because they're some of the best people I know.

## Chapter 10

# SONG AND ALBUM DISCUSSIONS

Hearing Quincy explain what was going on around him when he arranged, conducted, and produced some of the best music of all time is a treat. In these sessions, the specified track was played to elicit a response from Quincy. And respond he did. Q realized that he hadn't thought of some of these details for many, many years.

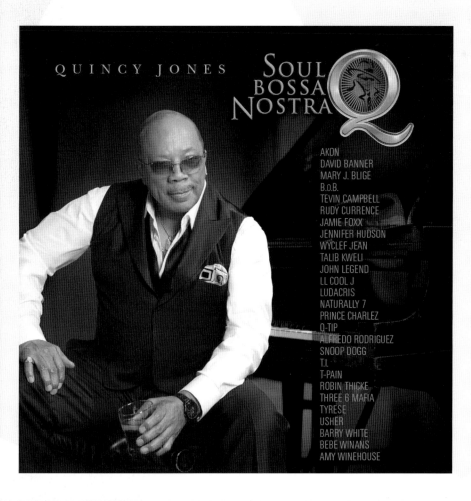

QUINCY JONES — SOUL BOSSA NOSTRA Q

AKON
DAVID BANNER
MARY J. BLIGE
B.O.B.
TEVIN CAMPBELL
RUDY CURRENCE
JAMIE FOXX
JENNIFER HUDSON
WYCLEF JEAN
TALIB KWELI
JOHN LEGEND
LL COOL J
LUDACRIS
NATURALLY 7
PRINCE CHARLEZ
Q-TIP
ALFREDO RODRIGUEZ
SNOOP DOGG
T.I.
T-PAIN
ROBIN THICKE
THREE 6 MAFIA
TYRESE
USHER
BARRY WHITE
BEBE WINANS
AMY WINEHOUSE

# "SOUL BOSSA NOVA," from *Big Band Bossa Nova*

## Track Listing

1. Soul Bossa Nova
2. Boogie Stop Shuffle (issued as "Boogie Bossa Nova")
3. Desafinado
4. Manha de Carnaval (Morning of the Carnival)
5. Se E Tarde Me Pardoa (Forgive Me If I'm Late)
6. On the Street Where You Live
7. Samba de Una Nota So (One Note Samba)
8. Lalo Bossa Nova
9. Sere Nata
10. Chega de Saudade (No More Blues)
11. A Taste of Honey (previously unissued), Quincy Jones (arr, cond), with big band including: Clark Terry (tpt);

From album liner notes: "Its influence on jazz will be lasting," Quincy Jones said cautiously of bossa nova. Of course, Jones's gift for rich orchestrations and bossa nova's floating yet supple rhythms were bound to meet on record. And with Lalo Schifrin and Latin American percussionists (and Jim Hall on two tracks), success was guaranteed.

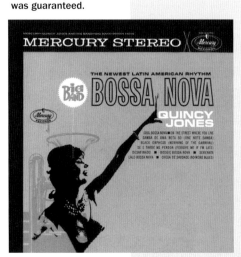

## Personnel

Bass—Chris White
Drums—Rudy Collins
Flügelhorn—Clark Terry
Flute—Jerome Richardson, Rahsaan Roland Kirk
Flute [Alto]—Jerome Richardson
Guitar—Jim Hall
Percussion—Carlos Gomez, Jack Del Rio, José Paula
Piano—Lalo Schifrin
Saxophone [Alto]—Phil Woods
Saxophone [Tenor]—Paul Gonsalves
Trumpet—Clark Terry
Woodwind—Jerome Richardson
Recorded August and September 1962
Produced by Quincy Jones.

**Q:** "Soul Bossa Nova" was recorded in 1962. That's unbelievable.

**Bill Gibson:** It sounds as if you liked to experiment with textures and different kinds of sounds. How did that come about?

**Q:** I was always trying new sounds and combinations of sounds. Sometimes I'd stumble onto sounds by accident, too. Early on in my writing and arranging career, in 1951, I did a chart called "Kingfish" for Lionel Hampton's band. When we were trying the chart out, Jerome Richardson had been playing lead alto but he had to go take a telephone call. Bobby Plater covered the lead part; when Jerome came back, he picked up his flute and doubled the trumpet part up an octave, which is how we ended up doing the chart. It's a great sound. I loved experimenting with voicings and colors. I loved the sound of five saxes playing five different notes, and all the variations that can be created in different voicings and cross-voicings. I love to mix it up. And I like to experiment with different combinations of instruments, like using muted violas with four alto flutes and a trumpet with a stem-out Harmon mute—each new combination is like a new instrument.

**BG:** How long did it take you to write "Soul Bossa Nova"?

**Q:** Twenty minutes. Sometimes it just flows out as fast as you can write it.

**BG:** Tell me about the percussion sounds in this arrangement.

**Q:** That was pure Brazilian influence. Half of that rhythm section was Brazilian; we used the cuíca and many of the things we ran into when we were down there. That's a perfect example of how we would absorb the culture of the different people we met around the world.

**BG:** A lot of the stuff on this album is very symphonic sounding, with nice big warm chords. I also noticed that you are progressing through different textures, even within like sections. For instance, on "Soul Bossa Nova," the recurring upbeats on the "and" of beats 2 and 4 change a little each time; sometimes the voicings are open, and other times they're tighter clusters.

**Q:** Variations in chord voicing and the use of different textures are my passion. As a trumpet player, I especially like experimenting with brass voicing. Changing the texture and density helps keep the arrangement from stagnating can help hold the listener's attention. After I found the piano when I was a kid, I used to stay after school and just play. I played every instrument in the brass section from tuba to trumpet.

**BG:** Where was this recorded?

**Q:** New York, at A&R with Phil Ramone. We did everything during that time at A&R, and to this day, they can't match the sounds we were getting. When they used "Soul Bossa Nova" as the theme song for the Austin Powers movies, they wanted to rerecord everything but just weren't able to replicate the original, either sonically or musically. There were some things that we did with cross-voicings in the trombones, and then Phil Ramone had really mastered the art of recording big bands. There was magic in a lot of that stuff we did in New York with Phil, because there was such a powerful balance of technique and art.

**BG:** In your arrangements, do you consciously use traditional compositional techniques?

**Q:** No. You should have that so much as a part of your DNA that it comes when you call it. You have to be very familiar with it. If you have to think consciously about these concepts and principles, you have a problem.

## On Q
# Phil Ramone

I won't say I was ahead of my time, but I certainly was more adventurous than a lot of the other engineers. When they tried to copy "Soul Bossa Nova," they couldn't get it right because of the crazy echo stuff we had developed at A&R and the tricky orchestration.

We were using the first EMT German plate reverb. We acted as EMT's showroom for Harvey Radio in New York. They weren't selling well because Columbia, RCA, and Decca wouldn't buy them. The EMT plate was simply a large metal plate suspended by springs in a box that was about 4 feet tall, 8 feet wide, and 12 inches deep and it weighed about 600 pounds! Bill Schwartau was one of our engineers. He said to me, "We've got to tune these things. When we get 'em right, they'll sound great." And he was right. I learned how to adjust the springs and get them set up so they sounded fantastic. It wasn't long until people from CBS and other studios started showing up and asking to see what we were doing. Also, we had the EMT right in the studio, because we didn't have room for it anywhere else.

We had also developed a good setup for recording larger groups. We set the brass in circles, with the trumpets and 'bones in front of the drummer—so close you couldn't breathe. The bassist was right next to the drummer, and the guitar was right next to the bass. And then, if there were strings, they were in the corner of the room in the back. It wasn't a football field, but it was laid out kind of like that. The saxes were behind the trumpets and trombones in a semicircle.

In the beginning, I took a lot of heat from the musicians. They'd finish a take, come into the control room, and sneer, "I don't hear me. There's no second trumpet. What's the deal? Don't you like second trumpets?" That's really why I started putting them in a circle. If they could balance themselves better than I could, there was no reason to have four mics. So I used one omnidirectional mic, usually a Neumann U 47, U 67, or U 87— one on the trumpets and one on the 'bones. I didn't use an EQ, I just chose the right mics.

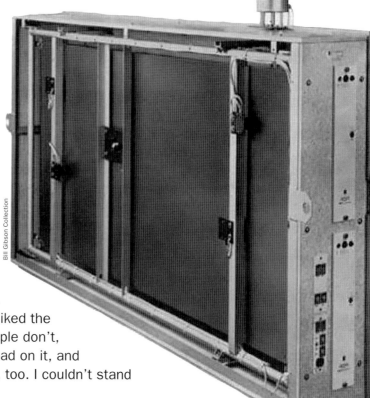

Bill Gibson Collection

It ended up that I liked the U 87 best; other people don't, but I do. I used the pad on it, and padded it at the wall, too. I couldn't stand brass distortion. I thought that was the biggest insult of all. I used Sony C37 tube mics in the beginning. They handle woodwinds and saxes, and you could hang them. I had one mic per sax and would adjust if they were going to double. Quincy always wrote doubles for flutes, and there were solos to keep track of, and if Jerome Richardson or somebody would switch to alto flute or tenor flute or C flute and I didn't capture it, my name was "Mud."

# "BABY CAKES,"
# From *Quincy's Got a Brand New Bag*, Featuring Ray Charles on B-3 (1963)

## Track Listing

1.  Ain't That Peculiar (Smokey Robinson, Marvin Tarplin, Warren "Pete"Moore, Robert Rogers)
2.  I Got You (I Feel Good) (Quincy Jones)
3.  I Hear A Symphony (Lamont Dozier, Brian Holland, Eddie Holland)
4.  A Lovers Concerto (Sandy Linzer and Denny Randell)
5.  Baby Cakes (Quincy Jones)
6.  Mohair Sam (Dallas Frazier)
7.  Something About You (Lamont Dozier, Brian Holland, Eddie Holland)
8.  Boss Bird (Robert William Scott)
9.  Hang On Sloopy (Wes Farrell, Bert Russell)
10. Fever (Eddie Cooley, Otis Blackwell)
11. Harlem Nocturne (Earle Hagen)
12. Papa's Got A Brand New Bag (James Brown)

## Personnel

Engineer—Joe Adams, Ray Charles, Rudy Hill (2)
Piano—**Bobby Scott
Piano, Organ—**Michael Rubini, **Ray Charles
Guitar—**Arthur Knight, **Rene Hall
Bass—*Ben Tucker, **Carol Kaye

Drums—*Grady Tate
Percussion—**Gary Coleman
Bongos/Bongos—*Ray Barretto
Flute—*Jerome Richardson
Saxophones [Alto]— **Jackie Kelso (Alto),
*Jerome Richardson (Tenor),
**Jewel Grant (Baritone)
Trumpet—**Bobby Bryant, Joe Newman
Trombone—**Urbie Green (Tenor ),
**Kenny Schroyer (Bass)

*Performed on tracks 3, 8, 9, 11
**Performed on tracks 1, 2, 4, 5, 6, 7, 10, 12

Recorded at RPM International Studios, Los Angeles, California,
November 22, 24, and 27, 1965.

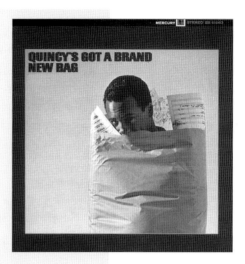

**BG:** So tell me about "Baby Cakes."
**Q:** That's what Ray used to call the girls, "Baby cakes."
We recorded that record in Ray's studio on Washington
Boulevard: RPM Studios. That's where he had his studio
and his offices; they're still there.

**BG:** What was going on in your life at this time?
**Q:** I had just gotten back from four years of getting my
booty kicked during an overseas tour. I had already cut
Lesley Gore in '63. I had seen the Beatles and the Rolling Stones get started a year earlier in 1964. That was the
year after I started conducting with Frank! I was
mixed between being vice president for Mercury
Records and scoring my first movie, *The Pawnbroker*.
I was in transition. I finally quit Mercury Records when
they offered me $1M for a 20-year contract. I quit and
went to L.A. to break into movies—didn't even have a
guarantee. Percy Faith's son was my manager and he
wouldn't let me do B movies, so we held out for the right
A movies to come along.

**BG:** What was the motivation behind this project?
**Q:** You just do projects. You get signed and you do it.
Back then, it wasn't like you took a year. You had to do
four three-minute songs a session, and the sessions
went for three hours, including three ten-minute breaks.

**BG:** Did you have to have it all charted out before you went into the studio?

**Q:** I had a lot of stuff charted, but I also left it open. If you put down a good foundation, you can only go so far wrong. These aren't the kind of voicings that you get from a head chart. The chord structure was all just waiting for Ray, like giving Ray a wet kiss.

# FRANK SINATRA
## *Sinatra at the Sands with Count Basie and the Orchestra*

### Track Listing

1.  Come Fly With Me (Sammy Cahn, Jimmy Van Heusen)
2.  I've Got a Crush on You (George & Ira Gershwin)
3.  I've Got You Under My Skin (Cole Porter)
4.  The Shadow of Your Smile (Johnny Mandel, Paul Francis Webster)
5.  Street of Dreams (Victor Young, Samuel Lewis)
6.  One for My Baby (And One More for the Road) (Harold Arlen, Johnny Mercer)
7.  Fly Me to the Moon - In Other Words (Bart Howard)
8.  One O'Clock Jump (Count Basie)
9.  Frank Sinatra Monologue
10.  You Make Me Feel So Young (Josef Myrow, Mack Gordon)
11.  All of Me (Seymour Simons, Gerald Marks)
12.  The September of My Years (Jimmy Van Heusen, Sammy Cahn)
13.  Get Me to the Church on Time (Alan Jay Lerner, Frederick Loewe)
14.  It Was a Very Good Year (Ervin Drake)
15.  Don't Worry 'Bout Me (Ted Koehler, Rube Bloom)
16.  Makin' Whoopee (Walter Donaldson, Gus Kahn)
17.  Where or When (Richard Rogers, Lorenz Hart)
18.  Angel Eyes (Earl Brent, Matt Dennis)
19.  My Kind of Town (Sammy Cahn, Jimmy Van Heusen)

20. Sinatra Closing Monologue
21. My Kind of Town – Reprise (Sammy Cahn, Jimmy Van Heusen)

## Personnel

Frank Sinatra
Count Basie and the Orchestra
Arranged and conducted by Quincy Jones
Produced by Sonny Burke
Engineered by Lowell Frank
Tape editor—Lee Herschberg

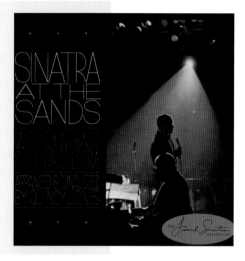

# On Q
# Phil Ramone

Picture this incredible moment: You're at the Sands; you've never met Frank Sinatra; and your best friend is on the stage leading the band. Q is on stage, he kicks off the intro, and you hear the announcer, "Ladies and Gentleman, Francis Albert Sinatra." Frank comes out, starts singing, and you can't hear him! Four bars, six bars, eight bars, and nothing! Frank just drops the mic and walks off stage. And the lesson to be learned was, "If the third trombone mic doesn't work, so be it. But never miss the star. Never."

I still live by that rule. That's why I always had two mics next to him. I was also recording Aretha Franklin once, and a friend of mine told me to put two mics on her—a condenser and a dynamic—because she might distort the condenser but not the dynamic. A lot of times, you only get one shot at the best take. "So," he said, "make sure they're in phase and make *sure* you're riding the gain. If that U 47 folds, you're got the EV 666 as a backup."

To this day, I keep telling the guys who are so concerned about how much digital information they need, "You need less information and more quality on her than you can ever imagine. Pad the crap out of the mic and don't be an idiot."

**BG:** As the arranger, you had to have the final version of the song in your head, before the band even saw the charts. Do you use a piano when you're arranging, or do you just hear the parts and write them down?

**Q:** Sometimes I use a piano; sometimes I don't. If there's a complicated voicing that I'm trying to get, I use the piano. But an orchestra's not like a piano. Sometimes you don't have time to get to a piano. I remember writing "Fly Me to the Moon" in my hotel room in Lake Tahoe and I didn't have a lot of time. There was no piano, so I had no choice but to sit down at the table and just tear it up.

**BG:** Tell me about Frank Sinatra, the musician.

**Q:** His phrasing was just like the phasing that a great horn soloist would use. It kind of starts on the beat, but just lays back throughout the phrase. It's very cool. And Frank was able to respond to the band's energy. That's what was great. At the same time, the band's responding to him—that's when it's happening. That's when the collective creativity is engaged. There's nothing like it in the world. It's what I was talking about before; it's *ubuntu*. The collective is always greater than the individual. You can take that to the bank! Apply it to everything you do.

In 1964, at the age of 31, I arranged and conducted the *Sinatra at the Sands: with Count Basie and the Orchestra* album, but Sonny Burke produced the recording. He had it set up so that you couldn't even see the equipment. You didn't even know what was going on. It felt like it was just another show, so far as the audience could tell. Sonny recorded four of the shows, come what may, and then picked the best parts and put them all together. Everything that was on that record happened live: all of the ad-libs, all of the vocals, the band, and everything. There were no overdubs. This was one of the highlights of my musical life, in fact I think the three of us all felt the same way.

**BG:** Did Frank have any monitoring system for live performances at the time of the Sands show?

**Q:** No, he just sang. They didn't use monitors then. It was just straight up: the singer had a microphone and sang along with the band. Even when we recorded, it was very real. He did no overdubbing; there was none of that BS. He'd just stand there and sing. He'd be looking me dead in the eye, I'm looking him dead in the

Quincy Jones Collection

There was nothing like
working with Sinatra!

eye, and he's also looking at the rhythm section and the
band. It was real.

**BG**: That must have been incredible for you, at around
31 years old, to be working with Sinatra and Basie!
**Q**: It was too much fun. To design the structure and
everything just for Basie's soul, and then have him love
it, was out of this world! He just loved it, man. There's
no greater feeling than when somebody like that says,
"Hell, yeah!" And Frank always responded very honestly
to whatever it was. He'd say, "Maybe it's too dense up
here," or something, and in ten minutes I'd fix it. I was
ready for him. I had to be, because he didn't play—he
was very serious about his music. Frank said it was one
of the most enjoyable and most musical experiences he
ever had in his life, and that's saying a lot.

   We were so close. It just doesn't get any better
than that: Count Basie and Sinatra, please! Forget it!
We couldn't wait to get to work at night, every night.
Basie practically adopted me when I was 13! When

215

Frank passed away, Tina gave me his ring that he wore for 40 years. It has his family crest on it—I don't even need a passport in Sicily. They know! It's amazing. Until the day he died, Frank was like my brother. And he cared about his friends. I would get a call from him, "What the hell are you doing sitting in a hotel writing music on Thanksgiving? I'm coming and picking you up and bringing you to my house for dinner." And he did that on Thanksgiving and Christmas, all the time. Sometimes we'd fly to Vegas afterwards and work at The Sands with Basie. He taught me a lot about family.

# *L.A. IS MY LADY*

## Track Listing

1. L.A. Is My Lady (Lyrics: Alan & Marilyn Bergman Music: Quincy Jones & Peggy Lipton)
2. The Best Of Everything (Fred Ebb, John Kander)
3. How Do You Keep The Music Playing (Lyrics: Alan & Marilyn Bergman Music: Michel LeGrand)
4. Teach Me Tonight (Sammy Cahn, Gene De Paul)
5. It's All Right With Me (Cole Porter)
6. Mack The Knife (Marc Blitzstein, Bert Brecht [original German lyric], Kurt Weill)
7. Until The Real Thing Comes Along (Mann Holiner, Albert Nichols, Sammy Cahn, Saul Chaplin, L.E. Freeman)
8. Stormy Weather (Ted Koehler, Harold Arlen)
9. If I Should Lose You (Leo Robin, Ralph Rainger)
10. A Hundred Years From Today (Joe Young, Ned Washington, Victor Young)
11. After You've Gone (Henry Creamer, Turner Layton)

## Personnel

Produced and conducted by Quincy Jones

Engineers: New York: Phil Ramone (record & mix) assisted Stanley Wallace, Jimmy Santis
Digital recording engineer: Roger Nichols
assisted by Gus Skinas and David Smith

Los Angeles: Allen Sides (8) and additional sound sources assisted by Mark Ettel and Steve Crimmel
Digital recording engineer: Scott Spector: digital recording engineer
Remix engineer and additional sound sources: Don Hahn, Elliot Scheiner assisted by Clif Jones
Mastered by Bernie Grundman at Grundman Mastering
Recorded April 13th, 16th, and 17th at A&R Recording Studios in New York City, and May 17th at Ocean Way Recording Studios and Village Recorders in Los Angeles.

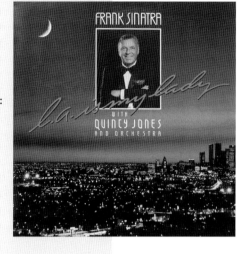

## Arrangers

Quincy Jones (1), Dave Matthews (1), Jerry Hey (1), Torrie Zito (1, 4), Joe Parnello (2, 3), Sam Nestico (5, 7, 8, 9, 10), Frank Foster (6, 11)

Soloists: Bob James (1), George Benson (1, 5, 6), Ralph MacDonald (1), Frank Wess (2), Joe Parnello (3), Major "Mule" Holley (6), Urbie Green (6, 10), Joe Newman (6, 7), Lionel Hampton (6, 11), Lee Ritenour (8)

Piano/Rhodes: NY: Bob James, Joe Parnello, Sy Johnson; LA: Randy Kerber
Synthesizer: NY: Ed Walsh, Bob James; LA: Craig Huxley, Randy Kerber
Guitar: NY: George Benson, Tony Mattola
Bass: NY: Ray Brown, Gene Cherico, Bob Crenshaw, Marcus Miller, Major "Mule" Holley; LA: Neil Stubenhaus
Drums: NY: Steve Gadd, Irv Cottler; LA: Ndugu Chancler, John Robinson
Percussion: NY: Ralph MacDonald Vibes:
NY: Lionel Hampton
Trumpets: NY: Alan Rubin, Joe Newman, Randy Brecker, Lew Soloff, John Faddis; LA: Oscar Brashear, Gary Grant, Jerry Hey, Snookie Young
Trombones: NY: Wayne Andre, Urbie Green, Dave Taylor, Benny Powell; LA: George Bohanon, Lew McCreary, Bill Reichenbach, Bill Watrous
Saxophones: NY: George Young, Frank Wess, Frank Foster,

Michael Brecker, Ron Cuber; LA: Larry Williams, Buddy Collette, William Green, Kim Hutchcroft, Jerome Richardson
French Horns: NY: Peter Gordon, John Clark, Jerry Peel; LA: David Duke, Sidney Muldrow, Henry Sigismonte
Tuba: NY: Tony Price; LA: James Self
Harp: NY: Margaret Ross; LA: Amy Sherman
Concertmaster, NY: Harry Lookofsky

**BG:** You did three albums with Frank, with your duties ranging from arranger/conductor, to producer, to label executive. Was there a difference in the type of interactions you had with him on each of those projects?

**Q:** Whatever has to happen, has to happen. There's no technique for that. I can only respond to what's going on at each moment in any session. They're all different. It's my job to know music in general, to know the music I'm producing, and to know and love the artist. When those things are all happening at once, then the producer has something to offer. I did three albums with Sinatra and Basie; it was different on every album.

The last album I did with Frank, *L.A. Is My Lady*, was in 1984. It was the most complicated. I had started Qwest Records in 1980. By 1984 we had so many hit records out that when Frank came to me and said, "It would be cukoo for us to do another album, Q," I told him that I would love to record another album with him; but I also told his attorney, Mickey Rudin, that I wanted to do it on my label. Frank's response was, "What?! Mickey, you're giving him too much power!" It was understandable because I had started as his arranger and conductor, but we both knew nothing could even remotely change the love we had for each other. I finally owned my own record company, Qwest Records, in a joint venture with Steve Ross and Time-Warner. At that time and we owned the '80s because we had George Benson, James Ingram, the Brothers Johnson, *The Dude*, the *ET* soundtrack, *Back on the Block*, *We Are the World*, and the biggest-selling record in the history of music with Michael Jackson's *Thriller*, not to mention that I was coproducing *The Color Purple* with Steven Spielberg! And the Grammys were just flying in. But Frank was such a pro. He was in my office the next morning at 10 o'clock. I said, "Let's re-hearse tomorrow at 10 o'clock. Meet me there."

I wanted to film him recording "L.A. Is My Lady." I knew he was going to object to it, so we shot the opening scene from the roof, at night, when he was getting out of the car and going into the studio. I had guys getting out first and they were jittery about what was going on and everything. It was like something straight out of *The Godfather*. We were recording at A&R Studios at 799 Seventh Avenue in New York, and Phil Ramone was engineering. Phil and I had planned it out, and so when Frank walked into the building, the lights were very bright in the hallway. Then when he walked into the studio, we'd still have enough light to shoot the footage we needed but he'd feel like there was less light than there actually was. We also had two key lights up above him because I knew he was gonna say, "Turn that damn key light off!" And he did, but we had another in place so, even though we turned one light off, we were still covered. The cameramen were sneaking around the studio like rabbits, moving when he wasn't looking and freezing in place when he'd look up. It was quite an experience. It was great, man. We released the video as *Frank Sinatra: Portrait of an Album*. Even though he didn't really want us to shoot it, he was happy afterward.

Frank was still the consummate professional, and he never lost that ability to phrase like a horn player. When we were doing "Teach Me Tonight," the trombone section almost couldn't play at one point because they couldn't believe he was phrasing just like Lester Young!

We did an original song, called "L.A. Is My Lady," that I wrote with Alan and Marilyn Bergman and Peggy Lipton. On Frank's last take, during the instrumental section at the end, he looked me straight in the eye and ad-libbed, "Well, I think I'll have to unpack my bags and hang around here a little while longer." What an amazing man. What an incredibly amazing artist.

219

## On Q

# Phil Ramone

I had been producing records for a while, but when Quincy asked me if I'd be his engineer on *L.A. Is My Lady* with Frank Sinatra, I said, "Yeah. Frank … in New York? Yeah, absolutely!" Q told me he was going to put together a band and that we'd rehearse in the afternoon and record in the evening." I said, "What more could you ask?"

We were recording at A&R in New York, but the building was slated to have the iron ball hit it two weeks after Frank left. I went to all the construction crews, and I said, "The Old Man gets here at 5:30 or 6:00. You should be done, but would you please not put the jackhammers against the building. I need you not to do that. I don't know how to tell you not to work, but could you work the *other* side of the building and not next to me?" I used the trump card and said, "It's Frank Sinatra, guys. He hasn't been near a studio in ten years." I said, "This is quite an honor, and it's a fitting good-bye for this ship that we've been in for so long." They were fine, especially if I could get them some autographs—you know how it goes.

So everything looks fine, and Frank arrives. I've got a rcd carpet out to the street and I'm doing my little craziness to make sure the last-minute details are covered. The elevators are locked off so only he can get in, and the elevator man is ready to go. Everything is set.

Frank comes up and he looks around and says, "Where's my drummer? I've got to have my drummer!" Steve Gadd was on the stand and ready to go, but he wasn't Irv Cottler, who played for Frank for so long. And then Frank said, "Where's Ray Brown? Where the hell is my bass player?!" And then, "Where's my pianist?" Q was like, "Oh my God!" Well you've never seen a crew build a second drum kit as fast, and we were ready for two basses, just in case, and, fortunately, we had electric keyboards, Rhodes, and a couple of other instruments along with the grand piano. They were all set up in front of the control room kind of like a percussion section. And I thought I would die! We were all balanced and ready to go, and all of a sudden we had to rethink *everything*.

On top of the confusion when Frank showed up, I was

already doing things that you wouldn't normally do. I put my assistant out in the middle of the room with a monitor-mix console like you would use for stage monitoring. He handled all of the headphone mixes for the musicians. I told everyone, "I don't ever want to hear you guys ask me for anything. It's all about Frank. It's Frank and Q." So we tried a lot of new things.

So, I'm adjusting Frank's mic and he said, "Turn that damn key light off!" I said, "You know, the director has it there for your film. I'm not in charge of doing that." He said, "It's in my eyes; get rid of it." I told him I'd take care of it, so I went over to the director I said, "Your key light just left." And he said, "No, you can't do that." I said, "Yes he can." We went back and forth and Q got involved, and it wasn't an easy moment. Those kinds of things are never easy, but we worked it out.

# *WALKING IN SPACE*

## Track Listing

1. Dead End (Galt McDermot, Gerome Ragni, James Rado)
2. Walking In Space (Galt McDermot, Gerome Ragni, James Rado)
3. Killer Joe (Benny Golson)
4. Love and Peace (Arthur K. Adams)
5. I Never Told You* (Johnny Mandel, Arthur Hamilton)
6. Oh Happy Day (E. Hawkins)

*Arranged by Bob James.
All others arranged and conducted by Quincy Jones
Recorded at Van Gelder Studios, June 18 and 19, 1969
Engineer: Rudy Van Gelder

## Personnel

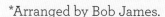

Piano: Paul Griffin (3), Bob James (1, 2, 4, 5, 6)
Guitar: Eric Gale (1–6), Toots Thielemans (1, 2, 5)
Bass: Ray Brown (1, 2, 3, 4, 6), Chuck Rainey (5)

Drums: Bernard Purdie (4, 6), Grady Tate (1, 2, 5, 3)
Trumpet/Flügelhorn: John Frosk (1, 2, 4, 5, 6), Freddie Hubbard (1–6), Lloyd
Michels (3, 4, 6), Marvin Stamm (1–6), Dick Williams (3), Snooky Young (1, 2, 4)
Saxophone/Flute/Reeds: Joel Kaye (1–6), Roland Kirk (1–6), Hubert
Laws (1–6), Jerome Richardson (1–6)
Trombone: Jimmy Cleveland (1–6), George Jeffers (1, 2, 4), J. J. Johnson (3, 4, 6), Norman Pride (4, 6), Alan Raph (3, 4, 6), Tony Studd, (1–6)
Kai Winding (1, 2, 5)
Vocals: Hilda Harris, Marilyn Jackson, Valerie Simpson, Maretha Stewart
Harmonica: Toots Thielemans (1, 2, 5)
Solos: Roland Kirk (2), Hubert Laws (2, 4),
Jerome Richardson (5), Eric Gale (all guitar),
Freddie Hubbard (all trumpet/flugelhorn),
Jimmy Cleveland (2), Valerie Simpson (2),

In September of 2008, astronaut Leland Melvin and hip-hopper Pharrell Williams presented a montage to me commemorating the playing of "Fly Me to the Moon" on the moon, and the fact that they used "Walking in Space" on Atlantis for wake-up music.

**BG:** Here's "Walking in Space" from your album *Walking in Space*. This was in 1969.

**Q:** In 1969, by coincidence, they played the Sinatra-Basie song we did together, "Fly Me to the Moon," on the moon. In September of 2008, astronaut Leland Melvin and hip-hopper Pharrell Williams presented a montage to me commemorating the playing of "Fly Me to the Moon" on the moon and the fact that they used "Walking in Space" on the space shuttle Atlantis for wake-up music.

This record was a tribute to the musical *Hair*, and it was actually produced by Creed Taylor for CTI and A&M. I arranged and conducted the record, controlling the musical development while Creed acted as a sounding board and handled the organization and details for the label. I recorded this album when I stopped doing movies for a while.

I was frustrated with movies because, at the time, the audio was all laid back to the optical track on the film. When the transfers were made from magnetic tape to optical, you'd get what they called the "Academy rolloff." Everything below a hundred cycles dropped off, and there was no high end, either; you couldn't hear crap! I was doing about eight movies a year, and I was so frustrated I was about ready to get out of the business. Plus, I wanted some freedom to just do an album. *Walking in Space* was my first chance in a long time to forget about film discipline and just let the guys play the charts and jam: Roland Kirk, Freddie Hubbard, Herbie Hancock, Toots Thielemans, and the rest of the best.

## Q on Dolby

I'll never forget, we went up to Fox one night. I was sitting with Elton John, who I've known since he was 17. All the music people were there, and they were talking about a new recording process. Ashley Boone, the marketing guy for Fox said, "This is going to revolutionize films. It's called Dolby." And Dolby did change everything, because it had the high and lower strata and it turned the audio back into 3D. It did revolutionize movies, starting with *Star Wars*, *Saturday Night Fever*, and *Turning Point*.

I just wanted to stretch out and be free from the limitation of synchronization in the movie business. Along with Isaac Hayes's "By the Time I Get to Phoenix" [on *Hot Buttered Soul*] and Miles Davis's *Bitches Brew*, this record was one of the foundational records of black FM radio. We had long tracks and I just wanted to be free and loose—no clothes on!

**BG:** Explain how you worked with Hubert Laws on the title song.
**Q:** We'd just talk. I know my players—that's the key. First of all, you'd write out the melody and the chords to have a talk about it to let him know what you're looking for. It's like impromptu sculpting with the music.

**BG:** Who's playing the Rhodes?
**Q:** That's Bob James. I found him when he was 19 years old at a jazz contest up in Ann Arbor at Notre Dame; Henry Mancini and I were two of the judges. The win-

ners were Bob James and Michael Lang. I promised a record deal with Mercury for the winner of the contest, so I did Bob James's first album, and then got him a job playing for Sarah Vaughn. Man, he's the best! He had just come out of school. I just love Bob; he's a great human being, too.

**BG:** Tell me about Valerie Simpson.

**Q:** *Walking in Space* is one of her very first records, but I met her a few years before when she was just 18 or 19 years old and I was vice president at Mercury. Valerie, her husband, Nick Ashford, and Joshie Armstead were, and still are, great Motown writers. Even though Motown had signed Valerie as a writer, they hadn't recorded her as a singer. I did the first few records with her as a solo singer, then Motown jumped all over her, telling me, "She's ours, leave her alone!" She and Nick are two of the most soulful human beings, closest friends, and greatest songwriters I've ever known. It was love at first sight. They've got it together. Valerie is so spiritual and so balanced. Both she and Nick are 360-degree human beings. I've known them a long time. "I'm even hooked on the food and music at their New York restaurant, Sugar Bar."

**BG:** Did you do anything to create the vibe for her in the studio when she was singing?

**Q:** That's what it's about with everybody. Love helps you know who they are. Creating the ambiance and the atmosphere to support exactly what's supposed to be done creatively. If you create the right ambiance, establish the appropriate setting, and if everything that's around paints an inspiring picture, the artist will be pulled into the correct state of mind. If I've built the right ambiance, then she'll put her interpretation on top of that. It's the very best when you provide the foundation and the artists can express themselves; they can contribute what they have, because you're not strangling them by being too rigid and controlling. I learned that from Duke Ellington. He told me, "Let everybody have their own, but do it together." That's how we create a collective benefit to form the whole.

# SMACKWATER JACK

## Track Listing

1. Smackwater Jack
   (Carole King-Gerry Goffin)
2. Cast Your Fate to the Wind
   (Vince Guaraldi)
3. Ironside (Quincy Jones)
4. What's Going On (Marvin Gaye,
   Al Cleveland, Renaldo Benson)
5. Theme from the "Anderson Tapes"
   (Quincy Jones)
6. Brown Ballad (Ray Brown)
7. Hikky Burr (Quincy Jones, Bill Cosby)
8. Guitar Blues Odyssey: from Roots to Fruits
   (Quincy Jones)

Produced by: Quincy Jones,
Ray Brown, and Phil Ramone
Recording Engineers: Phil Ramone, assisted by John Curcio,
Tommy Vicari, and George Clobin
Mastering: Kevin Reeves
Recorded at A&R Studios, New York, NY

## Personnel

Arranger, conductor: Quincy Jones
Co-arranger (5): Marty Paich
Woodwinds: Jerome Richardson, Hubert Laws, Pete Christlieb
Trumpets and Flügelhorns: Ernest Royal, Eugene Young,
Marvin Stamm, Joe Newman, Buddy Childers, Freddy Hubard
Trombones: Wayne Andre, Garnett Brown, Dick Hixon, Alan
Raph, Tony Studd
Piano: Bob James, Bobby Scott, Jakie Byard, Monty Alexander, Joe Sample, Dick Hyman
Organ: Jimmy Smith
Moog: Paul Beaver, Edd Kaleoff
Guitar: Arthur Adams, Eric Gale, Freddie Robinson, Joe Beck,
Francesca Robinson, Jim Hall Guitar, whistle (human),
harmonica: Toots Thielemans

Bass: Ray Brown, Chuck Rainey, Bob Crenshaw, Carol Kaye
Drums: Grady Tate, Paul Humphrey Percussion: Larry
Bunker, George Devens
Vibes: Milt Jackson
Violins: Harry Lookofsky
Vocal Group (1, 4): Valerie Simpson, Maretha Steward,
Marilyn Jackson, Barbara Massey, Joshie Armstead

## Soloists

Quincy Jones (1)—vocal
Eric Gayle (2)—guitar
Bobby Scott (2, 5, 6)—piano
Marvin Stamm (2)—Flügelhorn
Jerome Richadson (3)—Soprano Sax
Freddie Hubbard (3, 4, 5, 7)—Flügelhorn
Hubert Laws (3, 4, 7)—flute
Toots Thielemans (4, 5, 6, 7, 8 [parts 3, 5, & 6])—guitar,
harmonica, whistler
Milt Jackson (4, 5)—vibes
Jim Hall (4, 6, 8 [part 2])—guitar
Harry Lookofsky (4)—violins
Edd Kalehoff (5)—Moog
Bill Cosby (7)—vocal
Eric Gale (7, 8 [parts 1, 4, 7, &9])—guitar
Joe Beck (8 [part 8])

Artwork and Design: Andy Kman—production coordination
Ralph J. Gleason—liner notes Hollis King—art direction Jim
McCrary—photography Isabelle Wong—design Craig Braun—
design, concept Roland Young—creative director

**BG:** On *Smackwater Jack* it seemed like you were a little more experimental. There's a violin with delay and chorus on "What's Goin' On," and you have a synthesizer on "Ironside." Were you intentionally trying to push the boundaries a little bit more?

**Q:** I always push the boundaries as far as I can! There are 16 violins on "What's Going On." They're all played by Harry Lookofsky; the part is based on a transcribed harmonica solo by Toots Thielemans I'm serious, man! This is one of Phil Ramone's first coproductions, and I can't believe I let him talk me into singing on this one.

There are 16 violins played by Harry Lookofsky based on a transcribed harmonica solo by Toots Thielemans on "What's Going On."

It's interesting to have been around from disc to DAT—from 78 mono disks to digital multitrack DATs. In 1999, I was on the front page of *USA Today* with Bill Gates and Steve Case. In the article, they asked us, "What single piece of technology affected your genre the most?" I said, "The Fender bass," because it changed everything. We had the first one. Leo Fender brought it to Monk Montgomery in 1953, just before we were going overseas with Lionel Hampton. We didn't know what it was, so we used it on jazz records. The album *Work of Art, with The Art Farmer Septet,* was the first recording that used the Fender bass guitar. Without the Fender bass there'd be no rock 'n' roll and no Motown, because it locked up with the electric guitar, which had been around since 1939. Those two instruments together said, "Okay, I've finally found my buddy." That was the formation of something we'd never had before: the electric rhythm section. There is so much that couldn't have happened without that!

It was the same thing with the synthesizer; it changed everything, too. It's astounding to have seen it. I used it on "Ironside," one of the tracks on *Smackwater Jack*. That was the first synthesizer the public had ever heard. Bob Moog brought it in and we used it right away. The sirenlike sound at the beginning of the *Ironside* theme is Paul Beaver on that Moog synthesizer. That was in 1967, and Walter Carlos [later, Wendy Carlos] came out with *Switched-On Bach* two years after.

When we did "Ironside," the producers said, "We want this for the Midwest people who are in wheelchairs and stuff. So don't make it too hip." I went along with it and tried to do a version closer to their way. Then I went and recorded a much hipper version on *Smackwater Jack*. They ended up buying my version and using it on the air, instead of the one they had asked for. Robert Moog had asked me why no black artists were using his synthesizer. I told him it was because if you can't bend the notes, it ain't gonna sound funky. He quickly developed a pitch bender and a portamento wheel. Stevie Wonder, who was recording next door to me at the Record Plant, was on it like a hornet. He did four Grammy-winning records with it in a row.

# SOUNDS ... AND
## Stuff Like That!!

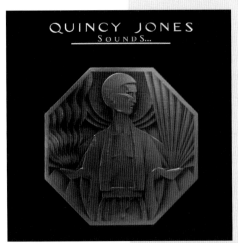

## Track Listing

1. Stuff Like That (Quincy Jones, Valerie Simpson, Nickolas Ashford, Eric Gale, Steve Gadd, Richard Tee, Ralph MacDonald)
2. I'm Gonna Miss You In The Morning (Quincy Jones, Tom Bahler, Ralph MacDonald)
3. Love, I Never Had It So Good (Quincy Jones, Tom Bahler, Patti Austin, Richard Tee)
4. Tell Me A Bedtime Story (Herbie Hancock)
5. Love Me By Name (Lesley Gore, Ellen Weston)
6. Superwoman: Where Were You When I Needed You (Stevie Wonder)
7. Takin' It To The Streets (Michael McDonald)

## Personnel

Producer: Quincy Jones
Arranged by Johnny Mandel,
Leon Pendarvis, Quincy Jones, Sy Johnson, Tom Bähler
Engineered and mixed by Bruce Swedien
Mastered by Bernie Grundman

Rhythm Section
Percussion: Ralph MacDonald
Drums: Steve Gadd
Bass: Anthony Jackson
Guitar: Eric Gale, David T. Walker (1), Melvin "Wah Wah" Watson (7)
Piano & Organ: Richard Tee
Synthesizer Keyboard Bass programming: Clark Spangler

Vocal soloists: Nick Ashford (1), Valerie Simpson (1), Patti Austin (2, 3, 5, 6), Luther Vandross (2, 7), Charles May (3), Gwen Guthrie (7)

Instrumental Solists: George Young (1), Tom Scott (2, 6), Michael Brecker (3, 7), Anthony Jackson (3), Hubert Laws (4), Herbie Hancock (4, 5, 6), Harry Lookofsky-H. Hancock transcription by Sy Johnson (4), Eric Gale (5)

New York Horn Section:
Trumpets: Jon Faddis, Virgil Jones
Bass Trombone: Alan Raph
Saxophones: George Young, David Tofani, Harold Vick, Howard Johnson

L.A. Horn Section:
Trumpets: Chuck Findley, Snooky Young, Oscar Brashear, Bill Lamb
Trombones: Chauncey Welsch, Robert Payne, Jimmy Cleveland, Donald Waldrup, Bill Watrous, Charles Loper
French Horns: Henry Sigismonti, David Duke, Sidney Muldrow, Arthur Maebe, Aubrey Bouh
Saxophones & Flutes: Hubert Laws, Bud Shank, Bill Perkins, Jerome Richardson, Buddy Collette
Tubas: Tommy Johnson, Roger Bobo
Synthesizer & Vocorder: Performed and Programmed by Michael "Lily" Boddicker

L.A. String Section
Violins: Israel Baker (Concertmaster) Nathan Ross, Marvin Limonick, Sheldon Sanov, John Wittenberg, Arnold Belnick, Jerome Reisler, Harry Bluestone, Wilbert Nuttycombe, Carl LaMagna, Betty LaMagna, Connie Kupka
Violas: David Schwartz, Myer Bello, Samuel Boghossian, Leonard Selic
Cello: Dennis Karmazyn, Gloria Strassner
Harp: Gayle Levant

New York Super Singers
Tom Bähler (Director), Patti Austin (Concertmistress), Gwen Guthrie, Lani Groves, Vivian Cherry, Yolanda McCullough , Luther Vandross, Zach Sanders, Bill Eaton, Frank Floyd

## "Stuff Like That"

**Q:** That's Richard Tee on the Rhodes. Incredible! We had some good bands, man. This was in 1978. We had done *Roots* the previous year in 1977, and we did *The Wiz* and *Off the Wall* the following year in 1979.

**BG:** So tell me about how this came together.

**Q:** To me, putting music together is like casting a movie. You don't just throw it together—you think about the players and where they fit in the big picture. Valerie and Nick were right for this, but Chaka was the right choice for the middle bridges.

God gave me the vision to feel musical potential before anybody else sees it—I've grown confident in that.

**BG:** Was most of this stuff charted out?

**Q:** No. You do your rhythm section stuff first, and then you have a framework to build on. When you're writing for symphony or a large brass ensemble, you have to write everything down. But if you want to capture the musicians' creative personalities, you have to leave some room in the structure and the arrangement. When you hear Richard Tee in this song, his part is so distinctive. That's his contribution—his part of the life in the song. Not to mention Eric Gale, Chuck Rainey, and Steve Gadd. Their personalities should be present. And Greg Phillinganes and Jerry Hey need to be included. With so much great talent, why wouldn't you want to make room for their input? You want to get everyone working together. That's what makes it great. Take it all: the great arrangements and the great people. Adding all of the people together is just exactly like arranging to me. It's arranging whether it's on the paper or off.

The perfect example of this "off-the-paper" arranging was when I scored *The Bill Cosby Show*. We did 56 episodes with no scores. I wrote down the lead sheets with all the leitmotifs, and every week we'd have a different guest musician. I'd have Oscar Peterson in one week, and the next week I might ask Milt Jackson, or Roland Kirk, or Jimmy Smith or Cannonball or McCoy Tyner. I also had a solid rhythm section with Ray Brown and those guys. With that level of talent, we could just make it up on the spot! That's dangerous living, but by then I wasn't afraid of anything. And those episodes came out great. That's how we would get "Whooo Lawd! Hikky-Burr, Hikky-Burr," and stuff like that.

During one of our takes I heard all this gobbledygook in the background, and I said, "What the hell is that?" It was Cosby, who was supposed to be shooting the episodes on the soundstage, but instead he's sitting up there with a bassoon, man, trying to play Coltrane. I said, "Bunions, come on, man!" I gave him a cowbell, and he just started in with, "Whooo Lawd! Hikky-Burr!" That's what it's about. It's when your mind is open and you can turn on a dime. You're not locked in anything. You can move and go wherever it goes.

That rhythm section on *Sounds ... and Stuff Like That!!* was called Stuff. It consisted of Steve Gadd [drums], Eric Gale [guitar], Richard Tee [keys], and Chuck Rainey [bass]. They were great. We did a lot of records together.

Johnny Mandel did the strings and French horn arrangements. Johnny is one of the best arrangers that ever lived. He and I go way back. He was with Basie when I was with Lionel Hampton. And we've been friends that long. In fact, we talked recently and he said, "Q, I think that we're gonna be two guys that somehow managed to evolve from infancy to Alzheimer's without passing grownup." I got a doctorate from the University of Pennsylvania, and Alan Greenspan was there. I had to do a speech at a reception after the ceremony. I said, "I bet there's not one person in this room knows that this man, Alan Greenspan, played tenor sax in Henry Jerome's band in 1945 sitting next to Stan Getz and Johnny Mandel." Man, they were shocked! He said, "How the hell did you know that?" I said, "Johnny told me." They were in the band together in 1945!

# THE BROTHERS JOHNSON

**Q:** After I went on the road with them following my aneurysm, I started to feel a very individualistic personality when the two of them played together. Louis Johnson's rock-solid thumping style was influenced by Larry Graham, the bass player from Parliament-Funkadelic. George and Louis just had incredible musical personalities, and their feel for songwriting also got better and better. They worked with Rod Temperton on their last couple of albums, *Blam!* and *Light Up the Night*. They kicked ass!

231

**BG:** Did you have to give them much guidance in the studio?

**Q:** Yeah, they needed a lot of help in the beginning, and we gave it to them. Almost everybody needs a little help here or there, just to shape and form the arrangement! It's the producer's job to help the artist discover the most powerful structure and feel for each song. Adding a section here or a solo there or shortening or lengthening a song is just part of the process. Rod did the same thing, once he came aboard to help cowrite some songs during *Blam!*

**BG:** Were those your horn arrangements?

**Q:** No, that's Jerry Hey. Jerry is a wonderful man. Shortly after that, he was working on arrangements for me. I started pushing him into writing for more strings. I loved throwing him in the water with strings and stuff, because that's what they did to me when I was younger. He caught on immediately and was quickly tearing it up! He's doing movies now; he can do anything. Jerry's son, Andrew, is one of the most talented kids I've ever met in my life. I'm not finished with him yet.

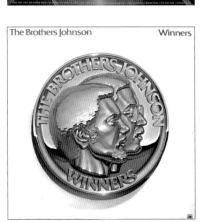

**BG:** There always seems to be a focal point throughout your productions. It never seems like the band is just aimlessly making their way through the chart. Is that intentional?

**Q:** Yeah, that's definitely intentional. That's the flavor in the arrangement; it's called thematic unity. The ear gets used to a certain sound. If you don't change that sound, the ear goes to sleep. That's what it's about: variation, surprise, momentum, inspiration, and so on. And it's about holding on to the listener's attention. When everything fits together and draws the audience from the beginning to the end, that's when it's right.

I draw on traditional musical concepts and techniques. There's a reason Beethoven has lasted so long. He utilized thematic development, retrograde inversion, counterpoint, leitmotifs, and everything he could to compose music that drew his audience in. These concepts are very important to the creative process! And it's subconscious; people aren't even aware of what's going on. There's a similar concept called image systems that's used in movies.

## Image Systems

We react to every image, visual or auditory, symbolically. We instinctively sense that each object has been selected to mean more than itself and so we add a connotation to every denotation. When an automobile pulls into a shot, our reaction is not a neutral thought such as "vehicle"; we give it a connotation. We think, "Huh. Mercedes ... rich. Or, "Lamborghini ... foolishly rich." "Rusted-out Volkswagen ... artist." "Harley-Davidson ... dangerous." "Red Trans-Am ... problems with sexual identity." The storyteller then builds on this natural inclination in the audience.

The first step in turning a well-told story into a poetic work is to exclude 90 percent of reality. The vast majority of objects in the world have the wrong connotations for any specific film. So the spectrum of possible imagery must be sharply narrowed to those objects with appropriate implications.

In production, for example, if a director wants a vase added to a shot, this prompts an hour's discussion, and a critical one. ... Like all works of art, a film is a unity in which every object relates to every other image or object.

[The] writer empowers the film with an image system, or systems . . . An *image system* is a strategy of motifs, a category of imagery embedded in the film that repeats in sight and sound from beginning to end with persistence and great variation, but with equally great subtlety, as a subliminal communication to increase the depth and complexity of aesthetic emotion.

—*from* Story: Substance, Structure, Style, and the Principle of Screenwriting, *by Robert McKee (iT Books, 1997).*

**BG:** I see many of the same names on the credits for the Brothers Johnson that I see on your Michael Jackson productions.

**Q:** That's the family that came together over the years. At that time the technical and production family was

233

Bruce Swedien, Rod Temperton, Jerry Hey, and me. We added to the family when we needed to, but you could usually count on that being the core. It was the same with the band and singers. We were all in love with music, hanging out, and each other. If you're going to work together for several days and nights in a row, 24/7, you better love the people you're with.

# "STOMP!" FROM
## *Q's Juke Joint*

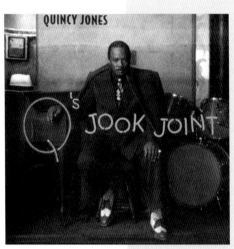

"Stomp !" from Q's Juke Joint
Music and Lyrics by Louis Johnson,
George Johnson, Valerie Johnson, and
Rod Temperton.
Intro and Link by Melle Mel.
Raps by Coolio, Yo·Yo, Shaquille O'Neal,
and Luniz)
Produced by Quincy Jones

© 1980 State of the Arts Music
ASCAP adm. by WB Music Corp. Kidada
Music BMI adm, by Warner-Tamerlane
Publ. Corp.

## Personnel

Featured Artists: The cast of "Stomp"/The Yes/No Productions: Luke Cresswell, Fiona Wilkes, Carl Smith, Fraser Morrison, Everett Bradley, Mr. X, Melle Mel, Coolio, Yo-Yo, Chaka Khan, Charlie Wilson, Shaquille O'Neal, and Luniz

Arranged by Quincy Jones, Rod Temperton, and Jerry Hey
Drum Programming: Erik Hanson, QDIII
Drums: John Robinson
Synth Bass: Greg Phillinganes
Keyboard Solo: Herbie Hancock
Keyboards: Rod Temperton, Randy Kerber
Guitar: Paul Jackson, Jr.

Synth Programming: Simon Franglen, Erik Hanson, Randy Kerber
Trumpets: Jerry Hey, Gary Grant
Trombone: Bill Reichenbach
Saxophones: Larry Williams, Kim Hutchcroft
Background Vocals: Patti Austin, Siedah Garrett, Mervyn Warren, Will Wheaton; Portrait (Michael Angelo Saulsberry, Eric Kirkland, Kurt Jackson, Irving Washington III); Style (Reginald Bell, Rodney Chambers, Richard Redd, Andre Scott)

**BG**: Tell me about "Stomp!"
**Q**: Listen to Louis, man. He is a killer! We had some good times in the studio. It's so important to get the basic components right when you start the session. The tempo, key, and feel have to be right, or you're wasting your time. I'll let the band play through the arrangement a few times, and then I'll have everybody come into the control room and take a listen. It's all about making sure we're in the pocket; that's where God takes you, because there's just one tempo that's right. If it's in the pocket, we're ready to continue on.

**BG**: Normally, the snare and claps would be on beats 2 and 4, but you have them on 1, 2, 3, and 4. Why is that?
**Q**: You're playing off the onomatopoeia, off the title of the song—*stomp, stomp, stomp, stomp*. It goes back to thematic unity again. The more connected the ingredients in your production, the more powerful it is. Many people don't think about the lyrics and how they should match the groove, or they put a lot of random stuff together that doesn't mean anything to the music. We need structure and intelligent musical ingredients. There is a lot of freedom once you establish a good foundation and a set of guidelines for your work. And, there's nothing new about a straight four-beat groove. Basie had four-on-the-floor with the kick drum 70 years ago, and then in disco it came back. It even goes back to the drums behind the flamenco dancers and the Berbers, and African and Arabic influences. Just like the fact that there are only 12 notes, there are only so many beats and rhythmic combinations. They recur throughout musical history and across genres with certain accoutrements added or taken away, but there's only so much you can do.

# THE DUDE

## "Just Once"

Written by Barry Mann and
Cynthia Weil

## Personnel

Jerry Hey—horn arrangements,
trumpet
Quincy Jones—rhythm and
vocal arrangements
Johnny Mandel—synthesizer
and string arrangements
Patti Austin—backing vocals
Abraham Laboriel—bass
Gerald Vinci—concertmaster
John Robinson—drums
Ernie Watts, Kim Hutchcroft—
flute, saxophone
Steve Lukather—guitar
James Ingram—lead vocals
Paulinho Da Costa—percussion
David Foster—piano (acoustic,electric)
Robbie Buchanan—piano (acoustic), synthesizer (string)
Ian Underwood—synthesizer
and string programming
Greg Phillinganes—synthesizer
Bill Reichenbach—trombone
Chuck Findley—trumpet

**BG:** Let's talk about *The Dude*.
**Q:** *The Dude* was recorded in 1980 and released in 1981, just a couple years before *Thriller* and a couple years after *Off the Wall*. This was my last record on A&M. We started out just planning on giving them a drum album, but we decided to just go all the way, and it worked. We got 12 Grammy nominations, and it was James Ingram's introduction to the music world.

**BG:** Let's listen to "Just Once." Did you write out that piano intro?

**Q:** No, that's David Foster, one of the best pianists ever. He came up with that intro. Everybody dug down and contributed something amazing. Thing is, you pick at it until it's well. There really can't be a defined sequence of events in producing music, because it's an art that's just based on your influences and background. It's what your humanity is about that counts. If you want to be a great producer, live your ass off. Play hard and work hard. Give everything 150 percent, and when it rains get wet! Then your soul will tell you what to do—when to use your classical background, or jazz, or whatever because it's part of you. I can't think about all that stuff in a session. What am I gonna do, stop the session and look at everything through a classical filter or Motown? I just have to do it and react. I think of Rod when we got Vincent Price to narrate *Thriller*. Vincent Price was Peggy's friend. I was just thinking, wouldn't it be hot to have the king of the thrillers narrate this song, and then Vincent gets there and I call Rod and say, "Rod, man, we need some more words for this!" And he's in the taxicab on the way to the session coming up with a masterpiece with the 40,000 years of funk and everything. That's it! He was prepared. We were all prepared! Vincent nailed it right on the money! Rod nailed it! *Thriller* speaks for itself. If you want to be great, get your booty prepared!

When you started the playback, I immediately thought Lou Horowitz. He is a director/producer, who was going to direct *We Are the Future*, a multinational event that I presented in 2004 at Circus Maximus, in Rome, Italy. When he went over to look at things, Lou went all over Rome, capturing video footage. Later he combined that footage with "Just Once" and, through his combination of the images with the song, completely transformed it into a song about world peace! He turned it into a political statement—transformed every word into a message about world unity: "I guess my best wasn't good enough. Just once, can we finally do it right." Every line was transformed to where it could easily be about Palestine and Israel instead of a man and a woman.

237

WE ARE THE FUTURE
YOU ARE THE ANSWER •

A NIGHT OF MUSIC AND HOPE
FEATURING
ALICIA KEYS
OPRAH WINFREY
ANGELINA JOLIE
CARLOS SANTANA
JOSH GROBAN
NAOMI CAMPBELL
ZUCCHERO
ANDREA BOCELLI
AND MORE

From the video *We Are the Future:*
*You Are the Answer*

*Peace is possible and children are the answer if we give them the tools to create better lives. Abandon them, and chaos and hate will rule their future.*
—Quincy Jones

In the last two decades war has killed or disabled over 8 million children, 12 million have been left homeless. On average 30,000 children die every day of preventable causes. On May 16th, 2004, visionary artist Quincy Jones, Ambassador Uri Savir, and peace activist Hani Masri launched *We Are the Future* with a star-studded concert at the historic Circus Maximus in Rome. Masri, a Palestinian, had approached Quincy and said he was working with an Israeli, Savir. They wanted Quincy to be their third partner. Lending their voice to this great cause were international superstars Alicia Keys, Josh Groban, Oprah Winfrey, Herbie Hancock, Carlos Santana, Zucchero, Angelina Jolie, Naomi Campbell, Andrea Bocelli, and a host of entertainers, world-class athletes, political leaders, and dignitaries.

At the heart of *We Are the Future* is an ambitious goal to change the cycle of violence that is more prevalent now than at any other time in world history. *We Are the Future* is a sustainable plan to give help and hope to the children struggling to survive in hostile surroundings. The foundation will establish children's centers that provide much-needed humanitarian aid for immediate problems. The centers will go further by investing in the future of each child that comes through its doors. It will provide programs in nutrition, health care, sports, the arts, education, and leadership.

**BG:** Did you have to do much with James to get that performance?
**Q:** You have to work on tempo. It's like sculpting to just get the tempo right. It's a process. When you do a few takes and see how it feels. We might slow it down or speed it up or transpose it until we get it right. When

SONG AND ALBUM DISCUSIONS

it's right, everybody knows it. There are a lot of different skills that work together in the process of recording and building a song: orchestration, arranging, composing, and more. Rod is a great songwriter. When he's right there, helping build the song, he can make minor changes that instantly make a big difference. Jerry Hey is an amazing musician and arranger. When something's not just right, he can fix it on the spot. Bruce is an amazing engineer; when he's in control, you know for sure that everything is covered sonically. When everyone's practicing their core skill, we know we have a chance of getting something great.

**BG:** Was this all done with a click track?
**Q:** I've always used a click track. It's the only way you can really make sure that you can edit between takes or even within the same take.

# *BODY HEAT*

## Track Listing

1. Body Heat (Q. Jones, L. Ware, B. Fisher, S. Richardson)
2. Soul Saga: Song of the Buffalo Soldier (R. Brown, Q. Jones, T. Bahler, J. Greene)
3. Everything Must Change (B. Ighner)
4. Boogie Joe, the Grinder (Q. Jones, D. Grusin, T. Bahler)
5. Everything Must Change–Reprise (B. Ighner)
6. One Track Mind (Q. Jones, L. Ware)
7. Just a Man (Valdy)
8. Along Came Betty (B. Golson)
9. If I Ever Lose This Heaven (L. Ware, P. Sawyer)

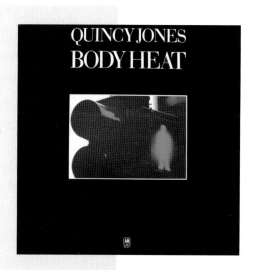

## Personnel

**Produced by Quincy Jones and Ray Brown**
Engineer by Phil Schier
Mixed by Phil Schier and Quincy Jones
Arranged by Quincy Jones, Tom Bahler, Dave Blumberg

Keyboards—Dave Grusin, Herbie Hancock, Richard Tee, Bob James, Billy Preston, Mike Melvoin

Guitars—Dennis Coffey, Arthur Adams, Phil Upchurch, Eric Gayle, Wah Wah Watson, David T. Walker

Drums—James Gadson, Paul Humphrey, Bernard Purdy, Grady Tate

Percussion—Bobbye Hall

Bass—Chuck Rainey, Melvin Dunlap, Max Bennett

Horns—Hubert Laws, Jerome Richardson, Chuck Findley, Frank Rosolino, Clifford Solomon, Pete Christlieb

Harmonica—Tom Morgan

Synthesizer—Robert Margouleff, Malcom Cecil

Vocal group—Tommy Bahler, Joe Greene, Jesse Kirkland, Jim Gilstrap, Carolyn Willis, Myrna Matthews, Minnie Riperton, Quincy Jones, Leon Ware

Vocal effects—Al Jarreau (2, 9)

Vocal soloists—Leon Ware (1, 9), Bruce Fisher (1), Jim Gilstrap (2), Minnie Riperton (9), Quincy Jones (7), Bernard Ighner (3, 5)

**BG:** Let's listen to a little bit of "If I Ever Lose This Heaven" from *Body Heat*.

**Q:** This was right before I had my aneurysm in 1974. That's Leon Ware and Minnie Riperton singing melody together. Leon was one of the songwriters, too—very talented guy. This was one of Minnie's first records, and also one of Al Jarreau's first. Al was doing vocal percussion and vocals.

**BG:** This tune has such a relaxed feeling. Obviously you could tighten anything up as much as you want, but when you compare "If I Ever Lose This Heaven" to "Ai No Corrida," it's a lot looser and much more relaxed, plus the intonation isn't quite as precise. Is that all intentional to create a certain feeling?

**Q:** You're right, it's more raw, and "Ai No Corrida" is just nailed to the cross—it's tight! Sometimes, it doesn't want to be tightened up. It can be okay to just let it be what it wants to be. It's amazing the way Hubert Laws and Frank Rosolino just nail their solos. It's ridiculous, man. That's what happens when you get people who can really react to what they hear—it takes it to a new level. But it always comes back to the same thing: there are only 12 notes, but people use them in so many different ways. And everything depends on the song or the story.

If you have talented and gifted musicians, you have to put some trust in whatever's happening naturally. Sometimes it's okay to let something be a little loose, if it has life—a life of its own. It's important that everything be alive in some way. It's possible to tighten the life out of a piece of music. I know how to tighten or loosen a piece of music, or I can go anywhere in between; I've been working on that since I was 13 years old. When you record a lead vocal or an instrumental solo, there's usually a take that just feels the best. Even if there's a flaw somewhere, everybody in the room can tell it's the most musical—that's the one to use. Fortunately, modern technology lets us fix most flaws so we can enjoy the best of both worlds.

# "AI NO CORRIDA"

**BG**: Let's listen to "Ai No Corrida." In the intro, was that eighth-note rhythmic sequence on the keyboard written, or did the player come up with it on the session?
**Q**: No, it was written out. It was by design. This is another great song! Rod Temperton brought this one to me, but Chas Jankel and Kenny Young wrote it. When Rod brought it in, I originally thought it was talking about someone named Carita, like "I know Mary" or "I know Shirley." I thought it was "I know Carita"! When we were at the press conference while on tour in Japan for *The Dude* in 1982, this little old lady told me that the literal interpretation is "for the love of a bullfight." It's half Spanish and half Japanese. Anyway, I was shocked when I found out that this lady had just been released from prison. When she found her lover with another girl, she cut off his genitals and wore them around her neck! She was just released after 30 years, and was sitting right there!

# BACK ON THE BLOCK

## Track Listing

1. Prologue - 2 Q's Rap (Big Daddy Kane)
2. Back on the Block (Q. Jones, R. Temperton, S. Garrett, C. Semenya, Ice-T, Melle Mel, Big Daddy Kane, Kool Moe Dee)
3. I Don't Go for That (I. Prince)
4. I'll Be Good to You (G. Johnson, L. Johnson, S. Sam)
5. The Verb to Be (M. Warren)
6. Wee B. Dooinit – Acappella Party (Q. Jones, S. Garrett, I. Prince)
7. The Places You Find Love (G. Ballard, C. Magness, C. Semenya)
8. Jazz Corner of the World (Kool Moe Dee, Big Daddy Kane)
9. Birdland (J. Zawinul)
10. Setembro - Brazilian Wedding Song (I. Lins, G. Peranzetta)
11. One Man Woman (I. Prince, S. Garrett, H. Roberts)
12. Tomorrow - A Better You, Better Me (G. Johnson, L. Johnson, S. Garrett)
13. Prelude to the Garden (J. Calandrelli)
14. The Secret Garden (Q. Jones, R. Temperton, S. Garrett, El DeBarge)

Producer: Quincy Jones
Associate producer: Rod Temperton
Engineer: Bruce Swedien
Additional recording: Bernie Kirsch, Don Cobb, Dave Frazer, Brad Sundberg
Assistant engineers: Rail Rogut, Don Kunz, Dana Jon Chappelle, Kevin Becka
Mastered by Bernie Grundman

## Personnel

Rhythm Section
Keyboards: Greg Phillinganes (2, 4, 10, 11), Ian Prince (3, 4, 9, 10, 11), David Paich (4, 7, 10), Randy Kerber (7, 12), Larry Williams (7, 9, 13, 14), Jerry Hey (7)
Fender Rhodes: George Duke (10), Greg Phillinganes (12, 14)

Synthesizer pads: Herbie Hancock (10), David Paich (10)

Synthesizer programming: Steve Porcaro (2, 4, 7, 10), Larry Williams (3, 4, 7, 11, 13, 14), Ian Underwood (3, 4, 10), Michael Boddicker (4, 7, 9), Randy Kerber (7), Rhett Lawrence (7), Michael Casey Young (9)

Synthesized Korg Pepe: Josef Zawinul (2)

Guitar: George Johnson (4), Michael Landau (7), Paul Jackson, Jr. (7), Steve Lukather (12, 14)

Bass: Louis Johnson (2, 4, 7), Nathan East (9), Neil Stubenhaus (12, 14)

Drums: Harvey Mason (4), John Robinson (7, 12, 14)

Drum sounds: Bruce Swedien (4, 12)

Drum programming: Rod Temperton (1), QD III (2), Quincy Jones (2, 10), Michael Boddicker (2)

Percussion: Bill Summers (2, 7, 8), Paulinho Da Costa (7, 10), Ollie Brown (12)

Timbales: Sheila E. (11)

Vocal percussion, body slaps, mouth sounds: Bobby McFerrin (6), Quincy Jones (6)

Vocorder: Ian Prince (6)

African percussion: J. C. Gomez (2)

Hand Claps: Quincy Jones (2, 9), Rod Temperton (2, 9), Ian Underwood (2, 9), Ian Prince (6)

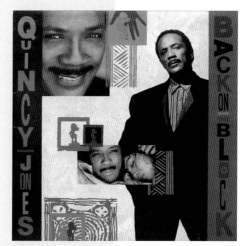

Horns

Trumpet: Jerry Hey (9), Gary Grant (9)

Saxophone: Larry Williams (9), Gerald Albright (10, 12)

Trombone: Bill Reichenbach (9)

Rappers: Ice-T (2), Melle Mel (2), Big Daddy Kane (2), Kool Moe Dee (2)

Soloists

Featured soloists: Herbie Hancock (3, 7, 10), James Moody (8, 9), Miles Davis (8, 9), George Benson (8, 9, 10), Sarah Vaughn (8), Dizzie Gillespie (8, 9), Ella Fitzgerald (8), Josef Zawinul (8), Gerald Albright (10, 12), George Duke (10, 11), Sheila E. (11), El DeBarge (14), James Ingram (14), Al B. Sure! (14), Barry white (14)

243

Vocals
Lead vocals: QD III (1), Quincy Jones (1), Tevin Campbell (2, 12), Siedah Garrett (3, 6, 7, 11), Ray Charles (4), Chaka Khan (4, 7), Ella Fitzgerald (6), Al Jarreau (6), Bobby McFerrin (6), Take 6 (6), Sarah Vaughn (6), Kool Moe Dee (8), Big Daddy Kane (8)

Featured vocalists
Ella Fitzgerald (9), Sarah Vaughn (9), Take 6* (10), Sarah Vaughn (10)
Spoken word: Mervyn Warren (5)

Background vocals
Andrae Crouch Singers** (2, 7), Siedah Garrett (2, 3, 4, 7, 11, 14), Caiphus Semenya (2), Nadirah Ali (3), Ian Prince (3), James Gilstrap (4), James Ingram (4, 7), George Johnson (4), Louis Johnson (4), Phil Perry (4), Syreeta Wright (4), Edie Lehman (6, 7), Peggi Blu (7), Howard Hewitt (7), Jennifer Holliday (7), Clif Magness (7), Dionne Warwick (7), Luther Vandross (7), Children's Choir*** (12), El DeBarge (14), Al B. Sure! (14)

*Take 6 consists of: Alvin Chea, Cedric Dent, Mark Kibble, Claude McKnight, David Thomas, and Mervyn Warren
**Andrae Crouch Singers, conducted by Andrae and Sandra Crouch, consist of: Andrae Crouch (2, 7), Sandra Crouch (2, 7), Rose Banks (2, 7), Jean Johnson-McGrath (2, 7), Alfie Silas (2, 7), Vonciele Faggett (2, 7), Tammi Gibson (2, 7), Howard McCrary (2, 7), Perry Morgan (2, 7), Maxi Anderson (7), Jackie Gouche (7), Pattie Howard (7), Geary Lanier Foggett (7), Derrick Schofield (7)
***Children's Choir, conducted by Rose Banks and Siedah Garrett, consists of: Alex Harris, Reginale Green, McKinley Brown, Donovan McCrary, Kwame James, Kenneth Ford, Shane Shoaf, Tyren Perry, Chad Durio, Jania Foxworth, Charity Young, Tiffany Johnson

Arrangements
Vocal arrangement: Quincy Jones (2, 4, 6, 7, 10, 14), Andrae Crouch (2, 7), Mark Kibble (6, 10), Siedah Garrett (6, 14), Rod Temperton (6, 14), Ian Prince (6), Caiphus Semenya (7)
Assistant produced and arrange: Jerry Hey (12)

Rhythm arrangement: Quincy Jones (2, 4, 6, 7, 8, 9, 10, 11, 12, 14), Rod Temperton (2, 9, 14), Bill Summers (2, 8), QD III (2), Ian Prince (6, 9, 11), Clif Magness (7), Glen Ballard (7), Greg

Phillinganes (10), Jerry Hey (12)

Synthesizer string arrangement and composition:
Jorge Calandrelli (13), Jerry Hey (14)

Horn arrangement: Jerry Hey (9), Quincy Jones (9)

Conductor: Quincy Jones (7)

**BG**: Where does rap music come from?

**Q**: Rap comes from way back. It comes from the word imbongi, which is a poet/praise shouter who is the go-between from the leader to the people. In 1994 Nelson Mandela had an imbongi at his inauguration, but they go a long way back in African history. It also goes back to the *griots* that Alex Haley talks about in *Roots*—the oral historians. It's old, man! It also comes via all of the American black music and the Inkspots, and the Mills Brothers, and even Motown; they all have talking things. Even though it wasn't rhythmic rap, you can still see the connection. The first time I heard them really go for it was in Gil Scott-Heron and the Last Poets. They were a gang in New York, in the late '60s during the Nixon Administration, that got in trouble with the government when they made an album of politically oriented poetry. They were very influential. And then there were also the Watts Prophets, who I had on my *Mellow Madness* album in 1975.

They were some of the pioneers, and then there started to be all kinds of stuff coming out of the South Bronx, and then the Sugar Hill Gang came out with "Rapper's Delight" in 1979. During that evolution, I took my son to meet LL Cool J, Beastie Boys, Run DMC, and all those guys. Rick Rubin had all those guys at Def Jam [Records]. I met with Rick in 1985, right after they first opened with "Walkin' in the Rain" and "My Adidas." I knew rap was going to be big.

**BG**: What are the fundamentally important elements in great rap music?

**Q**: There are beats and rhymes. The beats play a big part in it. A lot of guys just do beats, which is the rhythmic track you work from. Bebop and hip-hop are virtu-ally the same, because it's all improvised. The rappers

Bill Gibson Collection

improvise just like jazz musicians; they're unbeliev-able! I've worked with about 50 rappers, and the session usually goes like, "Heavy D, did you listen to the tape first?"—because you always send the tape out to singers so they get familiar with the music. And then Heavy D says, "No. Can I hear the tape one time?" He listens to it one time and writes the whole goddamn thing right there. I'm talking about with incredible syncopation and everything, right there. Then he goes out and does one or two takes and puts it down. They are unbeliev-able, and they're so influential on the culture! I believe completely that with informed and caring content, rap could revolutionize education.

It's just like jazz! They call it freestylin', but it's the same thing as bebop. It's just jammin', and there's no mystery there. Just like back in 52nd Street and the beboppers. It's the same kind of attitude towards improvisation; it's free. They can really tear it up the first time down! It's just astounding. I remember when we were finishing up *Back on the Block*, which had four rappers on it: Melle Mel, Ice-T, Big Daddy Kane, and Kool Moe Dee. I came out to go to the bathroom one time and saw Big Daddy Kane over there in the corner. When he saw me, he came over and said, "Let me hear you use 'sterile' in a sentence." I knew what he was trying to do; he was trying to rhyme with "Ella Fitzgerald." They are clever, man, they really are. And they'll figure out some words that will blow your mind! They'll scare you to death.

**BG**: What are a rapper's core skills? What are their fun-damental tools?

**Q**: Improvisation. They'd be nothing if they didn't have that. Listen to Heavy D's rap on "Rock with You" with Brandy. It's unbelievable, man. And listen to Melle Mel, who is the king of rap as far as I'm concerned. He's not a wannabe. He's for real. And he'd never pimp the 'hood in his rhymes, never. He's done stuff like "White Lines (Don't Do It)" and "The Message." Those things are un-equaled to this day. They're like the masterpieces of rap, and they're all positive solutions for the 'hood.

**BG**: Tell me about the impact made by *Back on the Block*.

**Q**: That was amazing. *Back on the Block* helped bring rap into the mainstream, especially when we won the Grammy for Record of the Year! People were still mum-bling about rap not being credible, but I've been feeling the whole evolution of rap music for a long time.

Chapter 11

# IN THE STUDIO WITH Q

During the production of this book, I had the opportunity to see and archive Quincy in action, producing two separate projects: a recording of Alfredo Rodriguez playing "The Bare Necessities" (from the animated Disney feature *The Jungle Book*) and the theme song for the 2010 World Expo in Shanghai. Both sessions were at studios in which Quincy has produced benchmark projects over the years, and both were unique and incredibly instructive. It's one thing to talk about how Q produces music, but it's another thing to actually see the way he works and the way he interacts with his musical family.

Quincy is the master of his environment. When he walks into the studio, the bar immediately rises. His track record and history set the tone. His band and singers understand the importance of what they contribute to a Quincy Jones session. Nathan East put it best when he said, "You realize that every note that you strike on your instrument is going to go out to millions and millions of people—that it's going to be preserved and become part of history—you definitely feel that weight. It's a huge honor."

I came back from each session with photos, video footage, and audio and video interviews. It was a privilege to be included in the sessions, and it's an honor to be able to share it with Quincy's fans, friends, enthusiasts, and admirers. The accompanying DVD includes specially selected video and audio representations of these sessions. It's our hope that you will find them inspiring and compelling.

It doesn't take long to see the affection that Quincy's musical and technical teams have for him and for each other. Not only are these folks the most talented group of musicians around, but they are also some of the nicest and warmest people I've met. When Q speaks, people listen. And they seem to do so out of a genuine sense of respect and reverence. Through the interviews and interactions I've had with his musical family, I know that, although they don't hold him up as deity, they do give him their utmost attention, care, and respect.

Quincy is not nervous, hyperactive, or demanding in the heat of battle. He commands respect because he gives respect, he receives love because he gives love, and he gets amazing results because he is the result of amazing diligence, intellect, experience, and talent. Peter Chaikin noted that Quincy creates an environment in which greatness can happen. It's true. Quincy's response to that comment was brutally pragmatic, "Well, anything else would be counterproductive."

Every person in the studio expects to give their best effort, and they look forward to the results. The addiction to creativity is intense and cumulative. Quincy has built a team that functions at the highest level, with each member contributing and inspiring the other. Once that cycle is established and put in motion, magic can happen.

# ALFREDO SESSION at Capitol Records

When Quincy talks about Alfredo Rodriguez, we instantly feel his expectation of greatness for his new young protégé.

250

Bill Gibson Collection

This recording session involved a solo piano piece that Alfredo arranged around the theme song "The Bare Necessities." His performance is slated to be released to the public in a compilation of great jazz pianists performing Disney theme songs. Its stylistic scope ranges from a fiery Cuban influence to ragtime. In the intro section, Alfredo is playing the clavé part with his left foot on a pedal while he's playing the piano. Although his arrangement hangs off of a defined structure, much of this piece is improvisational. Alfredo leaves room for inspiration and spontaneity, but he has also worked hard on this piece to make sure the recording session is efficient and productive. He admits to spending ten hours one day on a 14-second section, but he has also been preparing for an hour-long concert at the same time!

The session took place at Capitol Studios, Studio A, in Hollywood, California, on March 25, 2009. The engineer was Steve Genewick. Steve is a house engineer at Capitol and has engineered or assisted on records for an amazing list of music-industry icons, including Quincy Jones, Barbra Streisand, Diana Krall, Chris Botti, Natalie Cole, Dave Coz, Al Jarreau, and many more.

**Bill Gibson**: Did you work with Alfredo much before he went in the studio to record "The Bare Necessities?"

**Q**: He is a real musician! You don't need to work things out with someone of that caliber. I may suggest some things, like, "Stay in the Cuban part a little longer," or "Make that double-up thing that you played in the

Bill Gibson Collection

middle a little longer." But you don't have to tell him anything, because he really gets it. He's there already. It's important that, as the producer, you're keeping the big picture in mind *and* that you work together with the artist toward the same goal. Collective collaborations are always better than an individual effort.

**BG**: I noticed that Alfredo was his own worst critic. He'd come into the control room to listen and evaluate, and he'd find little things that he wanted to fix here and there. Is it the same way with most of the great musicians you've produced?

**Q**: Not all of them, no. Sometimes it's hard and sometimes it takes a lot of interaction to get it right. It's always different. But Alfredo has a special edge because, firstly, he's the most dynamic pianist I've ever heard in my life. And, secondly, he understands music, including counterpoint, harmony, retrograde inversion, orchestration, and everything else. He studied seriously in the Cuban conservatory, and he has a rich background in his Yoruba and Hispanic roots. He's studied classical, salsa, jazz, and everything else. That's the way it should be! Once you learn that core skill, you've got the tools you need. Melody is God given, but you have to know the craft.

**BG**: Were you happy with how everything went with Alfredo at Capitol?

**Q**: You can't make any mistakes with him! The guys at Disney said, "For crying out loud! You didn't say you were gonna do this!" They loved it! They had never heard anything like it before. But that's how Alfredo is. No joke. Once he hits his stride, he'll be over the top!

## 2010 World Expo in Shanghai

This collaboration between Q and China's premiere composer, Tan Dun, was written for the 2010 World Expo in Shanghai. Quincy included Alfredo Rodriguez and Siedah Garrett in the musical and lyrical composition. Alfredo played piano in the rhythm section, and Siedah sang the melody and backing vocals.

The session took place at Westlake Studios, Studio D, in Los Angeles on February 2, 2010. Studio D was built specifically for Michael Jackson prior to the production of *Bad*; it was constructed to meet Bruce Swedien's technical requirements, Quincy's production standards, and Michael's artistic needs.

The participants in the session were:

Quincy Jones—producer/songwriter
Alfredo Rodriguez—piano/songwriter
Siedah Garrett—vocals/songwriter
Greg Phillinganes—keys
Paul Jackson, Jr.—guitars
Nathan East—bass
John Robinson—drums
Antonio Sol—vocals
Francis Buckley—engineer
Yue-Sai Kan—lyric and diction consultant
JoAnn Tominaga—contractor
Adam Fell—Vice President of Business Development, Quincy Jones Productions

The remaining strings, choir, and other parts will be added in China.

**BG:** When you're building the production, starting with the basic tracks, what are you thinking about first?

**Q:** I'm making sure the overall vision is coming together. I'm trying to find out if the song has the legs that I perceive that it does, because the whole thing is about a song and a story. Whether it's on a record or in a movie or on a television program, it's all about the song and the story. If you don't have a great song, even the best musicians can't make it great. That's the way it works. A great song can make anybody a star.

Bill Gibson Collection

**BG:** What are the ingredients in a great song?

**Q:** There are a lot of ingredients, but it comes down to making an emotional connection, defining the structure, and figuring out the most effective way to tell the story. There are thousands of ways to do it, but it comes down to portraying the vision and the melody. You've got to get the right blend of theory and melody. You have to really open your soul, your mind, your knowledge, and your passion. It rolls around, and I can't really describe what it is at first. I just know it when I hear it. Once it's identified, there are a lot of possibilities, and I know how to deal with those—that's not the hard part.

**BG:** During the session, I was in and out of the control room because I was interviewing your musical and technical team. I noticed that when the basic tracks were coming together, it sounded like A-list musicians playing extremely accurate tracks. However, when I came back into the control room at one certain point it really felt like great *music*. There was another component that went beyond accuracy. Is that what you're looking for when you're producing?

**Q:** That's part of my blood system, part of my DNA. I've been doing that since I was 13 years old. My life perspective is derived from trying to get a big band to play together musically: four trumpets, three trombones, five saxes, bass, drums, piano, and guitar. I have an orchestrator/composer's mind. I can't help it, man; everything goes through that filter whether it's politics or whatever.

Working with musicians is a give-and-take situation. Some producers play the authoritarian in the studio, saying, "Okay, it's got to go just like this." But I don't think music sounds as good when you do that. It sounds good to me when I'm hearing Greg Phillinganes's soul in there, along with what Nathan East, and John Robinson, or Louis Johnson, or Michael McDonald, or whoever is on the session brings to the table. You hear the difference, because they all have different personalities. If you love the people you're working with, you'll take the time and make the effort to understand their capabilities. You'll know their strengths, and you'll know how to put them to use. Not a lot of people understand that.

**BG:** How do you keep everybody motivated to give you their best performance?
**Q:** Man I don't know what it is—if they smell it on me, or I tell them, or I write it, or what. I just know that every time, I get it—I get the best they have to give. Maybe it's because I *really* believe in what I'm doing. Maybe that helps them believe in what they're doing. The musicians that I use are going to come in every time and jump on it, anyway. And, they know they can contribute their part to the creative flow. That environment produces the best music.

**BG:** What was your inspiration when you were composing "A Better City, a Better Life" for the 2010 World Expo? **Q:** It's a very complex tapestry of Chinese singers mixed with English-speaking singers. But we figured it out. No problem. We just took it step by step. But I worked together with Alfredo on the music and Siedah Garrett on the lyrics.

I got an idea on the plane on my way from Shanghai to Luxembourg. When you're in a conversation with the Chinese, they interject frequent statements of agreement by saying "Hata" and "Ung." It's their way of saying, "Yes," or "I understand," or "I agree," or "Okay." That's what they do when you start talking. They add, "Hata . . . hata . . . ung . . . ung." So I've composed an ostinato line that repeats, "Hata, ung … hata ung … hata ung, ung, ung …" That's *pure* Mandarin and it comes right after the English lyric, "Better city, better life." It's really structuring the Chinese language so it's part of the ostinato. Man, it works like a charm, and I like the way the contrapuntal

255

polyrhythmic layers work together. When I consulted with my good friend Yue-Sai Kan in Shanghai, she recommended the we use "Ala nong" instead, because it communicates more clearly with the Shanghai people and it means "You and me." We also added "Ebu, ebu, ebu," to the chorus, which means "step by step" in Shanghainese. It all works together very well, and it conveys just the message we were after. Marilyn and Alan Bergman wrote the lyrics, and Patti Austin sang it.

This is written so that a stadium full of people will catch on right away. I've always seen the difference between something like a song in a Broadway theater that comes out on a record or gets played on the radio, and something like this World Expo theme that needs to communicate immediately. With something on the radio, we can talk about an indoctrination period where, through repetition, people catch on and start to appreciate the music. In 1968 we did a song contest in Brazil in front of 250,000 people. There were 11 contestants, and those songs had to communicate *right then and there*. There was no talking about an indoctrination period. You have to have something that people can grab immediately—two times through, and they have to get it. That's exactly how this is, "Ala nong, Ala nong, Ala nong, nong, nong." If they can't get that, they're deaf! And it works with lyrics: "You gotta feed the world together," "Ala nong ..." or "Yes, I agree." It works.

# AFTERWORD

The scope of Quincy's impact on the musical world is staggering. He has led the way through several musical revolutions, an unprecedented feat in the popular-music world. Quincy's body of work in the arts and in humanitarian causes is awe-inspiring, and it's unlikely that one person ever again will have such a dramatic and positive impact on music and culture.

Quincy's background and unique gifts enabled him to form a career characterized by integrity and good taste mixed with a phenomenal instinct for commercial success—a perfect storm in the world of music. From the most modest of beginnings, he emerged highly motivated to succeed—and to spread goodwill as he shared his success with the world.

Sitting at the feet of the masters, Quincy was taken under their wings. He learned that music has its own soul and that each type needs to be treated with respect and performed with excellence. He also learned what it's like to play music with the best musicians on the planet—musicians who were virtuoso technicians and at the same time passionate trendsetters who played music for music's sake. He learned that money and music didn't always go hand in hand, and was happy enough making great music with great musicians.

Yet it was natural that he became a leader in the music industry. When he was at Garfield High School in Seattle, he played music—all types of music— constantly, and still does. As a big-band musician and arranger, Quincy pushed the boundaries, creating new textures, incorporating Latin and European influences, and finding different combinations of musicians to paint new musical portraits.

When rock 'n' roll emerged in the 1950's Quincy was already ahead of the curve, because he had grown up playing the music that evolved into rock 'n' roll, as well as jazz, schottisches, and any other style he could find to play. He recorded Big Maybelle singing "Whole Lotta Shakin Goin' On" in 1955, two years before Jerry Lee Lewis recorded it. His film scoring was so new and fresh that some directors made sure he was available before they cast the actors. He saw something in Michael Jackson that hadn't been tapped into yet—something that, cultivated by Quincy, enabled Michael to evolve into the biggest pop star of his era, the first black artist on MTV, and an artist with the biggest selling record of all time. Quincy also saw the rap revolution coming, recognizing the same kind of spirit and impact that he'd seen in bebop culture and in recording hip-hop artists before the movement took hold in mainstream America.

A constant leader in the music industry, Q continues to invest his heart and soul into new areas of creativity. He is always learning, always listening, and always willing to take a step in faith, believing that people have value, that music is powerful, and that when we move ahead with an agenda that serves a cause larger than ourselves, everything will work our for the better.

The following is a partial list of musicians with whom Quincy has worked as producer, arranger or band mate. Incredibly, it consists of nearly 1,000 musicians spanning multiple generations—some of the most influential players from the 1950s on. It is a testimony to the impact Quincy has had on a musical era and on the creative souls with whom he's built an amazing musical legacy.

**Arrangers**
Greg Adams
Tom Bähler
Kevin Becka
Dave Blumberg
Billy Byers
Dana Jon Chappelle
Frank Foster
Dave Grusin
Jerry Hey
Bob James
Sy Johnson
Don Kunz
Charlie Mariano
Dave Matthews
Sammy Nestico

Claus Ogerman
Marty Paich
Joe Parnello
Leon Pendarvis
Rail Rogut
Rod Temperton
Torrie Zito

**Bass**
Carlos Benavent
Max Bennett
Chuck Berghofer
Simon Brehm
Ray Brown
Sekou Bunch
Ron Carter

Buddy Catlett
Paul Chambers
Gene Cherico
Stanley Clarke
Bob Crenshaw
Art Davis
Richard Davis
Melvin Dunlap
George Duvivier
Nathan East
Arni Egillson
Jim Gilstrap
Catherine Gotthoffer
Lars Gullin
Percy Heath
Alton Hendrickson

Milt Hinton
Major Holley
Anthony Jackson
James Jamerson
Alphonso Johnson
Louis Johnson
Eddie Jones
Carol Kaye
Milton Kestenbaum
Abraham Laboriel, Sr.
Wendell Marshall
Bobby McFerrin
Marcus Miller
Charles Mingus
Red Mitchell
Monk Montgomery
Jaco Pastorius
Pat Patrick
Oscar Pettiford
Chuck Rainey
Ed Reddick
Mike Richmond
George Riedel
Neil Stubenhaus
Ben Tucker
Leroy Vinnegar
Bobby Watson
Chris White
Edgar Willis

## Cello

Seymour Barab
Paul Bergstrom
Ronald Cooper
Jesse Erlich
Dennis Karmazyn
Kermit Moore
Lucien Schmit
Alan Shulman
Jeffrey Solow
Gloria Strassner

## Clarinet

Arne Domnérus
Hanspeter Frehner
Christian Gavillet
Jimmy Hamilton
Bob Malach
Roger Rosenberg
Larry Schneider
Michel Weber

## Drums and Percussion

Art Blakey
Miko Brando
Leon "Ndugu"
   Chancler

Kenny Clarke
Billy Cobham
Vinnie Colaiuta
Rudy Collins
Bill Costa
Irving Cottler
Alan Dawson
Jack del Rio
Kenwood Dennard
George Deven
Zak Diouf
Sheila E.
Don Elliott
Bill English
Billy Gene English
Steve Ferrone
Teagle Fleming
Steve Gadd
James Gadson
Douglas Getschall
Carlos Goméz
Curley Hamner
Joe Harris
Paul Humphries
Osie Johnson
Jimmy Johnson, Jr.
James "J.J." Johnson
Egil "Bop" Johnson
Sonny Johnson
Harold Jones
Jo Jones
Gene Krupa
Mel Lewis
Ralph MacDonald
Shelly Manne
Stu Martin
Harvey Mason, Sr.
Cornelius Mims
Jose Paula
Sonny Payne
Charles Persip
Jeff Porcaro
Bernard "Pretty" Purdie
John "JR" Robinson
Buddy Rich
Ed Shaughnessy
Warren Smith
Arthur Taylor
Grady Tate
Ed Thigpen
Ron Tutt
Carlos Vega
Sam Woodyard
Bill Yottrell

## Engineer

Joe Adams
Peter Chaikin

Frances Buckley
Chris Brent
Ed Cherney
Terry Coffey
Bokie Coleman
Dave Collins
Tom Dowd
Humberto Gatica
Steve Genewick
Bernie Grundman
Don Hahn
Rudy Hill
Bones Howard
Norm Kinney
Jon Nettlesbey
Roger Nichols
Phil Ramone
Teddy Riley
Elliot Scheiner
Phil "Boogie" Schier
Al Schmitt
Bill Schwartau
Allen Sides
Bill Smith
Brad Sundberg
Bruce Swedien
Rudy Van Gelder
Tommy Vicari
Dave Way

## Flute

Pepper Adams
George Adams
Rolf Blomqvist
Julian Cawdry
Buddy Collette
Eric Dixon
Alex Foster
Hanspeter Frehner
Raymond Guiot
Terry Harrington
Kim Hutchcroft
Joel Kaye
Hubert Laws
Herbie Mann
Anne O'Brien
Bill Perkins
Jerome Richardson
Rahsaan Roland Kirk
Tom Scott
Bud Shank
Sahib Shihab
Les Spann
Ernie Watts
Larry Williams
Phil Woods
George Young

259

### French Horn
Ray Alonge
Aubrey Bouck
Alex Brofsky
James Buffington
Earl Chapin
John Clark
James A. Decker
David Duke
Jerry Folsom
Peter Gordon
Arthur Maebe
Tony Miranda
Sidney Muldrow
Bob Northern
Jerry Peel
Claudio Pontiggia
Alan Robinson
Willie Ruff
Henry Sigismonti
Rick Todd
Tom Varner
Brad Warnaar
Julius Watkins
Robert L. Watt
Gregory Williams

### Guitar
Arthur Adams
Elek Bacisk
Joe Beck
George Benson
Rolf Berg
Bill Bottrell
Dennis Budimir
Kenny Burrell
Larry Carlton
Dennis Coffey
David E. Williams
Tal Farlow
Barry Galbraith
Eric Gale
Grant Geissman
Freddie Greene
Jim Hall
Rene Hall
Allen Hanlon
Michael Hart
Thompson
Marlo Henderson
Sam Herman
Dann Huff
Danny Hull
Paul Jackson, Jr.
George Johnson
Arthur Knight
Michael Landau
Mundell Lowe

Steve Lukather
Randy Lukather
Billy Mackel
Wes Montgomery
Tony Mottola
Mary Osborne
Dean Parks
Carlos Rios
Lee Ritenour
Francesca Robinson
Freddy Robinson
Les Spann
Steve Stevens
David T. Walker
Tommy Tedesco
Toots Thielemans
Phil Upchurch
Eddie Van Halen
Melvin "Wah Wah"
   Watson
Wayne Wright

### Harp
Gloria Agostini
Dorothy Ashby
Gayle Levant
Dorothy Remsen
Margaret Ross
Xenia Schindler
Amy Sherman

### Keyboards
Tom Bahler
John Beasley
Paul Beaver
Michael Boddicker
Delmar Brown
Malcolm Cecil
Chick Corea
George Duke
Clare Fischer
David Foster
Gil Goldstein
Paul Griffith
Dave Grusin
Don Grusin
Herbie Hancock
Rob Hoffman
Jerry Hey
James Ingram
Bob James
Pete Jolly
Ed Kalchof
Artie Kane
Randy Kerber
Michael Lang
Don Lewis
Eddie Louis

Robert Margouleff
Mike Melvoin
David Paich
Jerry Peters
Greg Phillinganes
Bill Plummer
Billy Preston
Ian Prince
Bobby Scott
Richard Tee
Rod Temperton
Ian Underwood
Mervyn Warren
Larry E. Williams
Bill Wolfer
David "Hawk"
   Wolinski
Stevie Wonder
Casey Young
Michael Young
Joe Zawinul

### Oboe
Xavier Duss
Dave Seghezzo
Judith Wenziker
Tilman Zahn

### Organ
Eddie Louis
Billy Preston
Jimmy Smith

### Percussion
Nickolas Ashford
Ollie Brown
Eddie "Bongo" Brown
Paul Bryant
Larry Bunker
Lenny Castro
Paulinho Da Costa
George Devens
King Errisson
Gene Estes
Victor Feldman
J.C. Gomez
Martin Grupp
Bobbye Hall
Richard Heath
Milt Holland
Randy Jackson
Philip Leo Kraus
Shelly Manne
Bobbye Porter
Emil Richards
John Riley
Caiphus Semenya
Bill Summers

Tommy Vig
James Fee
Elliot Gilbert

**Piano**
Monty Alexander
Count Basie
Patti Bown
Jaki Byard
George Duke
Duke Ellington
Clare Fischer
David Foster
Paul Griffin
George Gruntz
Dave Grusin
Bengt Hallberg
Marvin Hamlish
Herbie Hancock
Dick Hyman
Bob James
Sy Johnson
Hank Jones
Jimmy Jones
Thad Jones
Randy Kerber
Lou Levy
Kevin Maloney
Dave McKenna
Bill Miller
Michael Omartian
David Paich
Joe Parnello
Carl Perkins
Oscar Peterson
Greg Phillinganes
Terry Pollard
Little Richard
Joe Sample
Lalo Schifrin
Bobby Scott
Horace Silver
Billy Taylor
Richard Tee
George Wallington
David "Hawk"
  Wolinski

**Rap/Vocals**
Akon
Big Daddy Kane
Ice-T
Kool Moe Dee
LL Cool J
Ludacris
Melle Mel
Miss Mia
Q-Tip

Queen Latifah
Ricky C.
Shaquille O'Neal
Snoop Dog
T-Pain
Talib Kweli
Three 6 Mafia
Wycef Jean

**Saxophones/
Woodwinds**
Pepper Adams
Julian "Cannonball"
  Adderley
Gerald Albright
Rolf Backman
Danny Bank
Bunny Bardach
Walter Benton
George Berg
Jerry Bergonzi
Georg Björklund
Michael Brecker
Don Byas
Benny Carter
Emilio Castillo
Pete Christlieb
Jeff Clayton
Al Cohn
Buddy Collette
Ronnie Cuber
Eric Dixon
Arne Domnérus
Johnny Ekh
Reiner Erb
Oscar Estell
Rune Falk
Harold Fick
Brandon Fields
Frank Foster
Charlie Fowlkes
Kenny Garrett
Herb Geller
Sal Giorgianni
Benny Golson
Paul Gonsalves
Bill Green
Gigi Gryce
Lars Gullin
Terry Harrington
Coleman Hawkins
Dan Higgins
Johnny Hodges
Kim Hutchcroft
Fred Jackson, Jr.
Budd Johnson
Howard Johnson
Walter Kane

Joel Kaye
Porter Kilbert
Rahsaan Roland Kirk
Ernie Krivda
Stephen Kupka
Hubert Laws
Walter Levinsky
Joe López
Charlie Mariano
Bjarne Nerem
Jack Nimitz
James Moody
Ted Nash
Oliver Nelson
Anthony Ortega
Cecil Payne
Romeo Penque
Art Pepper
Bill Perkins
Lenny Pickett
Seldon Powell
Gene Quill
Christian Rabe
Joshua Redman
Jerome Richardson
Charlie Rouse
Marshal Royal
Aaron Sachs
Clifford Scott
Tom Scott
Sahib Shihab
Eddie Shu
Zoot Sims
Clifford Solomon
Lucky Thompson
David Tofani
Ernie Watts
Stanley Webb
Frank Wess
Kirk Whalum
Larry Williams
Phil Woods
George Young
Josef Zawinul

**Synthesizer**
Glen Ballard
Brian Banks
John Barnes
Paul Beaver
Jorge Calandrelli
Christopher Currell
Craig Huxley
Rhett Lawrence
Eric Persing
Steve Porcaro
Greg Smith
Clark Spangler

261

Randy Waldman
Ed Walsh

**Trombone**
Wayne Andre
Dave Bargeron
George Bohannon
Garnett Brown
Billy Byers
Jimmy Cleveland
Henry Coker
George Cooper
Roland Dahinden
Glenn Farris
Paul Faulise
Curtis Fuller
Mic Gillette
Al Gray
Urbie Green
Al Hayse
Conrad Herwig
Dick Hixson
Quentin Jackson
George Jeffers
J.J. Johnson
Rod Levitt
Melba Liston
Charles Loper
Tom "Bones" Malone
Lew McCreary
Earl McIntyre
Tommy Mitchell
Grover C. Mitchell
Dick Nash
Robert Payne
Ake Persson
Benny Powell
Norman Pride
Alan Raph
Frank Rehak
Bill Reichenbach, Jr.
Frank Roelino
Frank Rosolino
Santo Russo
Andreas Skjold
Maurice Spears
Tony Studd
David Taylor
Bill Tole
Georg Vernon
Donald Waldrop
Bill Watrous
Chauncey Welsch
Kai Winding
Britt Woodman
C. Young
Reggie Young

**Trumpet**
Al Aarons
Cat Abron
Greg Adams
Cat Anderson
Louis Armstrong
John Audino
Hugh Bähler
Tom Bähler
Benny Bailey
Chet Baker
Rick Baptist
John Bello
Wayne Bergeron
Oscar Brashear
Randy Brecker
Garnett Brown
Ray Brown
Clifford Brown
Tom Bryant
Bobby Bryant
Norma Carson
Buddy Childers
Paul Cohen
George Cohn
John D'earth
Miles Davis
Al DeRisi
Harry "Sweets"
  Edison
Roy Eldridge
Sixten Ericksson
Rob Ericson
Rolf Ericson
Miles Evans
Jon Faddis
Art Farmer
Chuck Findley
John Frock
Dizzy Gillespie
Bernie Glow
Gary Grant
Al Grey
Larry Hall
Jerry Hey
Freddie Hubbard
George Jeffers
Arnold Johansson
Lonnie Johnson
Leonard Johnson
J.J. Johnson
Reunald Jones
Thad Jones
Virgil Jones
Jerry Kail
Bill Lamb
Warren Luening
Jimmy Maxwell

Lloyd Michaels
Danny Moore
Joe Newman
Dick Nixon
Jimmy Nottingham
Al Perisi
Ake Persson
Barry Powell
Don Rader
Alan Raph
Clyde Reasinger
Weine Renliden
Fip Ricard
Wallace Roney
Frank Rosolino
Ernie Royal
Alan Rubin
Manfred Schoof
Jack Sheldon
Lew Soloff
Marvin Stamm
Floyd Standifer
Tony Studd
Marvin Stunn
Clark Terry
Ack Van Rooyen
Harold Vick
Ron Wallace
Jack Walrath
Joe Wilder
Dick Williams
Walter Williams
Snooky Young
Gene Young

**Tuba**
Roger Bobo
Howard Johnson
Tommy Johnson
Harvey Phillips
Toni Price
James Self

**Vibraphone**
Gary Burton
Lionel Hampton
Milt Jackson
Brother Soul

**Viola**
Meyer Bello
Samuel Boghossian
Rollice Dale
Alex Nieman
Bob Ostrowsky
David Schwartz
Leonard Selic

## Violin

Israel Baker
Arnold Belnick
Harry Bluestone
Bobby Bruce
Elliott Fisher
Janice Gower
Stéphane Grappelli
Doug Kershaw
Connie Kupka
Betty LaMagna
Carl LaMagna
Marvin Limonick
Joseph Livoti
Harry Lookofsky
Erno Neufeld
Wilbert Nuttycombe
Jerome Reisler
Nathan Ross
Sheldon Sanov
John Santulis
Ralph Shaeffer
Sid Sharp
Joe Stepansky
Robert Sushel
Gerald Vinci
John Wittenberg

## Vocals

Nadirah Ali
Jocelyn Allen
Ernestine Anderson
Maxi Anderson
Joshie Armstead
Rodney Armstrong
Louis Armstrong
Nickolas Ashford
Patti Austin
Dan Aykroyd
Babyface
Tom Bähler
Rose Banks
David Banner
Holley Bass
Harry Belafonte
Reginald Bell
George Benson
Brook Benton
Mary J. Blige
Peggi Blu
Edwin Bonilla
Alexandra Brown
McKinley Brown
Jocelyn Brown
Bridgette Bryant
Lindsay Buckingham
Tevin Campbell
Kim Carnes

Rodney Chambers
Ray Charles
Alvin Chea
Vivian Cherry
Bill Cosby
Andraé Crouch
Sandra Crouch
Casey Cysik
Sammy Davis, Jr.
El DeBarge
Cedric Dent
Quincy Duke
Jermaine Dupri
Chad Durio
Bill Eaton
Billy Eckstine
Don Elliott
Gloria Estefan
Linda Evans
Geary Faggett
Voncielle Faggett
Rachelle Ferrell
Venetta Fields
Bruce Fisher
Ella Fitzgerald
Roberta Flack
Frank Floyd
Geary Lanier Foggett
Ken Ford
Jania Foxworth
Jamie Foxx
Aretha Franklin
Cheryl Gamble
Siedah Garrett
Tammie Gibson
Jim Gilstrap
Leslie Gore
Jackie Gouche
Diva Gray
Joe Green
Reggie Green
Joseph Greene
Gwen Guthrie
Hilda Harris
Alex Harris
Alex Hassilev
Richard Heath
Howard Hewett
Al Hibbler
Billie Holiday
Jennifer Holliday
Pattie Howard
Jennifer Hudson
Benard Ighner
James Ingram
Phillip Ingram
Marilyn Jackson
Michael Jackson

Kurt Jackson
Jackie Jackson
La Toya Jackson
Marlon Jackson
Randy Jackson
Tito Jackson
Al Jarreau
Mortonette Jenkins
Waylon Jennings
Billy Joel
Louis Johnson
Tiffany Johnson
Tamara Johnson
Jean Johnson-
   McRath
Geraldine Jones
Quincy D. Jones, III
Chaka Khan
Mark Kibble
Joey Kibble
Eric Kirkland
Jesse Kirkland
Cyndi Lauper
Peggy Lee
John Legend
John Lehman
Edie Lehmann
Yvonne Lewis
Huey Lewis
Kenny Loggins
Leanne Lyons
Clif Magness
Dean Martin
Barbara Massey
Myrna Matthews
Charles May
Big Maybelle
Letta Mbulu
Donovan McCrary
Howard McCrary
Yolanda McCullough
Claude McKnight
Paulette McWilliams
Helen Merrill
Bette Midler
Luis Miguel
The Mirettes
James Moody
Perry Morgan
Willie Nelson
Willie R. Norwood
Anita O'Day
Jeffrey Osborne
David Pack
DJ Paul
Phil Perry
Tyren Perry
Steve Perry

The Pointer Sisters
David Pridgen
Paul Pridgen
Lou Rawls
Richard Redd
Lionel Richie
Minnie Riperton
Smokey Robinson
Kenny Rogers
Diana Ross
Henri Salvador
Zachary Sanders
Michael Angelo
Saulsberry
Derrick Schoefield
Andre Scott
Shane Shoaf
Alfie Silas
Paul Simon
Valerie Simpson
Frank Sinatra
Sherwood Sledge
Bruce Springsteen
Stephanie Spruill

The Stairsteps
Barbra Streisand
Maeretha Steward
Scott Storch
Al B Sure!
Pepper Swinson
Tamia
Lisa Taylor
Robin Thicke
Eric Thomas
Debbie Tibs
Nate Turner
Tina Turner
Usher
Luther Vandross
Sarah Vaughan
Leon Ware
Mervyn Warren
Dionne Warwick
Lalomie Washburn
Dinah Washington
Irving Washington III
Oren Waters
Watts Prophets

The Wattsline Choir
Alex Weir
Wil Wheaton
Barry White
Steve White
Warren Wiebe
Joe Williams
Paulette Williams
Andy Williams
Carolyn Willis
Nancy Wilson
The Winans
BeBe Winans
Carvin Winans
Marvin Winans
Michael Winans
Ron Winans
Bill Withers
Syreeta Wright
Charity Young
Timo Yuro
Joe Zawinul

# APPENDIX

# I
## Discography

Key: PD-Producer, CD-Conductor, CP-Composer, AR-Arranger, MS-Music Supervisor, TRPT-Trumpet, VO-Vocal, P-Piano

**Adderley, Cannonball**

*Julian "Cannonball!" Adderley;* 1955, EmArcy: MG-36043 (CD; CP; AR)

**Alpert, Herb**

*You Smile, the Song Begins;* 1974, A&M: 3620 (AR)

**Anderson, Ernestine**

"After the Lights Go Down"/"Hurry, Hurry"; 1962, Mercury: 71960 (PD)

**Anthony, Ray**

*Standards;* 1954, Capitol: T663 (AR)

**Armstrong, Louis**

*Louis;* 1964, Mercury: MG-610BI (AR)

**Arnold, Harry**

*Harry Arnold + Big Band + Quincy Jones = Jazz!;* 1958, Metronome: MLP-15010 (CD; CP; AR)

**Austin, Patti**

*Every Home Should Have One;* 1981, Qwest: QWS-3591 (PD; AR)

*Patti Austin;* 1984, Qwest: 1-23974 (PD)

**Baker, LaVern**

"Game of Love"/"Jim Dandy Got Married," "Learning to Love"/"Substitute," "Humpty Dumpty Heart"/"Love Me Right"; 1957, Atlantic: 1136, 1150, 1176 (45s) (CD; AR)

**Barclay, Eddie**

*Et Viola;* 1957, Barclay: 82. 138 (AR);
*Twilight Time;* 1960, Barclay: SR-60167 (CP; AR)

**Bennett, Tony**

*The Movie Song Album;* 1966, Columbia: CS-9272 (CD; CP; AR)

**Benson, George**

*Give Me the Night;* 1980, Qwest: HS-3453 (PD; AR)

**Benton, Brook, a.k.a. Benjamin Peay**

"Can I Help It"/"The Kentuckian"; 1955, Okeh: (45 RPM) (AR)

*There Goes That Song Again;* 1961, Mercury: MG-20673 (CD; AR)

**Big Maybelle**

"Whole Lot-ta Shakin' Goin' On"/"The Other Night," "Such a Cutie"/"Ocean of Tears"; 1955, Okeh: (78 RPM, EPs) 7060/7066 (CD; AR)

**Brothers Johnson**

*Look Out for #1; 1976, A&M: SP-4567 (CD; CP; AR)*
*Right on Time; 1977, A&M: SP-4644 (CD; CP; AR)*
*Blam; 1978, A&M: SP-4685 (PD; AR; CP)*
*Light Up the Night; 1980, A&M: SP-3716 (PD; AR; VO)*

**Brown, Clifford/ Farmer, Art**

*Stockholm Sweetnin';* 1953, Metronome: MLP-15020 (CD; CP; AR)

**Brown, Clifford I A. Farmer, Sw. A-Str**

*Stockholm Sweetnin';* 1953, Metronome: MEP18 & 19 (10") (CD; CP; AR)

**Brown, Ray**

*Harold Robbins Presents Music from The Adventurers*; 1970, Symbolic: SYS-9000 (PD; AR)

**Cardinals**

"Sunshine," "Near You"/"One Love"; 1956, Atlantic: (78 RPM EPs, 1126) (AR)

**Carol, Lily Ann**

"Oh No!"/"So Used to You," "Ooh Poppa Doo"/"Everybody"; 1956, Mercury: (45 RPM)/70958X45 (CD; AR)

**Carroll, David**

*Happy Feet;* 1964, Mercury: SR-60846 (PD)

**Carroll, Diahann**

*Diahann Carroll Sings Harold Arlen's Songs;* 1956, Victor: LPM-1467 (CD; AR)

**Carter, Betty**

*Meet Betty Carter and Ray Bryant;* 1955, Epic: LN-3202 (CD; AR)

**Charles, Ray**

*The Great Ray Charles; 1956, Atlantic: SD-1259(CP; AR)*
*The Genius of Ray Charles; 1959, Atlantic: 1312 (AR)*

*Genius + Soul = Jazz;* 1960, Impulse: A-2 (AR)
*The Great Ray Charles;* 1956, Atlantic: SD-1259 (CP; AR)
*The Genius of Ray Charles;* 1959, Atlantic: 1312 (AR)
*Genius + Soul = Jazz;* 1960, Impulse: A-2 (AR)
*A Message from the People;* 1972, Tangerine: ABCX-755/TRC (CD; AR)

**Cleveland, Jimmy**

*Introducing Jimmy Cleveland and His All-Stars;* 1955, EmArcy: MG-36066 (CD; CP; AR)

**Clovers**

"Shakin," "I-I-I Love You," "So Young," "Pretty, Pretty Eyes," "Baby, Darling"; 1957, Atlantic: EP (AR)

**Count Basie**

*Basie—One More Time;* 1958, Roulette: SR-52024 (CP; AR)
*Basie-Eckstine, Inc.;* 1959, Roulette: SR-52029 (AR)
*String Along with Basie;* 1959, Roulette: R-52051 (CP; AR)
*Li'l Ol' Groovemaker...Basie!;* 1963, Verve: V6-8549 (CD; CP; AR)
*This Time by Basie: Hits of the '50s and '60s;* 1963, Reprise: R-6070 (CD; AR)

**Davis, Sammy/Count Basie**

*Our Shining Hour;* 1964, Verve: V6-8605 (CD; AR)

**Davis, (Wild) Bill Trio**

"Belle of the Ball," "Syncopated Clock," "Serenade to Benny"; 1955, Okeh (CP; AR)

**Double Six of Paris**

*The Double Six Meet Quincy Jones;* 1960, Columbia (Foreign): FPX 188 (CD; CP; AR)

**Eckstine, Billy**

*Mr. B. in Paris with the Bobby Tucker Orchestra;* 1957, Barclay (PD; CD; CO-AR)
*Billy Eckstine and Quincy Jones at Basin Street East;* 1961, Mercury: SR-60674 (PD; AR)
*Don't Worry 'Bout Me;* 1962, Mercury: MG-20736 (PD)
*The Golden Hits of Billy Eckstine;* 1963, Mercury: SR-60796 (PD)
*The Modern Sounds of Mr. B.;* 1964, Mercury: SR-609J6 (PD)

**Elliott, Don**

*A Musical Offering by Don Elliott;* 1955, ABC-Paramount: ABC-I 06 (CD; AR)

**Farmer, Art**

*A. Farmer Septet Plays Arrangements of G. Gryce and Q. Jones;* 1953, Prestige: P-7031 (CP; AR; P)

*Work of Art;* 1953, Prestige: PrLP-162 (10") (CP; AR; P)

*Last Night When We Were Young;* 1957, ABC Paramount: ABC-200 (CD; AR)

**Farnon, Robert**

*The Sensuous Strings of Robert Farnon;* Philips: PHM-200-038 (PD)

*Captain from Castile;* 1964, Philips: PHM-200-098 (PD)

**Fitzgerald, Ella**

*Ella and Basie;* 1963, Verve: MGV-4061 (CD; AR)

**Franklin, Aretha**

*Hey Now Hey (The Other Side of the Sky);* 1972, Atlantic: SD-7265 (PD; CD; AR)

*"Master of Eyes";* 1973, Atlantic: 2941 (PD; CD; AR)

**Gibbs, Terry**

*Terry Gibbs Plays Jewish Melodies in Jazztime;* 1963, Mercury: MG-20812 (PD)

**Gillespie, Dizzy**

*Afro;* 1954, Norgran: MG N-1003 (TRPT)

*Diz Big Band;* 1954, Verve: MGV-81 78 (EP) (TRPT)

*Dizzy Gillespie: World Statesman;* 1956, Norgran: MG N-I 084 (CP; AR; TRPT)

*Dizzy in Greece;* 1956, Verve: MGV-80 17 (CP; AR; TRPT)

*Dizzy on the French Riviera;* 1962, Philips: PHM-200-048 (PD)

*New Wave;* 1962, Philips: PHM-200-070 (PD)

**Gordon, Joe**

*Introducing Joe Gordon;* 1954, EmArcy: MG-26046 (10") (CP; AR)

**Gore, Lesley**

*I'll Cry if I Want To;* 1963, Mercury: MG-20805 (PD)

*Boys, Boys, Boys;* 1964, Mercury: MG-2090 I (PD)

*Girl Talk;* 1964, Mercury: MG-20943 (PD)

*California Nights;* 1967, Mercury: MG-61120 (PD)

*Love Me by Name;* 1976, A&M: SP-4564 (PD; CD; AR; KB; VO)

**Gryce, Gigi**

*"Jazz Time Paris"* Vol. 10; 1953, Vogue: LD 173 (AR; CP; TRPT; P)

**Hamlisch, Marvin**

"If You Hadn't Left Me (Crying)"/"One"; 1976,
A&M: 1775-S (45 RPM) (PD; CD;AR)

**Hampton, Lionel**

"Kingfish"/"Don't Flee the Scene Salty"; 1951,
M.G.M.: 11227 (78 RPM) (CP; AR; TRPT)

**Hathaway, Donny**

*Come Back, Charleston Blues* (Soundtrack); 1972,
Atco: SD-70 I 0 (CP; MS)

**Hendricks, Jon**

"Flyin' Home"/"Happy Feet," "Cloud Burst";
1955, Decca: EP (AR)

**Hodeir, Andre**

*Jazz et Jazz;* 1963, Philips: PHS 600-073 (TRPT)

**Horn, Shirley**

*Shirley Horn with Horn;* 1963, Mercury:
MG-20835 (PD; CD; AR)
"For Love of Ivy"; 1968, ABC: 11108 (45 RPM)
(PD; CP; CD)
"If You Want Love (main theme from the film
*A Dandy in Aspic)"/"*The Spell You Spin"; 1968,
Bell: B-727 (45 RPM) (CD; CP; AR)

**Horne, Lena**

*The Lady and Her Music—Live on Broadway;*
1981, Qwest: 2QW-3597 (PD)

**Hunter, Lurlene**

*Lonesome Gal;* 1955, RCA Victor: LPM-1151
(AR; CD)

**Ingram, James**

*It's Your Night;* 1983, Qwest: 1-23970 (PD; CP;
AR; P; VO)
*Never Felt So Good;* 1986, Qwest: 1-25424 (PD)

**Jackie and Roy**

*Bits and Pieces;* 1957, ABC Paramount: ABC-163
(CD; AR)

**Jackson, Michael**

*Off the Wall;* 1979, Epic: FE-35745 (PD; AR)
*E. T. The Extra-Terrestrial* (Soundtrack); 1982,
MCA: MCA-70000 (PD)
*Thriller;* 1982, Epic: QE-38 I 12 (PD; CP; AR)
*Bad;* 1987, Epic: OE-40600 (PD; AR)

**Jackson, Milt**

*Plenty, Plenty Soul;* 1957, Atlantic: 1269 (CP; AR)
*The Ballad Artistry of Milt Jackson;* 1959, Atlantic:
SD-1342 (CD; CP; AR)

**Jacquet, Illinois**

*Illinois Jacquet Flies Again;* 1959, Roulette: 97272 (CP; AR)

**Jacquet, Russell**

"They Tried"/"Port of *Rico";* 1953, Network (AR; VO; TRPT)

**Jo, Damita**

*This One's for Me;* 1964, Mercury: MG-20818 (PD; CD)

**Johnson, J.J.**

*Man and Boy* (Soundtrack); 1971, Sussex: SXSB-70 II (PD; MS)

**Jones Boys**

*The Jones Boys;* 1956, Period: SPL-121 0 (CP; AR; FLH)

**Jones, Quincy**

*Lullaby of Birdland;* 1955, RCA Victor: LPM-1146 (CD; AR)

*The Giants of Jazz;* 1955, Columbia: CL-1970 (CD; CP; AR)

*This Is How I Feel About Jazz;* 1956, ABC Paramount: ABC-149 (CP; AR)

*Go West, Man;* 1957, ABC-Paramount: ABC-186 (PD)

*The Birth of a Band;* 1959, Mercury: MG-20444 (CP; AR)

*The Great Wide World of Quincy Jones;* 1959, Mercury: SR-60221 (CD)

*I Dig Dancers;* 1960, Mercury: SR-60612 (CD; CP; AR)

*Around the World;* 1961, Mercury: PPS-60 14 (CD; CP; AR)

*Newport '61;* 1961, Mercury: SR-60653 (CD; CP; AR)

*The Boy in the Tree* (Soundtrack); 1961, Mercury-Sweden: EP-60338 (EP) (CD; CP; AR)

*The Great Wide World of Quincy Jones—Live (in Zurich)!;* 1961, Mercury: 195J-32 (CD; AR)

*The Quintessence;* 1961, Impulse: A-II (CD; CP; AR)

*Big Band Bossa Nova;* 1962, Mercury: MG-20751 (CD; CP; AR; PD)

*Quincy Jones Plays the Hip Hits;* 1963, Mercury: SR-60799 (CD; AR)

*Golden Boy;* 1964, Mercury: MG-20938 (CD; CP; AR)

*I Had a Ball;* 1964, Mercury: MG-21 022 (PD; AR)

*Quincy Jones Explores the Music of Henry Mancini;* 1964, Mercury: MG-20863 (CD; AR)

*The Pawnbroker* (Soundtrack); 1964, Mercury: SR-61011 (PD; CD; CP; AR)

*Mirage* (Soundtrack); 1965, Mercury: MG-21025 (CD; CP; AR)

*Quincy Plays for Pussycats;* 1965, Mercury: MG-21 050 (CD; AR)

*Quincy's Got a Brand-New Bag;* 1965, Mercury: MG-21 063 (PD; CD; AR)

*The Slender Thread* (Soundtrack); 1966, Mercury: MG-21070 (CD; CP)

*Walk, Don't Run* (Soundtrack); 1966, Mainstream: S-6080 (CD; CP)

*Enter Laughing* (Soundtrack); 1967, Liberty: LOM-16004 (CD; CP)

*In Cold Blood* (Soundtrack); 1967, Colgems: COM-107 (CD; CP)

*In the Heat of the Night* (Soundtrack); 1967, United Artist: UAL-4160 (CD; CP)

*The Deadly Affair* (Soundtrack): 1967, Verve: V-8679-ST (CD; CP)

*For Love of Ivy* (Soundtrack); 1968, ABC: ABCS-OC-7 (CD; CP)

*Bob & Carol & Ted & Alice* (Soundtrack); 1969, Bell: 1200 (PD; CD; AR; CP)

*John and Mary* (Soundtrack); 1969, A&M: SP-4230 (PD; CP; CD)

*MacKenna's Gold* (Soundtrack); 1969, RCA Victor: LSP-4096 (PD; CD; CP; AR)

*The Italian Job* (Soundtrack); 1969, Paramount: PAS-5007 (CD; CP)

*The Lost Man* (Soundtrack); 1969, Uni: 73060 (PD; CP)

*Walking in Space;* 1969, A&M: SP-3023 (CD; AR)

*Cactus Flower* (Soundtrack); 1970, Bell: 120 I (PD; CD; CP; AR)

*Gula Matari;* 1970, A&M: SP-3030 (CP; AR; CD)

*They Call Me Mister Tibbs!* (Soundtrack); 1970, United Artist: UAS-5241 (PD; CD; CP)

*Dollars* (Soundtrack); 1971, Reprise: MS-2051 (PD; CD; CP; AR)

*Smackwater Jack;* 1971, A&M: SP-3037 (PD; CD; CP; AR; VO)

*The Hot Rock* (Soundtrack); 1972, Prophesy:
SD-6055 (PD; CD; CP; AR)
*You've Got It Bad, Girl;* 1972, A&M: SP-3041
(PD; CD; CP; AR; VO)
*Body Heat;* 1974, A&M: SP-3617 (PD; CD; CP;
AR; VO)
*Mellow Madness;* 1975, A&M: SP-4526 (PD; CD;
CP; AR; KB; TRPT; VO)
*I Heard That;* 1976, A&M: SP-3705 (PD; CD; CP;
AR; KB; VO; TR; PT)
*Roots;* 1977, A&M: SP-4626 (PD; CP; AR; CD)
*Sounds...and Stuff Like That;* 1978, A&M: SP-4685
(PD; CP; AR)
*The Wiz* (Soundtrack); 1978, MCA MCA2-14000
(PD; CD; CP; AR; AD; MS; KB)
*Live at the Budokan;* 1981, A&M: AMP-28045
(PD; CD; CP; AR; KB)
*The Dude;* 1981, A&M: SP-372 I (PD; CP; AR; VO)
*The Birth of Band—Vol. 2;* 1984, Mercury: 195J-30
(CP; AR)
*The Color Purple* (Soundtrack); 1985, Qwest:
25389-1 (PD; CD; CP; AR)
*Back on the Block;* 1989, Qwest: 26020-1
(PD; CD; CP; AR; VO)
*Miles & Quincy Live at Montreux;* 1991, Warner
Bros.: 45221) (PD; CD)
*Q's Jook Joint;* 1995, Qwest: 45875 (PD; CD; CP; AR)
*Q, Live in Paris Circa 1960;* 1996, Qwest: 46190;
(PD; CD; CP; AR)
*From Q with Love; 1999, Qwest: 46490 (PD; CD;
CP; AR)*
*The Quincy Jones–Sammy Nestico Orchestra:
Basie and Beyond;* 2000, Qwest: 47792 (PD; CD;
CP; AR)
Q: *The Music of Quincy Jones;* 2001, Rhino:
R2-74363 (PD; CD; CP; AR; TRPT; VO; P)
*Original Jam Sessions 1969* with Bill Cosby; 2004,
Concord Jazz: 2257 (PD)
*Strawberry Letter 23* Featuring Akon; 2010,
Qwest (PD)

**Jones, Quincy/Farmer, Art**

*Quincy Jones and Swedish-American All-Stars;*
1953, Prestige: PrLP-172 (10") (CD; CP; AR)

**Jones, Thad**

*Mad Thad;* 1956, Period: SP1208 (CD; AR)

**Jordan, Louis**

*Somebody Up There Digs Me (Greatest Hits);* 1956, Mercury: MG-20242 (PD; AR)

**King Pleasure**

"Don't Get Scared"/"Funk Junction," "I'm Gone"/"You're Crying"; 1954, Prestige: 913/908 (78 RPM), EPs (CD; CP; AR)

**Kirk, Roland**

*Kirk in Copenhagen;* 1964, Mercury: 20894 (PD)

**Krupa, GeneIFeaturing Roy Eldridge, Anita O**

*Drummer Man;* 1956, Verve: MGV-2008 (AR)

**Laws, Hubert**

*Hubert Laws—Quincy Jones—Chick Corea;* 1985, CBS Masterworks: M-39858 (CD)

**Lee, Peggy**

*Blues Cross Country;* 1961, Capitol: ST-1671 (CD; CP; AR)

*If You Go;* 1961, Capitol: T-1630 (CD; AR)

**Little Richard**

*It's Real;* 1961, Mercury: MG-20656 (CD; CP; AR)

**Lookofsky, Harry**

*Miracle in Strings;* 1954, Epic: EG-7081 (EP) (CP; AR)

*The Hash Brown Sounds;* 1962, Philips: PHM-200-018 (PD)

**Mardigan, Art**

*The Jazz School;* 1954, Wing: MGW-60002 (CP; AR)

**Mays, Willie/The Treniers**

"Say Hey (The Willie Mays Song)"; 1954, Okeh: 9066 (78 RPM) (CD; AR)

**McRae, Carmen**

*Carmen/Carmen McRae;* 1972, Temponic: TB-29562 (CD; AR)

**Merrill, Helen**

*Helen Merrill with Clifford Brown;* 1954, EmArcy: MG-36006 (AR)

*You've Got a Date with the Blues;* 1959, Metro-jazz: E-IOIO (CD)

**Moody, James**

*James Moody's Mood for Blues;* 1954, Prestige: PrLP-198 (CP; AR)

*Moody's Mood;* 1954, Prestige: PrLP-192 (10") (CP; AR)

*Wail, Moody, Wail;* 1955, Prestige: LP-7036 (CP; AR)

273

**Newman, Joe**

*Happy Cats;* 1957, Coral: 57121 (AR)

*Joe Newman Quinte at Count Basie's;* 1961, Mercury: SR-60696 (PD)

**Pettiford, Oscar**

*The New Oscar Pettiford Sextet;* 1951, Debut: DLP-8 (CP; AR)

*Basically Duke;* 1954, Bethlehem: BCP-1019 (10") (AR)

*Oscar Pettiford;* 1954, Bethlehem: BCP-1003 (10") (CP; AR)

*The Finest of Oscar Pettiford;* 1955, Bethlehem: BCP-6007 (CP; AR)

**Quinichette, Paul**

*Moods;* 1954, EmArcy: MG-36003 (CP; AR)

**Renaud, Henri**

"Meet Quincy Jones," "Dillon," "Wallington Special"; 1954, Vogue: EP (AR)

**Richmond, June**

"Sleep"/"Everybody's Doin' It," "Devil and Deep Blue Sea"/"Between the Devil and the Deep Blue Sea"; 1957, Barclay: EP-70105 (EP) (CD; AR)

**Ross, Annie**

"Jackie"/"The Song Is You"; 1953, Metronome: B-647 (78 RPM) (P)

**Rufus and Chaka**

*Masterjam;* 1979, MCA: MCA-5103 (PD; CP)

**Sachs, Aaron**

*Aaron Sachs Quintette;* 1954, Bethlehem: BCP-I 008 (10") (CD; CP; AR)

**Salvador, Henri**

"Blouse du Dentiste"/"Moi J'Prefere La Marche a Pied," "Trompette D'Occasion"/"Tous Les Saints"; 1958, Barclay: 70141 (EP)(CD; AR)

**Sandmen, The/Featuring Brook Benton**

"Ooh, Fool Enough to Love You," "Bring Me Love"; 1955, Okeh (AR)

**Scott, Bobby**

*Joyful Noises;* 1962, Mercury: MG-2070 I (PD)

*When the Feeling Hits You;* 1962, Mercury: SR-60767 (PD)

**Simon, Paul**

*There Goes Rhymin' Simon;* 1973, CBS: 32280 (AR)

**Sinatra, Frank**

*It Might as Well Be Swing;* 1964, Reprise: FS-I 0 12 (CD; AR)

*L.A. Is My Lady;* 1984, Qwest: 25145-1 (PD; CD; CP; AR)

**Sinatra, Frank /C. Basie / Q Jones**

*Sinatra at the Sands;* 1966, Reprise: 1019 (CD; AR)

**Starr, Ringo**

*Sentimental Journey;* 1970, Apple: SW-3365 (AR)

**Stitt, Sonny**

*Sonny Stitt Plays Arrangements from the Pen of Quincy Jones;* 1955, Roost: LP-2204 (CD; CP; AR)

**Summer, Donna**

*Donna Summer;* 1982, Geffen: GHS-2005 (PD; CP; AR; VO)

**Taylor, Billy**

*My Fair Lady Loves Jazz;* 1957, ABC Paramount: ABC-I 77 (CD; AR)

**Terry, Clark**

*Clark Terry;* 1955, EmArcy: MG-36007 (CP; AR)

*Clark Terry in the P.M.;* 1955, EmArcy: EP-I-6108 (EP) (CP; AR)

**Three Sounds**

*The Three Sounds Play Jazz on Broadway;* 1962, Mercury: MG-20776 (PD)

*Some Like It Modern;* 1963, Mercury: SR-60839 (PD)

*Live at the Living Room;* 1964, Mercury: MG-2092I (PD)

**Treniers, The *I* Featuring Willie Mays**

"Go! Go! Go!"; 1954, Okeh: 9127 (CD; AR)

**USA for Africa**

"We Are the World" (12" Single); 1985, Columbia: US2-05179 (PD; CD; AR)

**Various Artists**

*Save the Children;* 1973, Motown: M800-R2 (CD; AR)

*The Official Music of the 23rd Olympiad in Los Angeles;* 1984, Columbia: BJS-39322 (PD; CP; AR)

**Vaughan, Sarah**

*Vaughan and Violins;* 1958, Mercury: MG-20370 (CD; CP; AR)

*You're Mine, You;* 1962, Roulette: R-52082 (CD; AR)

*Sassy Swings the Tivoli;* 1963, Mercury:
SR -60831 (CD)
*Vaughan with Voices;* 1963, Mercury:
MG-20882 (PD)
*Viva! Vaughan;* 1964, Mercury: MG-20941 (PD)
*Sarah Vaughan Sings the Mancini Songbook;*
1965, Mercury: MG-21009 (PD)

**Wallington, George**

*George Wallington Showcase;* 1954, Blue Note:
BLP-5045 (10") (CP; AR)

**Washington, Dinah**

*For Those in Love;* 1955, Mercury: MG-360 II
(CD; AR)
*The Swingin' Miss D;* 1956, EmArcy: MG-36104
(CP; AR)
*I Wanna Be Loved;* 1961, Mercury: MG-20729
(CD; CP; AR)
*Tears and Laughter;* 1961, Mercury: SR-60661
(PD; CD)
*This Is My Story (Vol. 1 & 2);* 1962, Mercury:
*R-60765/60769 (CD)*
*The Queen and Quincy;* 1965, Mercury:
SR-60928 (CD)

**Watkins, Julius**

*French Horns for My Lady;* 1960, Philips:
PHM-200-001 (PD; AR)

**Watts, Ernie**

*Chariots of Fire;* 1981, Qwest: QWS-3637
(PD; CP; AR)

**White, Josh**

*At Town Hall;* 1961, Mercury: MG-20672 (PD)

**Williams, Andy**

*Under Paris Skies;* 1960, Cadence: CLP-3047
(CD; AR)

**Willis, Chuck**

"Come on Home," "I Can Tell," "Give Me a Break,"
"Search My Heart," "Ring-Ding-Doo"; 1955,
Okeh: 4-7062 (45 RPM, EP) (CD; AR)

**Yuro, Timi**

*The Amazing Timi Yuro;* 1964, Wing:
MG-20963 (PD)

# II
# Awards and Honors

## Grammy Awards

**National Academy of Recording Arts and Sciences**

1963    **Best Instrumental Arrangement**: "I Can't Stop Loving You" [Count Basie] (Reprise)

1969    **Best Instrumental Jazz Performance, Large Group or Soloist with Large Group**: "Walking In Space" (A&M)

1971    **Best Pop Instrumental Performance**: *Smackwater Jack* [album] (A&M)

1973    **Best Instrumental Arrangement**: "Summer in the City" (A&M)

1978    **Best Instrumental Arrangement**: "Main Title" Overture Part One; track from *The Wiz Original Soundtrack*–Quincy Jones [co-winner: Robert Freedman] (MCA)

1980    **Best Instrumental Arrangement**: "Dinorah, Dinorah" (George Benson) [co-winner: Jerry Hey] (Warner Bros.)

1981    **Best R&B Performance by Duo or Group with Vocal**: "The Dude"–Quincy Jones (A&M)
**Best Cast Show Album**: *Lena Horne: The Lady And Her Music - Live On Broadway* - Quincy Jones, producer [various composers and lyricists] (Qwest/Warner Bros.)
**Best Arrangement On An Instrumental Recording**: "Velas" (A&M) Track from *The Dude* - Quincy Jones, arranger [Johnny Mandel, synthesizer & string arranger]
**Best Instrumental Arrangement Accompanying Vocal**: "Ai No Corrida" (A&M) Track from *The Dude* [co-winner: Jerry Hey, instrument arranger]
**Producer of the Year (non-classical)**: Best Producer of 1981 - Quincy Jones

1983    **Record of the Year**: "Beat It" (Michael Jackson) (Epic/CBS) - Producer Quincy Jones [co-winner: Michael Jackson]

**Album of the Year**: *Thriller* (Michael Jackson) (Epic/CBS) - Producer Quincy Jones [co winner: Michael Jackson]

**Best Recording For Children**: *E.T. The Extra Terrestrial* album (MCA) Producer, Quincy Jones [co-winner: Michael Jackson, Narrator/Vocals]

**Producer of the Year**: Best Producer of 1983 - Quincy Jones [co-winner - Michael Jackson]

1984 **Best Arrangement Of An Instrumental**: "Grace" (Gymnastics Theme) - Quincy Jones [co-winner: Jerry Lubbock] *The Official Music of the 23rd Olympiad In Los Angeles* (Columbia)

1985 **Record of the Year**: "We Are the World" - USA For Africa (Columbia/CBS)

**Best Pop Performance By A Duo Or Group With Vocal**: "We Are the World" – single USA For Africa (Columbia/CBS)

**Best Music Video, Short Form**: "We Are the World" - *The Video Event USA for Africa* [co-winner: Tom Trbovich, video director]

1988 **Trustees Award**: Special award presented to Quincy Jones - arranger, composer, producer, conductor

1990 **Album of the Year**: *Back on the Block* (Qwest) Producer, Quincy Jones

**Best Rap Performance By A Duo Or A Group**: "Back on the Block" from *Back on the Block* (Qwest) [co-winners: Ice-T, Melle Mel, Big Daddy Kane, Kool Moe Dee, Quincy D. III]

**Best Jazz Fusion Performance**: "Birdland" from *Back on the Block*

**Best Arrangement On An Instrumental**: "Birdland" from *Back on the Block*

**Best Instrumental Arrangement Accompanying Vocal (s)**: "The Places You Find Love" from *Back on the Block*

**Producer of the Year (non-classical)**: Best Producer of 1990 - Quincy Jones

**Grammy Living Legend Award**

1993 **Best Large Jazz Ensemble Performance**: *Miles and Quincy Live at Montreux* (Warner Bros.)

1996 **MusiCares Person of the Year**: Special Humanitarian Award

2001 **Best Spoken Word Album**: *Q: The Autobiography of Quincy Jones*

278

# Grammy Nominations

### National Academy Recording Arts and Sciences

1960    **Best Arrangement**: "Let the Good Times Roll" [Ray Charles] (Mercury)
        **Best Jazz Performance, Large Group**: *The Great Wide World of Quincy Jones* (Mercury)

1961    **Best Performance By An Orchestra For Dancing**: *I Dig Dancers* (Mercury)

1962    **Best Performance By An Orchestra For Dancing**: *Big Band Bossa Nova* (Mercury)
        **Best Instrumental Arrangement**: *Quintessence* (Impulse)
        **Best Original Jazz Composition**: *Quintessence* (Impulse)

1963    **Best Instrumental Arrangement**: "I Can't Stop Loving You" [Count Basie] (Reprise)
        **Best Instrumental Jazz Performance, Large Group**: *Quincy Jones Plays the Hip Hits* (Mercury)
        **Best Performance By An Orchestra, For Dancing**: *Quincy Jones Plays the Hip Hits* (Mercury)

1964    **Best Instrumental Arrangement**: "Golden Boy" - String Version (Mercury)
        **Best Instrumental Performance, Non-Jazz**: "Golden Boy" - String Version (Mercury)
        **Best Instrumental Jazz Performance, Large Group or Soloist w/Large Group**: *Quincy Jones Explores the Music of Henry Mancini* (Mercury)
        **Best Original Jazz Composition**: "The Witching Hour"; track from *Golden Boy* (Mercury)

1967    **Best Original Score Written For A Motion Picture Or Television Show**: *in the Heat of the Night* (United Artists)

1969    **Best Instrumental Jazz Performance, Large Group Or Soloist With Large Group**: "Walking In Space" (A&M)
        **Best Original Score For A Motion Picture Or Television Show**: *MacKenna's Gold* (RCA)
        **Best Instrumental Theme**: *MacKenna's Gold - Main Title* (RCA)
        **Best Original Score For A Motion Picture Or A Television Show**: *The Lost Man* (Universal)

**Best Instrumental Arrangement**: *Walking In Space* (A&M)

1970 **Best Instrumental Arrangement**: *Gula Matari* (A&M)

**Best Instrumental Composition**: *Gula Matari* (A&M)

**Best Jazz Performance, Large Group Or Soloist W/ Large Group**: *Gula Matari* (A&M)

**Best Contemporary Instrumental Performance**: "Soul Flower"; track from *They Call Me Mr. Tibbs* soundtrack (United Artists)

1971 **Best Pop Instrumental Performance**: *Smackwater Jack* [album] (A&M)

1972 **Best Original Score Written For A Motion**: *$* Soundtrack (Reprise)

**Best Instrumental Arrangement**: "Money Runner"; track from *$* Soundtrack (Reprise)

**Best Pop Instrumental By Arranger, Composer, Orchestra**: "Money Runner"; track from *$* Soundtrack (Reprise)

1973 **Best Instrumental Arrangement**: "Summer in the City" (A&M)

**Best Pop Instrumental Performance**: *You've Got It Bad Girl* (A&M)

1974 **Best Pop Instrumental Performance**: "Along Came Betty"; track from *Body Heat* (A&M)

**Best Pop Vocal Performance By A Duo Or Group Or Chorus**: *Body Heat* (A&M)

1976 **Best Instrumental Composition**: "Midnight Soul Patrol"; single from *I Heard That* (A&M)

1977 **Best Arrangement For Voices**: "Oh Lord, Come By Here"; track from the *Roots* soundtrack (A&M)

**Best Inspirational Performance**: "Oh Lord, Come By Here" [James Cleveland]; track from the *Roots* Soundtrack (A&M)

**Best Instrumental Composition**: "Roots Medley (Motherland, "Roots" Mural Theme)" (A&M)

1978 **Best Instrumental Arrangement**: "Main Title" Overture Part One; track from *The Wiz Original Soundtrack* - Quincy Jones [co-nominee: Robert Freedman] (MCA)

**Best Instrumental Composition**: "End of the Yellow Brick Road" [Nick Ashford & Valerie Simpson]; single from *The Wiz* (A&M)

**Best Arrangement For Voices**: "Stuff Like That"; single from *Sounds...And Stuff Like That* (A&M)

**Producer of the Year (non-classical)**: Best Producer of 1978 - Quincy Jones

1979    **Best Disco Recording**: "Don't Stop 'Til You Get Enough" [Michael Jackson]; track from *Off the Wall* (Epic) [co-nominee: Michael Jackson]

**Producer of the Year (non-classical)**: Best Producer of 1979 - Quincy Jones

1980    **Best Instrumental Arrangement**: "Dinorah, Dinorah" (George Benson) [co-nominee: Jerry Hey] (Warner Bros.)

**Producer of the Year (non-classical)**: Best Producer of 1980 - Quincy Jones

1981    **Best R&B Performance by Duo Or Group With Vocal**: "The Dude" - Quincy Jones (A&M)

**Best Cast Show Album**: *Lena Horne: The Lady And Her Music - Live On Broadway* - Quincy Jones, producer [various composers and lyricists] (Qwest/Warner Bros.)

**Best Arrangement On An Instrumental Recording**: "Velas" (A&M) Track from *The Dude* - Quincy Jones, arranger [Johnny Mandel, synthesizer & string arranger]

**Best Instrumental Arrangement Accompanying Vocal**: "Ai No Corrida" (A&M) Track from *The Dude* [co-nominee: Jerry Hey, instrument arranger]

**Producer of the Year (non-classical)**: Best Producer of 1981 - Quincy Jones

**Album of the Year**: *The Dude* (A&M)

**Best Pop Instrumental Performance**: "Velas"; track from *The Dude* (A&M)

1982    **Producer of the Year (non-classical)**: Best Producer of 1982 - Quincy Jones

1983    **Record of the Year**: "Beat It" (Michael Jackson) (Epic/CBS) - Producer Quincy Jones [co-nominee: Michael Jackson]

**Album of the Year**: *Thriller* (Michael Jackson) (Epic/CBS) - Producer Quincy Jones, [co-nominee: Michael Jackson]

**Best Recording For Children**: *E.T. The Extra Terrestrial* album (MCA) Producer, Quincy Jones [co-nominee: Michael Jackson, Narrator/Vocals]

**Producer of the Year (non-classical)**: Best Producer of 1983 - Quincy Jones [co-nominee - Michael Jackson]

**Best R&B Instrumental Performance**: "Billie Jean" – (Instrumental version) [Michael Jackson]; track from *Thriller* (Epic)

**Best New Rhythm & Blues Song**: "P.Y.T. (Pretty Young Thing)" [Michael Jackson]; track from *Thriller* (Epic)

**Producer of the Year (non-classical)**: Best Producer of 1983 - Quincy Jones

1984 **Best Arrangement Of An Instrumental**: "Grace" (Gymnastics Theme) - Quincy Jones [co-nominee: Jerry Lubbock] *The Official Music of the 23rdOlympiad In Los Angeles* (Columbia)

**Best Rhythm & Blues Song**: "Yah Mo B There" [James Ingram & Michael McDonald]; single from *It's Your Night* (Qwest/Warner Bros.)

1985 **Album of the Year**: *We Are the World (USA For Africa/The Album)* [various artists] (Columbia)

**Record of the Year**: "We Are the World" - USA For Africa (Columbia/CBS)

**Best Pop Performance By A Duo Or Group With Vocal**: "We Are the World" – single USA For Africa (Columbia/CBS)

**Best Music Video, Short Form**: "We Are the World" - *The Video Event USA For Africa* [co-nominee: Tom Trbovich, video director]

1987 **Album of the Year**: *Bad* [Michael Jackson] (Epic)

**Producer of the Year (non-classical)**: Best Producer of 1987 - Quincy Jones [co-nominee: Michael Jackson]

1988 **Record of the Year**: "Man in the Mirror" [Michael Jackson]; single from *Bad* (Epic)

1990 **Album of the Year**: *Back on the Block* (Qwest) Producer, Quincy Jones

**Best Rap Performance By A Duo Or A Group**: "Back on the Block" from *Back on the Block* (Qwest) [co-nominees: Ice-T, Melle Mel, Big Daddy Kane, Kool Moe Dee, Quincy D. III]

**Best Jazz Fusion Performance**: "Birdland" from *Back on the Block*

**Best Arrangement On An Instrumental**: "Birdland" from *Back on the Block*

**Best Pop Instrumental Performance**: "Setembro (Brazilian Wedding Song)" [Quincy Jones & various artists]; track from *Back on the Block* (Qwest/Warner Bros.)

**Best Instrumental Arrangement Accompanying Vocal(s)**: "The Places You Find Love" from *Back on the Block*
**Producer of the Year (non-classical)**: Best Producer 1990 - Quincy Jones

1993     **Best Music Video, Long Form**: *Miles and Quincy Live at Montreux* [Miles Davis & Quincy Jones] (Reprise)
**Best Large Jazz Ensemble Performance**: *Miles and Quincy Live at Montreux* (Warner Bros.)

1996     **Best Instrumental Arrangement With Accompanying Vocal(s)**: "Do Nothin' Till You Hear From Me" [Phil Collins]; track from *Q's Jook Joint* (Qwest/Warner Bros.)

2001     **Best Spoken Word Album**: *Q: The Autobiography of Quincy Jones*
**Best Instrumental Arrangement**: "Soul Bossa Nova" [Quincy Jones & George S. Clinton]; track from *Austin Powers International Man of Mystery* and *The Spy Who Shagged Me* scores

# Grammy Participation Certificates

**National Academy Recording Arts and Sciences** (Grammy-winning recordings where Quincy Jones served as producer/arranger/conductor/composer/vocalist/artist)

1960     **Best Rhythm and Blues Performance:** "Let the Good Times Roll" [Ray Charles] track from *The Genius of Ray Charles* (Atlantic)/ Arranger/ Conductor
**Best Vocal Performance, Male:** *The Genius of Ray Charles* [Ray Charles] (atlantic)/ Arranger/Conductor

1963     **Best Performance by an Orchestra- For Dancing:** *This Time By Basie! Hits of the 50's & 60's* [Count Basie] (Reprise)/ Conductor/ Arranger

1965     **Song of the Year:** "The Shadow of Your Smile (Love Theme from *The Sandpiper*)" [Composers: Johnny Mandel & Paul Francis Webster] (Mercury)/ Producer
**Best Original Score Written for a Motion Picture or TV Show**: *The Sandpiper* [Robert Armbruster/ Conductor; Johnny Mandel/ Composer] (Mercury)/ Producer

1973     **Best R&B Vocal Performance, Female:** "Master of Eyes" (Single) [Aretha Franklin] (atlantic)/

Co-producer with Aretha Franklin

1977 **Best R&B Instrumental Performance:** "Q" [Brothers Johnson] track from *Right On Time* (A&M)/ Producer

1979 **Best R&B Performance, Male:** "Don't Stop 'Til You Get Enough" (Single) [Michael Jackson] track from *Off the Wall* (Epic)/ Producer

1980 **Best R&B Vocal Performance, Male***: Give Me the Night* (Album) [George Benson] (Qwest/ Warner Bros.)/ Producer/ Arranger

**Best R&B Instrumental Performance:** "Off Broadway" [George Benson] track from *Give Me the Night* (Qwest/ Warner Bros.)/ Producer

**Best Jazz Vocal Performance, Male:** "Moody's Mood" [George Benson] track from *Give Me the Night* (Qwest/ Warner Bros.)/ Producer/ Arranger

1981 **Best Pop Vocal Performance, Female:** *Lena Horne: The Lady and Her Music Live on Broadway* (Album) [Lena Horne] (Qwest/ Warner Bros.)/ Producer

**Best Rhythm & Blues Vocal Performance, Male:** "One Hundred Ways" track from *The Dude* [James Ingram] (A&M)/ Producer/ Artist

**Best R&B Performance by a Duo or Group with Vocal:** *The Dude* (A&M)/ Producer

1982 **Best Pop Instrumental Performance:** "Chariots of Fire" (Theme/ Dance Version) [Ernie Watts] track from *Chariots of Fire* (Qwest/ Warner Bros.)/ Producer

1983 **Best Pop Vocal Performance, Male:** *Thriller* (Album) [Michael Jackson] (Epic/ CBS)/ Producer

**Best Rock Vocal Performance, Male:** "Beat It" (Single) [Michael Jackson] track from *Thriller* (Epic/ CBS)/ Producer/ Arranger

**Best R&B Vocal Performance, Male:** "Billie Jean" (Single) [Michael Jackson] track from *Thriller* (Epic/ CBS)/ Producer

**Best New R&B Song:** "Billie Jean" [Songwriter: Michael Jackson] track from *Thriller* (Epic/ CBS)/ Producer

**Best Engineered Recording (Non-Classical):** *Thriller* (Michael Jackson/ Album) [Engineer: Bruce Swedien] (Epic/ CBS)/ Producer

1984 **Best R&B Performance by a Duo or Group with Vocal:** "Yah Mo Be There" (Single) [James

Ingram & Michael McDonald] track from *It's Your Night* (Qwest/ Warner Bros.)/ Producer/ Co-composer/ Arranger
**Best Video Album:** *Making Michael Jackson's Thriller* [Michael Jackson] (Vestron Music Video)/ Producer

1985    **Song of the Year:** "We Are the World" [Songwriters: Michael Jackson & Lionel Richie] track from *We Are the World* (Columbia/ CBS)/ Producer/ Conductor

1987    **Best Engineered Recording (Non-Classical):** *Bad* (Michael Jackson/ Album) [Engineer: Bruce Swedien & Humberto Gatica] (Epic)/ Producer

1990    **Best R&B Performance by a Duo or Group with Vocal:** "I'll Be Good to You" (Single) [Ray Charles & Chaka Kahn] track from *Back on the Block* (Qwest/ Warner Bros.)/ Producer/ Arranger/ Artist
**Best Engineered Recording (Non-Classical):** *Back on the Block* (Quincy Jones/ Album) [Engineer: Bruce Swedien] (Qwest/ Warner Bros.)/ Producer/ Artist

1992    **Best Contemporary Soul Gospel Album***: Handel's Messiah- A Soulful Celebration* (Album) [Various Artists]; Mervyn Warren, Producer (Reprise)/ Conductor

## American Music Award

1986    **Special Recognition**, *We Are the World*

## MTV Video Award

1984    **Special Recognition** (1st Annual MTV Video Awards Ceremony)

## Academy Awards

**Academy of Motion Picture Arts and Sciences**

1995    **Jean Hersholt Humanitarian Award** (Awarded to an individual in the motion picture industry who's humanitarian efforts have brought credit to the industry. Award presented by Oprah Winfrey During 67th Annual Academy Awards Telecast)

(In 1971, Quincy Jones conducted the orchestra for the 43rd Annual Academy Awards Telecast. In 1996, Jones served as Executive Producer and co-Producer with David Salzman of the 68th Annual Academy Awards Telecast)

## Academy Award Nominations

**Academy of Motion Picture Arts and Sciences**

1967  **Best Original Music Score**, from the film *In Cold Blood*
**Best Original Song**, "The Eyes Of Love" from the film *Banning* (Music by Quincy Jones, lyrics by Bob Russell; performed by Gil Bernal)

1968  **Best Original Song**, "For Love Of Ivy" from the film *For Love Of Ivy* (Music by Quincy Jones, lyrics by Bob Russell; performed by Shirley Horn)

1978  **Best Adaptation Score**, from the film *The Wiz*

1985  **Best Original Song**, "Miss Celie's Blues (Sister)" from the film *The Color Purple* (Music by Quincy Jones and Rod Temperton, lyrics by Quincy Jones, Rod Temperton, Lionel Richie; performed by Tata Vega)
**Best Original Score**, from the film *T he Color Purple*
**Best Picture** (producer), *The Color Purple*

## Golden Globe Nominations

**Hollywood Foreign Press Association**

1970  **Best Original Song, Motion Picture**, "The Time For Love Is Anytime" from the film *Cactus Flower* (Music by Quincy Jones, lyrics by Cynthia Weil; performed by Sarah Vaughan)

1973  **Best Original Score, Motion Picture**, *The Getaway*

1986  **Best Original Score, Motion Picture**, *The Color Purple*

## Emmy Awards

**Academy of Television Arts and Sciences**

1977     **Outstanding Achievement In Music Composition For A Series, Or A Single Program Of A Series**, *Roots – Episode I* (ABC) [co-winner: Gerald Fried for dramatic underscore]

## Emmy Nominations

**Academy of Television Arts and Sciences**

1970     **Outstanding Achievement In Music Composition**, *The Bill Cosby Show* (NBC)

1977     **Outstanding Achievement In Music Composition For A Series, Or A Single Program Of A Series**, *Roots – Episode I* (ABC) [co-nominee: Gerald Fried]

1995     **Outstanding Informational Series**, *The History of Rock 'n' Roll: Punk* (WBTD) (Executive Producers: Quincy Jones, David Salzman, Bob Meyrowitz, andrew Solt; Producers: Ted Haimes, Jeffrey Peisch)

1996     **Outstanding Variety, Music or Comedy Special**, *The 68ᵗʰ Annual Academy Awards* (ABC) (Executive Producer: Quincy Jones; Producers: Quincy Jones, David Salzman)

## Tony Award Nominations

**American Theatre Wing**

2006     **Best Musical**, *The Color Purple* (Oprah Winfrey, Scott Sanders, Roy Furman, Quincy Jones, Creative Battery, Anna Fantaci & Cheryl Lachowicz, Independent Presenters Network, David Lowy, Stephanie P. McClelland, Gary Winnick, Jan Kallish, Nederlander Presentations, Inc., Bob & Harvey Weinstein, andrew Asnes & Adam Zotovich, Todd Johnson

## Image Awards

**National Association for the Advancement
Of Colored People**

1972    **Big Band Album of the Year**, *Smackwater Jack*
1974    **Best Jazz Artist**, *You've Got It Bad Girl*
1975    **Best Jazz Artist**, *Body Heat*
1980    **Best Musical Score, Motion Picture**, *The Wiz*
1981    **Best Jazz Album**, *The Dude*
1981    **Album of the Year**, *Off the Wall*
1983    **Producer of the Decade**
1986    **Best Motion Picture**, *The Color Purple*
1990    **Best Album**, *Back on the Block*
1990    **Hall of Fame Award**
1996    **Outstanding Jazz Artist**, *Q's Jook Joint*
1996    **Entertainer of the Year**
1997    **Outstanding Jazz Artist**, *Q Live In Paris –
        Circa 1960*
2000    **Outstanding Jazz Artist**, *From Q, With Love*
2002    **Outstanding Jazz Artist**, *Q: The Musical
        Biography of Quincy Jones*

## Ebony Music Awards

**Johnson Publications**

1976    **Ebony Music Award – Best Composer, Jazz**,
        *I Heard That*
1976    **Ebony Music Award – Musician of the Year,
        Jazz**, *I Heard That*
1976    **Ebony Music Award – Big Band Leader, Jazz**,
        *I Heard That*
1976    **Ebony Music Award – Arranger of the Year,
        Jazz**, *I Heard That*
1978    **Ebony American Black Achievement Award
        for Music**, *Sounds...and Stuff Like That*
1982    **Ebony American Black Achievement Award
        for Music**, *Thriller*
1985    **Ebony American Black Achievement Award
        for Music**, *We Are the World*
1990    **Ebony American Black Achievement Lifetime
        Achievement Award**

## Recording Industry Awards

1964     **Edison Music Award**, MPVI – Edison
Foundation (International music award from
Netherlands, equivalent to Grammy Awards)

1970     **Edison Music Award**, MPVI – Edison Foundation

1972     **Edison Music Award**, MPVI – Edison Foundation

1978     **Edison Music Award**, MPVI – Edison Foundation

1979     **Edison Music Award**, MPVI – Edison Foundation

1979     **Most Popular Arranger/Producer/Composer**,
Black College Radio Convention

1982     **Golden Note Award**, American Society of
Composers, Authors and Publishers

1989     **Lifetime Achievement Award**, National
Academy of Songwriters

1990     **Heritage Award For Lifetime Achievement**,
Soul Train Music Awards

1990     **Nesuhi Ertegun – Cartier Man of the
Year**, MIDEM (International Music Market
Conference Held Annually In Cannes, France)

1994     **Golden Score Award**, American Society of
Music Arrangers and Composers

1997     **Vanguard Award for Lifetime Achievement**,
National Academy of Songwriters

1988     **Luminary Award**, American Society of Young
Musicians

1999     **Henry Mancini Lifetime Achievement Award**,
American Society of Composers, Authors and
Publishers

2003     **Tribute Honoree**, Los Angeles Jazz Society

2006     **BBC Jazz Award**, British Broadcasting Corporation

2007     **50$^{th}$ Anniversary Ambassador**, National
Academy of Recording Arts & Sciences

2007     **Ivor Novello International Award**, British
Academy of Composers & Songwriters

2007     **Leadership Award**, National Academy of
Recording Arts & Sciences

2007     **Grammy on the Hill Honoree**, National
Academy of Recording Arts & Sciences

2008     **Pied Piper Award**, American Society of
Composers, Authors & Publishers

2009     **American Eagle Award**, National Music Council

2010     **Walk of Fame**, Apollo Theater

2010     **Paul Acket Award for Lifetime Acheivement**,
North Sea Jazz Festival

## Film/Television Industry Awards

1993    **Trumpet "Living Legend" Award**, Turner
        Broadcasting Systems (For Outstanding Career
        Achievement)

1999    **Oscar Micheaux Award**, Producers Guild of
        America (For Outstanding Career Achievement
        as a Film and Television Producer)

2006    **Daimler/Chrysler – Behind the Lens Award**
        (For Outstanding Career Achievement in Film
        and Television)

2008    **Leadership Award**, National Association of
        Broadcasters Education Foundation

2008    **Humanitarian Award**, Black Entertainment
        Television

## Newspaper/Magazine Awards

1960    **Best New Arranger of the Year,** International
        Critics' Poll, *DownBeat Magazine*

1960    **Best New Big Band of the Year,** International
        Critics' Poll, *DownBeat Magazine*

1960    **Reader's Choice Award, Jazz Arranger/
        Composer of the Year**, *Jet Magazine* J
        ohnson Publications

1971    **Arranger of the Year,** Readers' Poll, *DownBeat
        Magazine*

1972    **Arranger of the Year,** Readers' Poll, *DownBeat
        Magazine*

1972    **Trendsetters Award**, *Billboard Magazine*

1973    **Arranger of the Year,** Readers' Poll, *DownBeat
        Magazine*

1974    **Arranger of the Year,** Readers' Poll, *DownBeat
        Magazine*

1980    **Producer of the Year**, *Billboard Magazine*

1982    **Trendsetters Award**, *Billboard Magazine*

1983    **Producer of the Year**, *Billboard Magazine*

1983    **Jazz Composer/Songwriter of the Year**,
        Playboy Music Award

1984    **Jazz Composer/Songwriter of the Year**,
        Playboy Music Award

1985    **Jazz Composer/Songwriter of the Year**,
        Playboy Music Award

| 1986 | **Jazz Composer/Songwriter of the Year**, Playboy Music Award |
|---|---|
| 1986 | **Record Producer of the Year**, Playboy Music Award |
| 1990 | **Entrepreneur of the Year**, USA Today/Financial News Network |
| 1994 | **Essence Lifetime Achievement Award**, *Essence Magazine* |
| 1996 | **Entertainer of the Year**, *Weekly Variety* |
| 1999 | **Influential Jazz Artist of the Century**, *Time Magazine* (Shared honor with Louis Armstrong, Duke Ellington, Charlie Parker, Miles Davis and Wynton Marsalis) |
| 2008 | **American Black Achievement Award**, *Ebony Magazine* |

## Humanitarian Awards

| 1991 | (In 1991, Quincy Jones and Courtney Ross founded *The Quincy Jones Listen Up Foundation* to address and confront the state of emergency that currently threatens the future of the world's youth; and to recognize and encourage youth who are achievers and support them in their pursuits) |
|---|---|
| 1971 | **Distinguished Service Award**, The Brotherhood Crusade (In recognition of commitment to addressing the socio-economic needs and concerns of america's urban communities) |
| 1982 | **Spirit of Life-"Man of the Year,"** City of Hope (In Recognition Of Ongoing Support On Behalf Of Cancer Research) |
| 1984 | **American Academy of Achievement Golden Plate** (Inducted into the Academy in recognition of personal and professional accomplishments which established him as a role model for America's youth) |
| 1986 | **Humanitarian of the Year**, TJ Martell Foundation (In recognition of ongoing support on behalf of leukemia, cancer and AIDS research) |

1986    **Norma Zarky Humanitarian Crystal Award**, Women In Film (In recognition for ongoing charitable contributions and efforts to improve the human condition)

1986    **Whitney Young, Jr. Award**, National Urban League (In recognition for commitment to enabling African-Americans to secure economic self reliance, parity, power and civil rights)

1991    **Angel Award**, Center for Population Options (In recognition of commitment to encouraging normal, positive and healthy attitudes towards sexual relationships between young adults)

1992    **Spirit Of Liberty Award**, People for the American Way (In recognition of work to promote and defend the values of the American way of life: fairness, equality, tolerance, opportunity and individual liberty)

1993    **Entertainment and Community Achievement Award**, NAACP Legal Defense Fund (In recognition of commitment to ensuring the legal civil rights of all individuals)

1994    **Distinguished Service Award**, Northside Center For Child Development (In recognition of commitment to addressing the socio-economic concerns of urban families)

1994    **Equal Opportunity Award**, National Urban League (In recognition for commitment to enabling African-Americans to secure economic self reliance and equal opportunity)

1995    **Horatio Alger Award**, Horatio Alger Association (In recognition of accomplishments and achievements succeeded in the face of adversity; and for encouragement of young people to pursue their dreams with determination and perseverance)

1996    **Time Warner Ambassador of Goodwill**, Time Warner Inc.(Designated Ambassador Of Goodwill By Time Warner Chairman and CEO Gerald Levin)

1996    **International Committee Award**, Intercambios Culturales (In recognition of work to promote arts education in third world nations)

1996    **1996 Honoree**, Young Audiences of America (In recognition of being an advocate of arts education for all children)

1996 **Humanitarian Award**, The H.E.L.P Group
(In recognition of commitment to helping
young people fulfill their potential to lead
positive, productive and rewarding lives)

1996 **Thurgood Marshall Lifetime Achievement
Award**, NAACP Legal Defense Fund
(In recognition of lifetime career achievements
and commitment to ensuring the legal civil
rights of all individuals. Shared award with
Clarence Avant)

1996 **Pioneer in Black Achievement Lifetime
Achievement Award**, the Brotherhood Crusade
(In recognition of lifetime career achievements
and commitment to addressing the socio-
economic needs and concerns of america's
urban communities)

1998 **Spirit Award**, Children's Defense Fund
(In recognition of commitment to addressing
the needs and concerns of children)

1999 **Ellis Island Medal of Honor**, National Ethnic
Coalition of Organizations (In recognition of
exemplifying outstanding qualities in both
personal and professional life, while continuing
to represent the richness of his heritage)

1999 **Media Spotlight Award for Lifetime
Achievement**, Amnesty International
(In recognition for commitment to promoting
human rights and social consciousness
throughout the world)

1999 **Seasons of Hope Award**, AMFAR
(In recognition for ongoing commitment to
AIDS research. award presented by Clive Davis)

2000 **Lena Horne Legend Award**, Citizens Committee
for New York (For outstanding career achievement
and commitment to improving the quality of life
in New York City and its neighborhoods. award
presented by Bill Cosby)

2002 **Building Hope Award,** Habitat for Humanity
2002 **Frances E. Williams Award,** Community Coalition
2004 **Uncommon Height Award**, National Council of
Negro Women
2005 **Spirit of Compassion Award**, UNICEF
2006 **Spirit of Hope Award**, Carousel of Hope
2007 **Mentor of the Year**, Harvard University School
of Public Health

2008    **Wisdom Award**, National Visionary Leadership Project

2008    **Sunflower Philanthropy Award**, Sunflower Foundation

2009    **Cultural Diplomacy Award**, The Aspen Institute

2009    **Global Citizen Award**, The Clinton Global Initiative

2010    **Exceptional Advocacy Award**, Global Down Syndrome Foundation

2010    **Chairman's Award for Community Service**, Ludacris Foundation

2010    **Salute To Greatness Award**, Martin Luther King, Jr. Center

## Arts and Humanities Awards

1990    **Honors Award**, Los Angeles Arts Council (For outstanding career achievement in the arts)

1994    **President's Committee on the Arts & Humanities** (Presidential appointment to address the needs and concerns regarding the nation's commitment to promoting the arts and humanities)

2001    **Ted Arison Award**, National Foundation for Advancement in the Arts (In recognition for commitment to promoting arts education. award presented by Mrs. Ted Arison)

2001    **Inducted into the American Academy of Arts and Sciences** (International learned society composed of the world's leading scientists, scholars, artists, businesspeople, and public leaders)

2008    **Jazz Masters Award**, National Endowment for the Arts

## City/State/Country/World Awards

(For outstanding career achievement and contributions to the world's culture)

1973    **Citation of Excellence**, Texas House of Representatives

1973    **Citation of Excellence**, Canadian National Exhibition

1974    **Special Recognition**, California State Assembly

294

1976    **In Special Recognition of 20<sup>th</sup> Anniversary in Music**, City of Philadelphia, PA

1980    **Hollywood Walk of Fame**, Hollywood, California

1982    **Key to the City**, Indianapolis, Indiana

1985    **Centennial Hall of Honor**, State of Washington

1990    **Living Treasure**, Governor's Arts Awards, State of California

1990    **Officier de la Legion d'Honneur**, Republic of France

1990    **Album of the Year Jazz Fusion**, Back on the Block, Japan Grand Prix

1991    **Alexander Pushkin Award**, Union Of Soviet Socialist Republics

1991    **Lifetime Achievement Award**, Rosedór de Montreux, France

1994    **Polar Music Prize**, Royal Swedish Academy Of Music (Considered the Nobel Peace Prize of Music. Award presented by Sweden's King Gustav)

1995    **Rudolph Valentino Award**, Republic Of Italy

1996    **Distinguished Arts & Letters Award**, French Ministry of Culture (Award presented by United States Ambassador to France Pamela Harrison)

1999    **Trophee des Arts**, French Institute Alliance Francaise

2000    **Crystal Award,** World Economic Forum Davos, Switzerland (Award presented by World Economic Forum founder, Professor Klaus Schwab)

2000    **Key to the City of Paris**, Paris, France

2000    **National Medal of the Humanities**, National Endowment of the Humanities, United States of America (Award presented by President William Clinton)

2001    **Marian anderson Award**, City of Philadelphia (In recognition of outstanding achievement as an artist and as a humanitarian)

2001    **Commandeur de la Legion d'Honneur**, Republic of France (Only American-born musician to hold honor. award presented by French President Jacque Chirac)

2001    **Kennedy Center Honoree**, Kennedy Center (For contributions to the cultural fabric of the United States of America)

2006    **Spirit of Los Angeles Award**, City of Los Angeles

| 2006 | **Culture and Arts Consultant 2008 Summer Olympic Games**, Beijing, China |
| 2007 | **Leadership in the Arts Award**, Congressional Black Caucus Spouses, United States |
| 2008 | **Pyramid Award**, Cairo International Film Festival (In recognition of lifetime achievement) |
| 2008 | **Lifetime Achievement Award**, Northwest African-American Museum |
| 2008 | **California Hall of Fame Inductee**, State of California |
| 2009 | **Lifetime Achievement Award**, Shanghai International Film Festival |
| 2009 | **City of Music Outstanding Achievement Award**, Seattle, WA |

## Honorary Doctorates/Academic Awards

| 1983 | **Honorary Doctor of Arts**, Berklee College Of Music |
| 1985 | **Honorary Doctor of Arts and Letters**, Howard University |
| 1990 | **Honorary Doctor of Philosophy**, Seattle University |
| 1991 | **Honorary Doctor of Arts**, Wesleyan University |
| 1991 | **Scopus Award**, Hebrew University |
| 1992 | **Honorary Doctor of Arts**, Loyola University |
| 1992 | **Honorary Doctor of Arts and Letters**, Brandeis University |
| 1993 | **Honorary Doctor of Philosophy**, Clark University, Atlanta |
| 1994 | **Legend In Leadership Award**, Emory University, Atlanta |
| 1995 | **Honorary Doctor of Letters**, Claremont University Graduate School |
| 1995 | **The UCLA Chancellor's Medal**, University of California – Los Angeles |
| 1996 | **Honorary Doctor of Fine Arts**, University of Connecticut |
| 1996 | **Magnum Opus Award for Lifetime Achievement**, USC School of Music |
| 1996 | **Lifetime Achievement Award**, The Thelonius Monk Institute of Jazz |
| 1996 | **Harvard Foundation Medal For Intercultural & Race Relations**, Harvard University |
| 1997 | **Honorary Doctor of Fine Arts**, Harvard University |

| | |
|---|---|
| 1997 | **Honorary Doctor of Fine Arts**, American Film Institute |
| 1999 | **Honorary Doctor of Fine Arts**, Tuskegee University |
| 1999 | **Honorary Doctor of Fine Arts**, New York University |
| 1999 | **Honorary Doctor of Fine Arts**, University of Miami |
| 1999 | **Frederick D. Patterson Award**, United Negro College Fund |
| 1999 | **Candle of Light Award**, Morehouse College |
| 2000 | **W.E.B. du Bois Medal**, Dept. of Afro-American Studies, Harvard University (In recognition of longstanding commitment to the Department of Afro-American Studies) |
| 2000 | **Quincy Jones Professorship Of African-American Music**, Harvard University ($3 Million Endowment Established By Time Warner Inc.) |
| 2007 | **George & Ira Gershwin Award**, University of California – Los Angeles |
| 2007 | **George Peabody Medal**, Peabody Conservatory of Music |
| 2007 | **Raymond & Esther Kabbaz Award**, Ly Lycee Francais de Los Angeles |
| 2007 | **Honorary Doctor of Humane Letters**, Morehouse College |
| 2008 | **Honorary Doctor of Music**, Washington University-St. Louis |
| 2008 | **Honorary Doctor of Arts**, University of Washington |
| 2008 | **Honorary Doctor of Music**, Princeton University |
| 2009 | **Honorary Doctor of Music**, The Julliard School |
| 2009 | **Honorary Degree**, Royal Welsh College of Music |
| 2010 | **Honorary Doctor of Music**, Jacobs School of Music – Indiana University |
| 2010 | **Honorary Doctor of Music**, New England Conservatory of Music |
| 2010 | **Honorary Doctor of Music**, Juilliard School of Music |

# INDEX